THE POETICS OF FASCISM

THE POETICS OF FASCISM
Ezra Pound, T. S. Eliot, Paul de Man

PAUL MORRISON

New York   Oxford
OXFORD UNIVERSITY PRESS
1996

Oxford University Press

Oxford   New York
Athens   Auckland   Bangkok   Bombay
Calcutta   Cape Town   Dar es Salaam   Delhi
Florence   Hong Kong   Istanbul   Karachi
Kuala Lumpur   Madras   Madrid   Melbourne
Mexico City   Nairobi   Paris   Singapore
Taipei   Tokyo   Toronto

and associated companies in
Berlin   Ibadan

Library of Congress Cataloging-in-Publication Data
Morrison, Paul (Paul A.)
The poetics of fascism : Ezra Pound, T. S. Eliot, Paul de Man / Paul Morrison.
p. cm.
ISBN 0–19–508085–8 (cloth)
1. Pound, Ezra, 1885–1972—Political and social views. 2. Fascism and
literature—History. 3. Eliot, T. S. (Thomas Stearns), 1888–1965—Political
and social views. 4. De Man, Paul—Political and social views.
5. Pound, Ezra, 1885–1972—Influence. 6. Eliot, T. S. (Thomas Stearns),
1888–1965—Influence. 7. Political poetry, American—History and criticism.
8. Modernism (Literature)—United States. 9. Literature,
Modern—20th century—History and criticism—Theory, etc.
10. Poetics.   I. Title.
PS3531.082Z7542   1995
811'.5209358—dc20   95–13418

Portions of chapter 2 originally appeared as, "'Jewspapers': Ezra Pound, Poststructuralism, and the Figure
of the Jew," in *Tainted Greatness: Antisemitism and Cultural Heroes,* ed. Nancy A. Harrowitz (Philadelphia:
Temple University Press, 1994); chapter 4 is a revised and expanded version of "Paul de Man: Resistance
and Collaboration," which appeared in *Representations* 32 (Fall 1990): 50–74.

Ezra Pound *The Cantos of Ezra Pound.* Copyright © 1934, 1938, 1948, 1962, by Ezra Pound. Reprinted
by permission of New Directions.
Collected Poems, 1909–1962 by T. S. Eliot. Reprinted with permission from Faber and Faber Ltd.

2 4 6 8 9 7 5 3 1

Printed in the United States of America
on acid-free paper

For my mother,
Elizabeth Joan Morrison

Acknowledgments

Modernism may still be with us historically—or so, in any case, I argue—but it is now, at long last, behind me professionally. I owe this postmodernism, the only variety I enthusiastically embrace, to the generous help and encouragement of the following individuals: John Burt, Stuart Blackley, Eleanor Cook, John Jay Crickett, Scott Derrick, Lee Edelman, William Flesch, Eugene Goodheart, Allen Grossman, David M. Halperin, Amanda Heller, Henry Krawitz, Alison Lane, Alan Levitan, Joseph Litvak, Elizabeth Maguire, Richard Meyer, Helena Michie, Linda Munk, Mary Nyquist, Henry Shaffer, Susan Staves, Arlyne Weisman and Christopher Wells.

Contents

THE POETICS OF FASCISM

1

MODERNISM
(for the Other People)

Modernism itself now occupies the position to which T. S. Eliot relegated Ezra Pound's "Hell":

> Mr. Pound's Hell, for all its horrors, is a perfectly comfortable one for the modern mind to contemplate, and disturbing to no one's complacency: it is Hell for the *other people,* the people we read about in the newspapers, not for oneself and one's friends.[1]

Only recently (or so it seems) we were still laboring to become Joyce's contemporaries; today "modern" is everything we no longer care to be. To my knowledge, no other age has ever thought of itself as "post" anything in quite so self-congratulatory a fashion, yet even from the safety of our side of the hyphen—the "post-modern," the "post-structuralist," or whatever—we may be protesting too much. Consider the titles of two influential studies: "the myth of the modern" (it didn't happen) and "the failure of modernism" (it did happen, but it didn't work).[2] A modernism that never was or never succeeded should hardly prove disturbing to anyone's complacency; yet the phrases themselves betray a curious defensiveness, a critical response in want of the composure the hyphen might be expected to afford.

   It is my intention to make that composure harder to sustain, to make modernism less comfortable for the postmodern mind to contemplate. My aims are twofold: to recover from the horror of Ezra Pound's and T. S. Eliot's political commitments, which are inseparable from their poetic accomplishments, the utopian impulses that inform them; and to deny the current theoretical regime, by which I mean poststructuralism/postmodernism, the "subversive" power it claims for itself. The two aims are related. The distance we have traveled from all things modern is not as great as is commonly supposed, and the direction has not always been positive.

To begin with the first: Pound's political commitments do not simply taint a greatness that nevertheless rises, phoenixlike, above them. And they are, of course, to be condemned. But the politics of condemnation is itself politically problematic. Pound's fascism and anti-Semitism have their origins in a profound and potentially revolutionary dissatisfaction with the liberal settlement; the anticapitalist, antibourgeois fervor that motivates both need not have assumed the reactionary form it did.[3] Condemnation cannot be relegated to the gentlemanly decorum of "it goes without saying"—there are still those for whom the fascism and anti-Semitism are only incidental blemishes—but neither can it be allowed to exhaust the issue, at least not if our relation to fascism is to progress beyond ritual condemnation.

As for the second of my two aims, poststructuralism is not the newest news in town, and few would characterize it as "the current theoretical regime." Yet there does seem to be a general consensus, the celebrated diversity of the contemporary theoretical field notwithstanding, that modern times are now comfortably behind us. And however we choose to characterize the divide, our historical moment is clearly given to a generalized distrust, which poststructuralism first theorized, of such reputedly modernist "virtues" as coherence, teleology, totalization, and the like (although the putative coherence of the term *modern* itself may be a retroactive projection from our side of the hyphen). Poststructuralism has suffered a remarkable free fall from institutional grace in recent years, and *postmodernism* is now the term of choice. Far from challenging the hegemony of what it appears to displace, however, the newer terminology may well guarantee it: a theoretical position (poststructuralism) becomes effectively irrefutable when it passes for a historical or quasi-historical dispensation (postmodernism). In any case, the condition of our contemporary (non)identity is precisely the measure of our distance from all things modern. Postmodernism: modernism for the other people and time.

The following study is divided into three chapters. The first two address the poetry and prose of Pound and Eliot, frequently, but not exclusively, as they relate to current theoretical orthodoxies; the third focuses on the "scandal" that has come to be attached to the name of Paul de Man. My governing concern is the interaction among modernism, fascism, and poststructuralism; my specific focus is the politics and poetics of the proper name. Here things divide rather neatly in two. I begin with Pound's commitment to a poetics of proper names, which he construes, following Aristotle (or later mistranslations of Aristotle), in opposition to an ethos of metaphoric displacement; I conclude with Paul de Man, arguably the most distinguished of U.S. poststructuralists, and hence a partisan of a movement that characterizes itself as a critique of the ideology of the proper, of what it takes to be the old metaphysical dream of anything beyond the endless play of tropological displacements. (Eliot occupies a middle position, both in what follows and in actual fact: committed to a theology of the proper, he nevertheless anticipates the poststructuralist critique of aesthetic versions of the same.) My governing concern and specific focus might seem only tangentially related—what has an ethos of tropological mobility or a politics of the proper name to do with the explicitly fascist?—but it is precisely the investment of fascism in issues of representation (an investment that the poststructuralist critique of "the rhetoric of totalitarianism" effectively perpetuates) that I wish to establish.

I say "explicitly fascist," but I have yet to define a term that notoriously resists definition. Gilbert Allardyce, for one, despairs of the possibility. The various movements conventionally termed fascist, he argues, do not in fact form a coherent category; the word itself is a specious totalization.[4] The historical referent is unproblematic (the Italian Fascists, unlike the majority of reactionary political movements in interwar Europe, actually designated themselves so), but a referent does not a definition make. And definition itself was a problem that "bedeviled the original Italian Fascists": they developed a "codified set of doctrines only ex post facto, some years after Mussolini came to power, and then only in part."[5]

The study of fascism need not, of course, replicate the conceptual confusion of its object, and not all scholars have despaired of the possibility of definition. Ernst Nolte, for example, has done much to establish the generic intelligibility of the term. He argues for the existence of a "fascist minimum," the lowest common denominators that unite Action Française, Italian Fascism, and National Socialism (but not, it will be noted, Soviet communism).[6] The thesis is helpful—for what it excludes as much as includes—although it is subject to critique on a variety of grounds. Because economic determinants are slighted, the importance Nolte attributes to the "leadership principle" risks reinscribing an inverse form of the fascist heroicization of the leader, thus reducing historical causality to a demonized version of the "great man" theory. Nolte fails to distinguish adequately, moreover, between the *Führerstaat,* Hitler's virtually unlimited power, and the very different situation that obtained in Fascist Italy. The tendency to privilege National Socialism in the construction of generic definitions of fascism is, of course, understandable. Few countires, then as now, were without reactionary elements; but fascist parties did not generally attain to the level of significant government participation, and only in Nazi Germany did the full horror of the movement manifest itself. Yet if understandable, the privileging of National Socialism is not therefore without an ideological agenda of its own.

Geoffrey Hartman, following Kenneth Burke, characterizes *Mein Kampf* as monological: like the historical atrocity over which he presided, Hitler's discourse is predicated on the suppression of a characteristically "liberal" or "parliamentary" play of differences.[7] The tendency to identify fascism with the "monological", reaffirms the opposition between the liberal-constitutional and the fascist-dictatorial state, which is itself an article of both liberal and fascist faith, but the binarism is generalizable only at the cost of suppressing "contrary voices" within and between fascist movements themselves. The Italy of the 1930s, for instance, was largely a juridical system of semipluralism—or "limited pluralism," as Juan Linz terms it— and formal law.[8] Giovanni Gentile, a leading theorist of Italian Fascism, introduced the term *totalitario* to characterize the ambitions of the new regime, but Italian Fascism was never in fact "totalitarian" in the ordinary sense of the word. Mussolini governed only with the tacit consent or collusion of nonparty elements—the church, the military, the organized business community—and his regime never fully escaped its various compromises. Victor Emmanuel III, not Il Duce, was the constitutional head of state, and the police force retained its independence from the party. The institutions of fascist culture were charged with promoting a sense of civic responsibility in the masses, but no specific form of artistic expression was ever deemed official. The reach of the new state was theoretically unlimited; in practice, however, its grasp was severely curtailed. Stanley Payne argues that fascist "totalitarianism" never extended "to total—or in most cases even approximate—day-by-day institutional control."[9] Contrary to conventional wisdom, which makes of fascism a dispensation different in kind from our own, it is entirely possible "to do the police"—or an unholy amalgamation of the quasi-constitutional and quasi-police state—"in different voices."

My own understanding of fascism is derived primarily from the manner in which it negotiates what are now termed, following Nolte, its "negations": antiliberalism and antimarxism (the conventional third, anticonservatism, seems to me of limited validity).[10] The double negation is potentially difficult to sustain: if the antidote to liberal capitalism is not marxism, what, then, is it? What is the positive content or promise that mediates between the two? Nolte argues that "without Marxism there is no fascism." The latter is "at the same time closer to and further from communism than is liberal anti-communism," if only because it "shows at least an inclination toward a radical ideology" (21). But the "inclination" is displaced, recontained, in what might be characterized, following Walter Benjamin, as an aestheticized marxism:

> Fascism attempts to organize the newly created proletarian masses without affecting the property structure which the masses strive to eliminate. Fascism sees its salvation in giving these masses not their right, but instead a chance to express themselves. The masses have a right to change property relations; Fascism seeks to give them an expression while preserving property. The logical result of Fascism is the introduction of aesthetics into political life.[11]

Communism collectivizes the means of production and the fruits of labor; fascism provides the illusion of collective experience through aesthetic means. The latter is most apparent in the elaborate political choreography to which it is given—the aesthetics of the mass rally, *sabato fascista,* and the like—but it is in no way restricted to it. For if the fascist aestheticization of the political involves a compensatory access to representation or expression, which is not to be confused with the liberal promise of an open exchange of ideas in an open marketplace, it is also given to a generalized effacement of the priority of the economic, in both its liberal and its marxist forms. Granted, the effacement is more apparent than real. Slavoj Žižek speaks of fascism as an "'attempt to change something so that nothing really changes' by means of an ideology which subordinates the economy to the ideological-political domain."[12] But the so-called domination of the political, then as now, serves only to mystify, rather than suspend, the contradictions inherent in capitalist development. Fascism intends a transformation of the relation of the self to the social no less radical than marxism. Unlike marxism, however, fascism responds to real needs with a pseudocommunity of the *Volk.* Fascism is a revolution conducted primarily on the level of the political, the cultural, the superstructural.[13]

Peter Drucker attributes the rise of European fascism to the death of *homo oeconomicus.* The dominant ideologies of the nineteenth century, laissez-faire capitalism and marxism, failed to command the imagination of the twentieth, as both presupposed a faith in the rationality of the economic order which was lost to the First World War and the Great Depression.[14] (Mussolini makes much the same point: "Fascism denies the materialist conception of happiness as a possibility, and abandons it to its inventors, the economists of the first half of the nineteenth century.")[15] But what Drucker terms a "death" is little more than a displacement, and the fascism he sees emerging from the ruins of laissez-faire capitalism and marxism was in fact a grotesque hybrid of the two. Fascism respected the basic sanctity of capitalist property relations, even as it labored to provide, in an aestheticized form of the marxist promise, an alternative to the fragmentation and alienation engendered by those relations.

The fate of Italian syndicalism, the precursor of fascist corporatism, is instructive. A. James Gregor characterizes the former as an "identifiable Marxist orthodoxy"; despite its special emphases, early syndicalism was "radically antistate, antinationalist, anticlerical, and antimilitarist. The focus of its argument was the class struggle, the irrespressible conflict between the two major protagonists on the contemporary scene: the bourgeoisie and the proletariat."[16] At the 1904 Socialist party congress at Brescia, for example, the syndicalists sought to reaffirm, in opposition to the party's capitulation to parliamentarianism, the "intransigently revolutionary character" of the proletariat organized in economic rather than political associations. Between 1907 and 1914, however, the movement increasingly deviated from both its marxist origins and its revolutionary aims. Enrico Corradini, a radical nationalist, simply denied the relevance of classical marxism to the historical reality of Italian development. Italy was itself a "proletarian nation"; the true class struggle inhered not within the socioeconomic structure of the nation proper, but between the industrialized, imperialist powers of the north and the backward, exploited countries of the south. Syndicalists more faithful to their origins argued the necessity of developing the industrial and economic potential of the peninsula as a prelude to the socialist state of the future. It was the historical task of the bourgeoisie to create an economic order that satisfied all the prerequisites for socialism, but Italy had yet to complete its bourgeois development. Thus, the proletariat was obliged to assume the historic responsibilities of the bourgeoisie, and anything that impaired Italy's economic development was construed as both ahistorical and counterrevolutionary.

But what was to be a transitional and strategic alliance between revolutionary aspirations and bourgeois historic tasks issued in little more than a modified parliamentarianism. In 1926 a national syndicalist system was formed for the regulation and development of all the major areas of economic life. Workers and employers were represented "organically" in different branches of national syndical groupings. In 1928 elections to Parliament were made indirect and corporate; ten years later a new Chamber of Fasces and Corporations formalized (much to Pound's delight) the corporate structure of occupational as opposed to political representation. Fascist corporatism effected a revolution on the level of representation—parliamentary democracies accommodate the abstract citizen; fascist suffrage is predicated on economic or professional function—but only to allow Mussolini to pursue a broadly capitalist path to modernization, all the more effectively for not seeming to abandon the mass base of the movement. (Real wages declined under both Mussolini and Hitler; profits increased).[17] The right to representation stands surrogate for the exercise of meaningful economic power, and the syndicalism that initially defined itself against socialist backsliding emerged as a full-fledged "marxist heresy,"[18] our century's only unique contribution to political philosophy: fascism.

The economic determinants of fascism cannot be slighted, but neither Mussolini nor Hitler attributed much significance to the economic as such. Both conceived of their regimes as belonging to an altogether different and higher plane of existence than laissez-faire liberalism or marxism. (From Mussolini's *Enciclopedia italiana* article: "[M]any of the practical expressions of Fascism—such as party organization, system of education, discipline—can only be understood when considered in relation to its general attitude toward life. A spiritual attitude. Fascism sees in the world not only those superficial, material aspects in which man appears as an individual, standing by himself, self-centered. . . ." In Nazi Germany the tension between the economic and the ideological found grotesque expression in the debate between the "pragmatists," such as Albert Speer, who viewed the concentration camps as a source of unlimited labor, and the "fundamentalists," who advocated the extermination of all "undesirables.")[19] Again, fascism respected the basic sanctity of capitalist property relations even as it labored to provide, in an aestheticized version of the marxist promise, an alternative to the alienation and fragmentation engendered by those relations. Fascism has been characterized as resistance to modernization and as an agent of it,[20] but Italian Fascism was ambiguously both. "Producers," Mussolini remarked, "represent the new Italy, as opposed to the old Italy of balladeers and tour-guides,"[21] and the new Italy was nothing if not invested in exploiting the industrial potential of the peninsula. Yet the new Italy was no less committed to the organic social relations that were themselves casualties of capitalist modernization. Hence the rejection of materialism and prudential egoism, but not the profit motive or private property, in favor of philosophical vitalism, organicism, and collectivism: capitalist property relations wedded to a precapitalist mode of social organization. Mussolini's refusal of the logic of binary opposition—"I am a reactionary and a revolutionary"[22]—is as good a characterization of Italian Fascism as any.

Now Ezra Pound would hardly seem guilty of this aestheticization of the political. On the contrary, he is most frequently accused of contaminating his poetic with a great deal of economic nonsense. The obsession with usury and the history of banking and money—recall those vast stretches of the *Cantos* that we read only reluctantly, if at all—is characteristically viewed as a politicization of art rather than an aestheticization of politics. Far from abandoning aestheticism, however, Pound's long "poem including history" actually renders it militant, in a manner perfectly consistent with the fascism to which it is given. Poststructuralist readings of Pound tend to attribute his fascism and anti-Semitism to a taste for fixity, totalization, and referential stability, everything that registers itself in his resistance to an ethos of tropological mobility. But the resistance is finally only local, and the local belies a generalized capitulation. Pound's economics never progressed beyond a concern with issues of monetary distribution and representation, the "poetics" of money, and the "poetics" became entangled in anti-Semitism, the tropological fantasy of a Jewish conspiracy. (As Theodor Adorno observes, bourgeois anti-Semitism works toward "the concealment of domination in production"; it characteristically focuses on the operations of finance capital, not capitalist modes of production.)[23] And if Pound never progressed beyond a concern with financial surfaces—the signifier rather than the signified, money rather than social labor[24]—it is not clear that we have progressed much beyond Pound.

Fascism "sees its salvation," as Benjamin styles it, "in giving the masses not their right, but instead a chance to express themselves." Poststructuralism, in turn, sees its subversive power in deconstructing expression. That is, the poststructuralist fetishization of the determining power of the signifier risks perpetuating the mystification it seeks to expose: an effective critique of fascism cannot be conducted on the level to which fascism itself would relegate critiques of the established order. Nor is it sufficient to reject Pound's demonology only to perpetuate the cultural and religious determinants of his symbolic economy. The Jew remains, in the discourse of poststructuralism no less than in Pound, *the* privileged figure for figuration, the paradoxical (non)referent for a semiotic order, at once linguistic and economic, which eludes referentiality. And while this is (emphatically) not to impute anti-Semitic motives, conscious or otherwise, to poststructuralism, it is to insist that the poststructuralist identification of the Jew with the nonteleological, nonreferential play of language unwittingly serves to naturalize the traditional (and traditionally disastrous) association of the Jew with the closed semiotics, the infinitely deferred finalities, of capitalist economies.

But what, then, of Eliot, who hovered ambiguously on the periphery of fascist and quasi-fascist movements—there is, for example, his admiration for Charles Maurras—but never fully committed himself to any? Eliot's dissatisfaction with the liberal settlement is at least as extreme as Pound's, yet it issues only in an archaic and archaizing Anglo-Catholicism. Why not fascism? Or communism?

Fascism is predicated on the substitution of an aesthetic consolation for the exercise of real economic power, and the postconversion Eliot is opposed to all forms of aesthetic consolation: he refuses to ask of art what religion alone can provide. Poetry belongs to the order of culture, and culture, in the sense of an autonomous sphere of human activity, is born of tropological displacement, the substitution of the lesser for the greater. Pater's aestheticism, for example, is but a diminished substitute for Arnold's humanism, and Arnold's humanism but a diminished substitute for religion. Pound is committed to the construction of the fascist city of man; Eliot awaits the coming of the City of God. (Hence he rejects all terrestrial fulfillments, fascist or communist.) The most poetry can hope to accomplish is to lead us, as Beatrice led Dante, to a place where something that is not poetry can be revealed. Words toward the Word, but a crucial synapse separates the two.

Eliot's ambitions for poetry are modest because his hopes for religion are extravagant: he attempts to revive for the modern world the premodern, precapitalist experience of the primacy of the theological, the properly collective energies of an older dispensation. But if religion is to underwrite a new communalism—*religio:* a binding together—it will be at the cost of all secular or aesthetic totalizations. The reconciliation of opposites effected by the romantic symbol, for instance, must be acknowledged for what it is, the parody form of the mystical union in the body of Christ. And it is here that Eliot and poststructuralism unexpectedly find common cause. The shared opposition to tropes of achieved interrelatedness, aesthetic totalizations, betrays a massive devaluation of cultural labor, a deeply antiutopian impulse. Eliot would have us see things as they are, see that they cannot be otherwise, and see that they will never suffice. Poststructuralism would have us see things as they are, see that they cannot be otherwise, and celebrate the impasse as the "radical."

Consider Slavoj Žižek's characterization of Ernesto Laclau and Chantal Mouffe's widely influential *Hegemony & Socialist Theory:*

It is the merit of Ernest [*sic*] Laclau and Chantal Mouffe that they have . . . developed a theory of the social field founded on such a notion of antagonism—on an acknowledgement of an original "trauma," an impossible kernel which resists symbolization, totalization, symbolic integration. Every attempt at symbolization-totalization comes afterwards: it is an attempt to suture an original cleft—an attempt which is, in the last resort, by definition doomed to failure. They emphasize that we must not be "radical" in the sense of aiming at a radical solution: we always live in an interspace and in borrowed time; every solution is provisional and temporary, a kind of postponing of a fundamental impossibility. The term "radical democracy" [part of the subtitle of Laclau and Mouffe's text] is thus to be taken somehow paradoxically: it is precisely *not* "radical" in the sense of pure, true democracy; its radical character implies, on the contrary, that we can save democracy only by *taking into account its own radical impossibility*. Here we can see how we have reached the opposite extreme of the traditional Marxist standpoint: in traditional Marxism, the global solution-revolution is the condition of the effective solution of all particular problems, while here every provisional, temporarily successful solution of a particular problem entails an acknowledgement of the global radical deadlock, impossibility, the acknowledgement of a fundamental antagonism.[25]

Žižek defines his own project in opposition to poststructuralism, particularly of the Derridean variety, but his sympathetic account of Laclau and Mouffe's theorization of the social field locates him firmly within the poststructuralist/postmodernist camp. Indeed, it is among the considerable merits of Slavoj Žižek that he makes explicit the political agenda of a movement that announces itself as the death knell of western metaphysics, but which, for all practical purposes, serves only to restrict the scope and efficacy of human action.

Radical democracy reaches the "opposite extreme of the traditional Marxist standpoint" for the simple reason that it begins from the opposite premise. Marx warns against a specious or overrapid universalization, a confusion of specific class and general human interests. Žižek cautions against an *"over-rapid historicization,"* a refusal of universalization that "makes us blind to the real kernel which returns as the same through diverse historicizations/symbolizations":

All the different attempts to attach this phenomenon [the demonic obverse of twentieth-century civilization, the concentration camp] to a concrete image ("Holocaust," "Gulag" . . .), to reduce it to a product of a concrete social order (Fascism, Stalinism . . .)—what are they if not so many attempts to elude the fact that we are dealing here with the "real" of our civilization which returns as the same traumatic kernel in all social systems? (50)[26]

But what is this if not a lyricism of evil? Eliot regretted the absence of a sense of original sin in the modern world, but Žižek (and others) effectively recuperate it for the postmodern. Certainly the inevitable failure of human effort before "the global radical deadlock" could as easily be attributed to the legacy of our first parents, to the theological "real" of our civilization which returns as the same through diverse historicizations and symbolizations. In any case, to pursue a "global solution-revolution" is to forget that all such projects are always already implicated in the totalitarianism that attends "symbolization, totalization, symbolic integration." Žižek's stated ambition is to "save" democracy by "taking into account its own radical impossibility." He succeeds, however, only in "saving" the term *radical* for the cause of local reformism. "Radical democracy" requires the threat of totalitarianism/totalization, yet neither fascism nor Stalinism exhausts the field of historical atrocities, and the one cannot be unproblematically reduced to the other.

Like Churchill, Žižek is committed to the politics of the lesser evil. Democracy may be "the worst of all possible systems," but, as the maxim has it, there is "no other system which would be better" (5). No matter, then, that the liberal settlement is far from perfect; given the available alternative—and when the middle is flanked by analogous totalitarianisms of the right and left, there is only one—the worst of all possible systems is easily recuperable as the best. Options are restricted in order to guard against the descent into totalitarianism—"the greatest mass murders and holocausts have always been perpetrated in the name of man as harmonious being, of a New Man without antagonistic tension" (5)—but the logic that informs Churchill's maxim has its own history. "Better Hitler than Léon Blum," as French businessmen were fond of saying in 1935.[27] (Blum, a socialist, threatened established economic interests with little more than an indigenous version of Roosevelt's New Deal.) Pound's Hitler is Blakean, "furious from perception,"[28] but Nazism was not above recommending itself as a simple stay against bolshevism, and de Man's wartime journalism is utterly innocent of visionary longing. The willful impoverishment of the utopian imagination is not an effective check against totalitarianism; the injunction is, after all, "never again," not "nothing to be done." Yet even "radical democracy" is committed to the impoverishment, for its claims are intelligible only in the context of a thoroughly fetishized and undifferentiated understanding of totalization/totalitarianism.

Fascism proper emerged as an object of intellectual inquiry in opposition to the cold war hegemony of "totalitarianism theory," the demonization of a thoroughly Stalinized communism as fascism by another name. (Hannah Arendt's *Origins of Totalitarianism* remains the most influential articulation of the theory; Nolte's *Three Faces of Fascism* and the early volumes of the journal *Das Argument* were the first significant challenges to it.)[29] By all reports the cold war is no longer with us, although its ideological agenda apparently survives intact: a theoretical position that indiscriminately takes arms against totalization as such (and this despite a professed commitment to the logic of *différance*) necessarily rehearses the cold war conflation of left and right, the better to preserve the "radicalism" of the middle. Again, it is to Žižek's credit that he acknowledges as much. "The opposite extreme of the traditional Marxist standpoint" is an antimarxism and not, as others would have it, a post-marxism. But an unwelcome irony passes unnoticed. The antimarxism that fueled the rise of European fascism continues to inform the contemporary critique of it.[30]

A case in point: it is not difficult to discern in de Man's early journalism consonance between the operations of fascistic power and the once most conventional of aesthetic categories, unity, coherence, teleology, and the like. It in no way follows, however, that the now equally conventional challenges to those categories—*différance,* dissemination, indeterminacy— are not consonant with their sociopolitical context. De Man's defenders can be conceded their central point: the mature work functions within the totality of the corpus as a retroactive critique of the earlier commitment to "symbolization-totalization," the earlier complicity with "the rhetoric of totalitarianism." But it does so at the cost of a radical anachronism. Fredric Jameson notes that the call to arms with which Jean-François Lyotard concludes *The Postmodern Condition*—"Let us wage war on totality . . . let us activate the differences"—has issued in a war that is itself well-nigh total.[31] The ability to think the political as a whole, with the curious exception of totalizing attacks on totalization, is itself a casualty of the decentered world of postnational consumer capitalism. The war has already been won. That battles continue to be fought (or staged) suggests that the enemy is not, as is sometimes claimed, a residual or innate fascism of the mind but the possibility of a collective praxis, a "global solution-revolution."[32]

Laclau and Mouffe argue that it is "the incomplete character of every totality" that leads them "to abandon, as a terrain of analysis, the premise of *'society'* as a sutured and self-defined totality. 'Society' is not a valid object of discourse. There is no single underlying principle fixing—and hence constituting—the whole field of differences" (111). Where the exploded concept of "the social" once was, a *"field of discursivity"* now is:

> This term indicates the form of its relation with every concrete discourse: it determines at the same time the necessarily discursive character of any object, and the impossibility of any given discourse to implement a final suture. On this point, our analysis meets up with a number of contemporary currents of thought which—from Heidegger to Wittgenstein—have insisted on the impossibility of fixing ultimate meanings. Derrida, for example, starts from a radical break in the history of the concept of structure, occurring at the moment in which the centre—the *transcendental signified* in its multiple forms . . .—is abandoned, and with it the possibility of fixing a meaning which underlies the flow of differences. (111–12)

How a system that constitutively produces differences eludes its own totalizing systemicity is not clear, although the ideological interests served by the substitution of overdetermined differences for a determinate antagonism is. It is entirely possible, as I have suggested, "to do the police in different voices." More often than not, however, the police state is invoked in order to construe the polyphonic as the "radical."

Consider the academic success of Mikhail Bakhtin's celebration of dialogism, heteroglossia, and the like, the positive ideal implicit in Geoffrey Hartman's characterization of *Mein Kampf* as monological. In the context in which Bakhtin's work was originally written and circulated, if not always published, the subversive power it attributes to the literary, particularly the novel, is plausible enough. Translated into the very different milieu of the liberal West, however, it quickly comes to underwrite the status quo. An understanding of literature as a polyphonic play of voices can do nothing to disrupt the parliamentarianism—Marx terms it a form of "cretinism"—that is at the heart of the liberal settlement. On the contrary, the contention that the novel is all generosity and accommodation, definable only in its resistance to definition, is itself the most compelling evidence of its bourgeois investments, of its collusion with the class that does not want to be named, or that would be known only in its resistance to nomination or definition.[33] The genre-that-is-not-one, the aesthetic dispensation that eludes ideological determination, merely returns to the class-that-is-not-one, the political settlement that embraces and enfolds all, an idealized image of its own infinitely plural self. To speak "somewhat paradoxically," in the manner of Žižek: the celebration of "open form" easily comes to underwrite a perfectly closed economy.

As does the political agenda of "radical democracy," the commitment to cultural practices that advance the interests of discrete "vocabularies," "perspectives," or "subject positions." Eliot, for example, would find little to object to in this politics of the local. *Notes Toward the Definition of Culture* argues for the preservation of marginal communities and peoples (Jews excepted) over and against the tendencies toward capitalist homogenization. Jameson, however, raises the "embarrassing historical possibility" that the contemporary tolerance of difference as a social fact—or, as I would formulate it, the contemporary fetishization of difference as a theoretical enterprise—is itself perverse testimony to the final triumph of the regime of the norm.[34] The theoretical projects now conducted in the name of difference seem very much of a piece; their sheer interchangeability suggests that they function best at a certain remove from the pressure any specific, concrete difference might be expected to exert. (Eve Sedgwick notes that "deconstruction, founded as a very science of *differ(e/a)nce,* has both so fetishized the idea of difference and so vaporized its possible embodiments that its most thoroughgoing practitioners are the last people to whom one would now look for help in thinking about particular differenc*es*. The same thing seems likely to prove true of theorists of postmodernism.")[35] Capitalism presupposes the production of specialists and the balkanization of knowledge; the elision or demonization of any global perspective can only serve the interests of an economic order that is itself defined by globalism, and so by a certain immunity to micropolitical "subversion." At best the politics of the local, the discourse of *différance,* compensates for what an increasingly global and globalizing socioeconomic order fails to provide, which is precisely differences that make a difference. At worst it actively works toward the expanded reproduction of that order by stigmatizing as "totalizing," and so "totalitarian," any effective challenge to it. The ubiquitous conviction that the working class is incapable of socialist consciousness or action is the most effective agent of ideological domination now commanded by capital. Not, however, the most refined. That distinction belongs to the thematization of class consciousness as a reductive, if not overtly reactionary, "totalization."[36]

The historical uniqueness of capitalism resides in its status as an "antisociety." Unlike the precapitalist world that Eliot sought to revive, which reproduced itself through various forms of cohesion or collectivity, the logic of capital is dispersive and atomizing.[37] But all this eludes poststructuralist scrutiny, which is incapable of acknowledging, little less subverting, a socioeconomic order that perpetuates itself through recourse to the logic of difference. It thus serves to reconcile us to the various impoverishments—broadly speaking, the want of collective energies and teleological purpose—that Pound and Eliot, in their different ways, sought to redress. The question asked of fascism proper must, then, be extended to the poststructuralist critique of it: How does a potentially revolutionary politics (for poststructuralism clearly intends as much) come to be recontained as an apology for business as usual?

2

EZRA POUND
The Poetics of Money

Ezra Pound translated poetry, a great deal of it. His command of the dozen or so languages from which he worked was not always, perhaps, everything it might have been, yet he remains among the most distinguished of modernist translators.[1] Pound cannot, then, be easily characterized as inimical to translation, and my attempt to do so in what follows might at first seem counterfactual, if not willfully perverse. Indeed, so great was his enthusiasm for translation that, at least in 1915, his utter innocence of the language to be translated in no way impeded his efforts at the same.

From which innocence came, of course, the notorious howlers of *Cathay*. "The River Song," to cite but one example, is a conflation of two poems, the result of Pound's apparent failure to recognize that the discursive title of a second poem was precisely that. Yet in what Pound might have characterized as its proper place, the original context of its appearance, *Cathay* was remarkable not only for its semantic blunders, its frequently inspired mistranslations, but for the fact that it made reference to anything remotely resembling a source text, semantic content that could in theory be translated. Composition "à la mode chinoise" was widely prevalent in the early days of the vers libre movement; Pound was unique only in having made contact, in however mediated a fashion, with an actual Chinese poem.[2] And even for Pound, the purpose of *Cathay* was not to transport an oriental "tenor" into an occidental "vehicle" but to renew the resources of the native medium itself, a point that Ernest Fenollosa, from whose notebooks Pound worked, makes explicit: "[T]he purpose of

16

poetical translation is the poetry, not the verbal definitions in dictionaries."[3]

There is an obvious paradox here: I have said that the purpose of translation was the renewal of the native medium, yet that renewal, as defined by Pound in particular and the imagist movement in general, was "the direct presentation of the thing," the contention, now much ridiculed by advanced theory, that a poem builds its effects out of things it sets before the mind's eyes by naming them. The renewal was thought necessary, again by Pound in particular and the imagist movement in general, given the rhetorical haze to which the late romantics had reduced the language. It is difficult to know, however, how the antidote, the reputed rigor and clarity of all things oriental, could be effective, at least given the situation as diagnosed by Pound. For *Cathay* makes its heliotropic progress to the Occident by way of translation, and it is not clear how translation, which presupposes a discursive or linguistic source, can revive the resources of a medium concerned with the direct presentation of a prediscursive or non-linguistic "thing." Nor is it clear how translation, which characteristically encounters its greatest difficulty with names, particularly proper names, can serve the interests of a poetic intent on "building its effects out of things it presents before the mind's eyes by naming them." (Pound takes considerable delight in noting that the phonetic translation of his name into Japanese "rendered back *ad verbum* into our maternal speech . . . gives for its meaning 'This picture of a phallus costs ten yen.'")[4] In "Separation on the River Kiang," Pound translates the common noun *kiang*, "river," as a proper noun, the name of a river, and he renders the common noun *ko-jin* as a proper name. The character he thereby invents, moreover, travels westward, which is the conventional movement of translation, of the *translatio imperii* and the *translatio studii*, although in the original the character who is not so named travels eastward. The blunders are relatively insignificant in themselves, and I introduce them here only to suggest the nature of Pound's quarrel (to risk a pre-posterous formulation) with the most influential of contemporary theories of translation: I mean poststructuralism, which posits a tradition of translation, the better to deconstruct it, that has as its ambition the unimpeded transference of semantic content. Yet if *Cathay* is remarkable in having made contact with an actual Chinese poem, it is totally unremarkable in its serene indifference to the integrity of semantic content. As Pound says of "logopeia," a word he uses in reference to *Homage to Sextus Propertius*, yet another of his translations that is untroubled by the priority of the signified, "Logopeia does not translate; though the attitude of mind it expresses may pass through a paraphrase" (*LE* 25).

The attitude of mind that characterizes translation as but incidentally concerned with paraphrasable content may seem idiosyncratic, yet it reflects the standard practice, if not the highly idealized theory, of translation in the postmedieval West. Keats's claim that he had never breathed the "pure serene of Homer's air" till he "heard Chapman speak out loud and clear" is orthodox ("On First Looking into Chapman's Homer"); Matthew Arnold's objection that Keats had not breathed anything other than Chapman's air (Keats had no Greek) is merely pedantic.[5] "Traduttore, traditore": the fame of the maxim is belied by the practice. True, current discontent with the implications of the word *translation*—its much bemoaned but largely illusory commitment to the priority of the signified— has led Derrida to advance "transformation" as the more adequate term.[6] This strategic mistranslation of *translation* is intended as both innovative and subversive, and so it is. But it is the innovation that founds the practice of vernacular translation (of which more presently) in the postmedieval West. Poststructuralism celebrates the ethos of metaphoric displacement as the destabilizing essence of all language; Pound descries it as a specific historical development. Pound's position is not now the fashion, but for that reason alone it can be placed in useful opposition to the current orthodoxy, binary opposition being itself a target of that orthodoxy.

Derrida has a point. The ideology of *translatio* understood as transformation—*translatio* is Quintilian's translation, or "transformation," of the Greek word *metaphora* (*Institutio Oratoria* 8.6)—once functioned in a progressive cause. In the hands of the early humanists, for example, it served to relocate the source of linguistic gravity and value, in opposition to the "tyranny" of a "transcendental signified," in the morphologies of national grammars, in language understood as the material production of sound. But the ideology of *translatio* has both an insurgent and a dominant phase, both a progressive and a reactionary historical life. And in its ascendent phase translation is one with the ideology of the personal and the competitive, the ethos of an emerging bourgeois order. Derrida holds the "transcendental signified" to be "the origin or alibi of all oppression in the world,"[7] but surely oppression also inheres in an order, at once linguistic and economic, in which signs are reduced to tokens without referential force or value. "From its servile role in which it [money] appears as mere medium of exchange, it suddenly changes into the lord and god in the world of commodities":[8] this is Marx, but it might easily be Pound. The displacement of the proper place of money is not a joy or fatality intrinsic to the nature of representation but a historically determined and motivated phenomenon. The emergence of the specific materialities of money, like "the symbols for words," have a history.[9] The ascendancy of what Pound terms "unconvertable paper" (Canto LXXXVIII),[10] for instance, corresponds historically to the development of abstract or nonreferential art.[11] Pound's economic project, which is to return the signs of wealth to their material basis in human productivity, in work done and goods produced, is one with his aesthetic project, which is to reestablish the lost connection between the order of words and the world, to repair the chasm between signifier and signified. He is thus opposed to the fetishization of tropological displacement, the compulsive mobility, that defines the ideology of *translatio* in its dominant phase.

I begin with a brief consideration of the emergence of vernacular translation in the early modern West. An exhaustive reading of the history of translation is beyond the scope of the present study—which is to say, beyond the competence of its author. Yet some rudimentary sense of context is necessary, if only to specify the nature of Pound's poetic radicalism, which, in a paradox sadly familiar to students of modernism, proves compatible with the most reactionary of politics. I address the tension within the *Cantos* between an Odyssean celebration of the portative and a Dantean or Confucian commitment to proper names and places, from which the latter emerges triumphant. Like Horkheimer and Adorno, Pound views (or comes to view) Odysseus as the "prototype of the bourgeois individual," that is, "the individual responsible to himself."[12] Odysseus succeeds, in Pound's astute reading of the poem, by virtue of a form of portative violence, polytropic language, in appropriating the goods of others. Dante's Ulysses, however, meets a watery grave. He too is a prototype of the bourgeois individual, although one who functions within a "communal society . . . still struggling to absorb the moral consequences of money and credit mechanisms into its religious view of the world."[13] The tension with Pound's poem is not, then, simply formal; rather, it is predicated on the clash between incompatible economies, antithetical understandings of the ethos of *translatio*. And since translation frequently involves the appropriation or "carrying over" of alien cultural goods and accomplishments (from the Latin *transfero*, "to transport" or "carry across"), I conclude my first section with a brief consideration of Pound's sinophilia, which represents an attempt, however problematic, to escape the ethnocentricism of western poetic practice.

I next turn to the Pisan Cantos, arguably the most enduring of Pound's accomplishments, albeit for the rather curious reason (or so I argue) that the lyric interlude heralds the collapse of the political ambitions of the poem that contains it. The late romanticism to which Pound was heir tended to reduce poetry to what *Hugh Selwyn Mauberley* calls the status of "friend and comforter."[14] If poetry bears any relation to the historical, it is on the order of the compensatory or redemptive. Jürgen Habermas characterizes bourgeois art as "the refuge for a satisfaction, even if only virtual, of those needs that have become, as it were, illegal in the material life process of . . . society."[15] Art consoles for what history fails to provide. And in the Pisan Cantos Pound translates what he had previously believed to be the historically possible, the construction of the fascist city of man, into the poetically plangent, a thoroughly metaphorical Italy of the mind. The romantic bower becomes the modernist prison—Pound wrote the poem in a cage six by six and a half feet—but the continuity with the self-enclosed logic of lyric is otherwise intact. Pound thought poetry should make something happen; he believed it was, or should be, of practical use to someone. His entire poetic, the apprentice work excepted, might be characterized as an attempt to recover the priority of use over exchange value for the modern world. But the Pisan Cantos (to put it badly) *not* only makes nothing happen; it abandons the desire to do anything. The extent to which the poem can be read as a palinode, as a recantation of the fascist project, has been grossly exaggerated. The lyric sequence admits to sins of omission, not commission. But it does offer assurances that it no longer has any designs on the world. It is thus greeted by the world with what *Mauberley* calls "well-gowned approbation / Of literary effort" (*P* 196), the Bollingen Prize in poetry.

Now there is obviously something problematic—or, again, willfully perverse—in advocating the wisdom, poetic or otherwise, of a virulent fascist and anti-Semite. The aesthetic cannot be divorced from the politics, and the full horror of the latter, to repeat a point that bears repeating, needs to be acknowledged. But the acknowledgment should not, indeed, cannot assume our own distance from, our innocence of, a politics that we have now happily left behind—modernism for the other people. Poststructuralist readings of Pound, for example, tend to construe his fascism and anti-Semitism as one with his resistance to the "flowers of rhetoric," particularly metaphor and its usurious excess. And as poststructuralism can hardly be accused of resistance to rhetoric, least of all to its own, it establishes its distance from Pound's politics in the very act of explicating them. But Pound's anti-Semitism and fascism are best understood not as a resistance to metaphor but as a failure to read or critique the culture of metaphor other than metaphorically. Pound's hell betrays a thoroughly tropological relation to the actual. And in this we are still his contemporaries.

Translatio, Translation, Transportation

Leonardo Bruni's *De Interpretatione Recta* (ca. 1426), the first formal treatise on translation in the Renaissance, argues for an ethics of translation in which the source text is "transformed" by the expressive fabric of the new; it thus introduces the verb *transformare* into theoretical discourse.[16] Derrida reintroduces it. The movement conventionally termed "interlingual translation," the movement *from* one language to another, Derrida renames the systematic "transformation" of one language *by* another.[17] And in so doing, he extends rather than challenges the orthodox understanding of translation in the postmedieval West. As Gianfranco Folena observes: if *translatare,* the common medieval word for "translate," implies a labor of fidelity to the signified, the translation of *translatare* into the neologisms of fourteenth-century civic humanism (*traducere, tradurre*) both implies and enacts an ideology in which the center of linguistic gravity is relocated in the morphologies of national vernaculars.[18] Derrida argues that "in effect, the theme of a transcendental signified took shape within the horizon of an absolutely pure, transparent, and universal translatability."[19] In historical fact, however, the practice of vernacular translation, as opposed to translation from Greek and Arabic sources into Latin, took shape within the horizon of national and individual challenges to the theme of a transcendental signified. Luther uses the verbs *übersetzen,* "to translate," and *verdeutschen,* "to Germanize," more or less indiscriminately: vernacular translation is at once the logical and historical analogue of an understanding of language as personal and national property. It became possible only with the waning of the Catholic and communal structures of the Latin Middle Ages, with the emergence of a bourgeois ethic of the original, the competitive, the individual, and the national.

To the extent that the political ideology of the Middle Ages was dominated by an Augustinian Neoplatonism that acknowledged no continuity between the cities of God and man, translation remained but a theoretical possibility. Eugene Vance notes that the Augustinian premise that true knowledge is a priori and is disclosed only from within, that language is properly mental rather than corporeal, cannot logically prohibit translation.[20] The Word of God might be housed in any historical language, as the Word is strictly transcendent in relation to all language, including Holy Scripture, which contains *signa translata,* "transferred" words or figurative language. Yet if Augustine does not (or cannot) explicitly prohibit translation, the dichotomy that structures his thought, as Vance also notes, effectively does: to proclaim the adequacy of the vernacular in relation to the sacred languages of Hebrew, Greek, or Latin is implicitly to diminish the distance separating the cities of God and man. Translation of the logos into the vernacular required a rather different understanding of the nature and validity of worldly activity, and changes in the ideology of translation were in fact closely linked to changes in the political attitudes of the Middle Ages. The assimilation of Aristotle's *Politics,* which was well under way by the time of Aquinas' commentary on it, was a decisive event. Aristotle insists that man is by nature a political animal, that the order of language plays a determining role in the order of politics.[21] Language, particularly the vernacular, attains a new legitimacy and a new corporeal center of gravity. To cite but two examples, both from Erasmus: the treatise on rhetorical *copia* associates verbal opulence attained through translation, especially from the Greek, with the recognition that material bounteousness, the art of getting wealth, is a natural and legitimate objective of the political order, a point documented by Terence Cave; and Erasmus' own translation of the Greek *logos* in John 1 by the word "sermo," as opposed to Jerome's "verbum," suggests a notion of divine oratory as colloquial fraternalism in Christ, expressed not only through the inner man, as it would be in a system of Augustinian Neoplatonism, but through the institutions of national grammars, a point argued by Marjorie Boyle.[22] Erasmus would not, then, accept the Derridean contention that "presiding over classical notions" of translation are "the separability of style and thought and the priority of the signified over the signifier," although he would have little difficulty with the notion that the richness of discourse resides, at least in part, in the fabric of the signifier.[23] True, Erasmus stands at the forefront of a new spirit of civic humanism, but then the historical specificity of Erasmus' position is precisely the point. Benedict Anderson argues that all "the great classical communities conceived of themselves as cosmically central, through the medium of a sacred language linked to a superterrestrial order of power. Accordingly, the stretch of written Latin, Pali, Arabic, or Chinese was, in theory, unlimited."[24] The print vernaculars of the early modern West could not pretend to the same universality, to which even Latin could only pretend; its universality always was a theoretical fiction. Yet in establishing a unified field of exchange below the level of the universal but above the idiosyncracies of spoken dialects, the new vernaculars effectively reached (or created) an unprecedented reading public. Between 1522 and 1546 some 430 editions of Luther's "Germanized" Bible translations, whole or in part, appeared in print; Luther himself became "the first best selling author *so known*."[25] Church Latin had been a truth language, the exclusive property of a trans-European intelligentsia. Luther's German was national and personal property. The translation of the former into the latter, the "making German" of the Word, was manifestly not a simple labor of fidelity to the signified.

But this is not the whole of Derrida's critique of what he takes to be the theme of "an absolutely pure, transparent, and unequivocal translatability." For if Derrida would rename or retranslate the word *translation* as "transformation," much in the manner that the early humanists translated *translatare* as "traducere" or "tradurre" or Luther substituted "verdeutschen" for *übersetzen,* so too would he redefine the problem of translation *between* texts or languages as a problem already *within* a single text or language. From the antithetical senses of the Greek word *pharmakon,* which means both "poison" and "remedy," Derrida argues that the "irreducible difficulty of translation" is "inherent in its very principle, situated less in the passage from one language to another . . . than already . . . in the tradition between Greek and Greek."[26] But again Derrida extends and legitimates a tradition that he alleges to challenge. Quintilian's translation of the Greek term *metaphora* as "translatio," for example, already implies the imbrication of "interlingual translation," or "the passage *from* one language *to* another," and "intralingual translation," or difference *within* the same language. Metaphor is *translatio* or translation; in Aristotle's formulation metaphor is the transference of a name that is "alien" or "alias" (*allotrois*), the "giving the thing a name that belongs to something else; the transference being either from genus to species, or from species to genus, or from species to species, or on grounds of analogy" (*Poetics* 1457b.6–9). Augustine's reflections on the presence of *signs translata* within Holy Writ, moreover, argue the imbrication of inter- and intralingual translation. The problem of housing the Word in any historical language, and hence the problem of translation between languages, cannot be divorced from the problem of figurative displacement within language. And if this is to argue the continuity of poststructuralism with a tradition it alleges to subvert, it is also a necessary prelude to my attempt to specify the scope of Pound's poetic radicalism. For it is against this ideology of the portative—as it is inscribed in both interlingual translation or translation proper and intralingual translation or metaphorical displacement—that Pound advocates a poetics and politics of tropological stability, of fixed addresses and proper names. "Name 'em, don't bullshit *ME*" (Canto LX-XIV): it is an injunction that Pound takes in earnest.

Yet Pound begins the *Cantos* with a translation, or with a translation of a translation, or with a translation of a translation of the great poem of *translatio,* the story of Odysseus Polytropos, the man of many turns or tropes: "And then went to the ship, / Set keel to breakers, forth on the godly sea . . ." Pound's source for Canto I is not the *Odyssey* but Andreas Divus' sixteenth-century translation or transformation of it. From Homer's Greek, through Divus' Latin, to Pound's archaic English, which "makes it new" by recovering what is old—the *Cantos* opens with an implicit thematization of the poetics of translation, the ostensibly self-effacing act by which the living give voice to the dead:[27]

> Pallor upon me, cried to my men for more beasts;
> Slaughtered the herds, sheep slain of bronze;
> Poured ointment, cried to the gods,
> To Pluto the strong, and praised Proserpine;
> Unsheathed the narrow sword,
> I sat to keep off the impetuous impotent dead,
> Till I should hear Tiresias.

The slaughter of sheep, the blood of the living: this is the precondition of the translation, the carrying over, of the voice of the dead.

But as with "On First Looking into Chapman's Homer," in which to experience the "Homeric serene" is to hear Chapman "speak out loud and clear," it is Divus, not Homer, who "speaks" in Canto I, who refuses, as the canto puts it, to "lie quiet." Pound is not subject to the critique of a Matthew Arnold, for unlike Keats or his own earlier self, he was fully capable of working from the original. He nevertheless chooses to work from Divus' highly corrupt Latin translation, as if to question the commitment of translation to the recuperation and transmission of "pure signifieds." Divus' poem, which is something of a sixteenth-century crib, bears only a tangential relation to the Homeric original—if the Homeric poem can be so characterized—and Pound's poem, which is dominated by the rhythms and diction of "The Seafarer," has only a tangential relation to Divus'. Indeed, one of the few lines in the canto that has a more or less direct relation to its source is Pound's translation of Divus' mistranslation of what is now considered an interpolated line, "A second time? why? man of ill star," the apostrophe by which Tiresias greets Odysseus in the underworld.

This curious suggestion of a double or previous descent, as if Odysseus traveled to the underworld with some regularity, might be explained as a simple accident of textual transmission. Divus unwittingly mistranslates an already corrupt text, which Pound perpetuates by translating Divus's mistranslation accurately.[28] But the accidents of textual transmission cannot always be distinguished from highly willful mistranslation, and in another poem no less innocent of the Homeric original than Pound's, Odysseus does descend to the underworld for a second time, although this time to stay. In book 26 of the *Inferno* Ulysses is placed in hell for the sin of *translatio,* understood as both the abuse of language or false counseling and the refusal of proper place, the inability to contain desire within the limits of the known or named or historical world:[29]

> Quando
> mi diparti' da Circe, che sottrasse
> me più d'un anno là presso a Gaeta,
> prima che sì Enëa la nomasse,
> né dolcezza di figlio, né la pieta
> del vecchio padre, né 'l debito amore
> lo qual dovea Penelopè far lieta,
> vincer potero dentro a me l'ardore
> ch'i' ebbi a divenir del mondo esperto
> e de li vizi umani e del valore. . . .[30]

Pound's highly indirect allusion to Odysseus'/Ulysses' second descent into the underworld suggests that the economy of *translatio* cannot be divorced from the larger economies it serves. In Canto LXVIII Pound registers John Adams's critique of Pope's translation of the Phaiakian episode in the *Odyssey,* which strategically makes Alkinoos, who is in Homer one prince among many, into an absolute monarch, and hence into an apology for absolutism in general: "There is nothing like it in the original / Mr Pope has conformed it to the notions / of Englishmen." And what is true of Pope's relation to Homer is no less true of Dante's; he too "conforms" things to the notions and interests of his own cultural situation. (Dante may have been innocent of the Homeric original, but he did know that there was nothing like death by water in it.) The *Commedia* posits an "economics of reference"—Ulysses and the false counselors are near-neighbors of the falsifiers of coins—that is at the furthest remove from an Odyssean ethos of unrestricted mobility. Indeed, there is a sense in which Ulysses must suffer death by water if Dante's cosmos is to remain intact. M. D. Chenu notes that the Roman Empire, which extended to the end of the world (*mundus*), was also the decisive episode at the end of the march of history (*saeculum*). All was providential preparation for the age of Christ; all was meaningful in terms of the temporality and geography of salvation. "When the ocean frontier was breached," Chenu argues, "history as well as geography changed; the medieval period was over."[31] But if Dante establishes his distance from the Odyssean—which is also, as it were, his defense against what was to come—Pound's indirect allusion to Dante marks a certain division within his poem. Like the volume *Cathay,* in which interlingual translation or translation proper is used against intra-lingual translation or metaphorical displacement, Pound's first canto can be read as both an Odyssean celebration of the portative and as Dantean containment of the excesses of metaphorical desire.

It is a tension that informs much of Pound's massive poem. Philip Kuberski allegorizes the *Cantos* as "a conflict between an Odyssean path of errancy, accumulation, and fortunate but undesigned homecoming, and a Confucian drive for directness, reduction, and unwavering purpose."[32] Kuberski's allegory, in turn, might be further allegorized as a conflict between an Odyssean misnaming or refusal of the name—"ou tis," "no one," as Odysseus calls himself in his confrontation with Polyphemus— and a Confucian drive toward *cheng ming*, the "principle of the rectification of names," which Pound gives as "Name for name, king for king" (Canto LXXXIX). Or, had I focused on the proleptic force of the Ovidian Canto II rather than the Homeric Canto I, the poem might be allegorized, following Herbert Schneidau, as a conflict between "two great values . . . derived from 'the tradition'—medieval exact distinctions and Ovidian multiplicity."[33]

A poem that eschews any "orderly Dantescan rising" (Canto LXXIV), that celebrates "the great periplum" that is wandering without foreknowledge, would seem to be of the party of Odysseus Polytropos. For Hanno, for Columbus, and presumably for Pound (even the Pound of the internment at Pisa), the Pillars of Hercules, the limit of the known or named world in Dante, are but the site of a new departure: "'[T]he great periplum brings in the stars to our shore.' / You who have passed the pillars and outward from Herakles / when Lucifer fell in N. Carolina" (Canto LXXIV). Appropriately, the poem that celebrates Odyssean errancy, the journey rather than its destination, also participates in the organizational principles of the *Odyssey*. Rock Drill concludes with a brief narrative of the breakup of Odysseus' raft and his return to the land of the Phaiakians, which is also the narrative site of the first canto. It thus binds Cantos I through XCV within the circle of Odysseus' wanderings, the *nostos* or return that is the most conventional of metaphors for aesthetic form. Yet the conclusion of Rock Drill—"That the wave crashed, whirling the raft, then / Tearing the oar from his hand, / broke mast and yard-arm / And he was drawn down under wave" (Canto XCV)—also suggests death by water, which is the fate of Dante's Ulysses. Thrones opens, like Canto I, with an incident taken from Homer, the story of the charmed scarf that Odysseus throws back into the water in an effort to propitiate *nostos*. It concludes, however, with an act analogous to Dante's abandonment of Virgil, although it is Homer who now occupies the position of Virgil: "You in the dinghy (piccioletta) astern there!" (Canto CIX). As Dante leaves Virgil when he moves from Purgatory to Paradise—"O voi che siete in piccioletta barca" (*Paradiso* 2.1)—so Pound leaves Homer and Odysseus as he moves toward his own Paradise. The Dante who enters the first canto only in the most indirect and mediated fashion—"A second time? why?"—emerges at the conclusion of Thrones fully in command of the field. And thereafter Odysseus is not a significant presence.

The triumph of Dante over Homer is ideological, not simply formal; indeed, the *Cantos* is open to purely formal analysis only to the extent that the poem fails in its ambition. Much has been written on the relationship between the accomplishments of the high modernists and the formalism of

New Critical aesthetics, but no poem has ever less resembled a well-wrought urn than the *Cantos,* and perhaps no poem, certainly no modern poem, has ever labored to intervene so overtly in the affairs of the world. (It is thus unfortunate that Pound's definition of epic, "a poem including history," has gained such general currency.[34] The *Cantos* does not simply "include" history as so much inert subject matter; rather, the poem hopes to effect a historical revolution.) The teleology specified in Canto LXXVII, for example, is a practical good: "Things have ends (or scopes) and beginnings." The various protagonists who come to occupy the forefront of the poem—Malatesta, Niccolo d'Este, Kung, John Adams—engage in a distinctly non-Odyssean form of "straight moving," which is one with their commitment to the work of historical renovation:

> pater patriae
> the man who at certain points
> made us
> at certain points
> saved us
> by fairness, honesty and straight moving
> ARRIBA ADAMS (Canto LXII)

Like Kung, Adams has no "twisty thoughts,"[35] no Odyssean propensity for the polytropic; rather, he endeavors to facilitate direct transmission, transportation, to make possible an orderly and honest "carrying over." Like Kung, moreover, who "demanded or commended a type of perception, a kind of transmission of knowledge obtainable only from . . . concrete manifestation" (*GK* 28), Adams is pragmatic, concerned with the efficacy of ideas, not their formal coherence or elegance. And, like Kung or Adams, so too Pound: "I have tried to write Paradise" (Canto CXVII). The line, like the project of the poem it concludes, is radically transitive.

The *Cantos* does not, then, occupy the ontologically discrete realm that is the category of the "aesthetic" in its modern or Kantian sense. Indeed, the poem rejects the entire compartmentalization of knowledge which Pound construes as our distinctly Aristotelian heritage: "Aristotle was so good at his job that he anchored thought for 2000 years. What he didn't define clearly remained a muddle for the rest of the race, for centuries following. But he did not engender a sense of social responsibility" (*GK* 39). Aristotle is credited with providing the West with the few clear definitions it possesses, but his true heritage is needless and artificial demarcations, the habit of mind that separates, say, a *Poetics* from a *Politics,* a *Politics* from an *Ethics.* Yet if Aristotle is the "master of those that cut apart, dissect and divide" (*GK* 343), there is a sense in which the Aristotelian divisions of knowledge did not hold in practice. The humanist assimilation of the *Politics,* to return to the earlier example, had repercussions beyond the strictly or narrowly political. The cult of verbal and vernacular opulence looked to the *Politics* as opposed to the *Poetics* for theoretical justification; because verbal opulence was itself construed as a form of material bounteousness, as personal and cultural wealth, the assimilation of the *Politics* challenged the compartmentalization of knowledge that the *Politics* itself presupposes.

Consider, in this context, Dryden's "Dedication" to his translation of the *Aeneid,* which explicitly acknowledges the imbrication of the aesthetic and the political, the poetic and the economic:

> If sounding Words are not of our growth and Manufacture, who shall hinder me to Import them from a Foreign Country? I carry not out the Treasure of the Nation, which is never to return: but what I bring from *Italy,* I spend in *England:* Here it remains, and here it circulates. . . . I trade both with the Living and the Dead, for the enrichment of our Native Language. We have enough in *England* to supply our necessity; but if we will have things of Magnificence and Splendour, we must get them by Commerce.[36]

This is very much a preface to Dryden's *Aeneid,* to a vernacular *Aeneid,* to England's *Aeneid.* The bourgeois ethic that the practice of vernacular translation both presupposes and promotes emerges as the appropriation of a text through translation as individual and national property, by an author and a national literature in something resembling the fully modern sense. Like most words for "translation" in Indo-European languages, *translatio* means both the linguistic transference of meaning and the economic transference of property.[37] And both are operable in Dryden: the heliotropic movement by which the *Aeneid* as poem comes to reiterate the "progress" of its protagonist—from Troy to Rome, from eastern origins to occidental fulfillments, from Virgil's Latin to Dryden's English—is continuous with other western appropriations of eastern goods. ("And if you CAN'T find *any* decent translations of Catullus and Propertius," Pound wrote to Iris Barry in 1916, "I suppose I shall have to rig up something."[38] Translations of Virgil were there for the asking, for unlike Propertius, Virgil is himself implicated in an ideology of imperial "translation.") "Immature poets borrow," a later admirer of both Virgil and Dryden remarks, "mature poets steal." The aphorism is Eliot's, although, as Franco Moretti notes, it could be taken for Lord Elgin's.[39] In its insurgent phase vernacular translation served to legitimize worldly activity: by bridging the gap between the sacred languages of Hebrew, Greek, and Latin and developing national vernaculars, it diminished the distance between the cities of God and man. In its ascendant phase, however, vernacular translation is implicated in the practices of "Commerce" in their explicitly capitalist and imperialist forms. Pound was intrigued by what he termed the "repeat" in history, the uncanny return of the same-but-different. And by a return to or repeat of Aristotle's *Politics,* a text much favored by the early humanists, Pound hoped to effect a revolution—at once aesthetic, political, and economic—no less extreme than that of the humanists, although with a difference. The humanists labored to relocate the source of linguistic and literary value in the signifier. Pound sought to return language to its signified, to reestablish the lost commerce between the order of language and the world.

In chapters 8 and 9 of the first book of the *Politics*, Aristotle distinguishes between two modes of economic organization: *oikonomike*, or economics "proper," and *chrematistike*, or "improper" wealth-getting. In the former, money functions solely as a mediating agent; its purpose is to facilitate the exchange of heterogeneous commodities; like metaphor it has an "eye for resemblances" or the capacity to mediate differences, but it is a means rather than an end. In an economy of wealth-getting, however, money itself is fetishized as a commodity; the agent of transference or translation becomes an "improper" source of value. The vocabulary of the *Politics* suggests that of the *Poetics*,[40] the Aristotelian divisions of knowledge notwithstanding. And it is precisely this imbrication of the economy of language by the language of economy that Pound takes in earnest: the etymological connection that binds "catachresis" and "chrematistics," abuses of language and economic abuses, is at the heart of his polemic against *translatio*.[41] Improper wealth-getting, or chrematistics, and improprieties of language, or catachresis, participate in an economy of circulation unrestricted by the referential, unencumbered by contact with a world of tangible goods and needs. For Pound, money properly functions "inside a system and measured and gauged to human / requirements" (Canto LXXVIII); it is only "a certificate of work done," without intrinsic value.[42] In its demonic form, however, "money carries within itself the structure of the need for luxuries in that it rejects any limitation upon the desire for it."[43] So too with the poetic "structure of the need for luxuries." Dryden's *Aeneid* answers to a taste for "Magnificence or Splendour" rather than need or "necessity." The practice of vernacular translation that begins as a challenge to Augustinian dichotomies, to the Augustinian denigration of worldly activity, emerges historically as a worldly "good" in itself, one with the practice of capitalist accumulation, imperialist appropriation, and conspicuous consumption.

Pound's figure for this aberrant economy, the figure who in himself unites an economy of catachresis and chrematistics, is the very character with whom he identifies early in the *Cantos*: Odysseus Polytropos. *Metaphora*, the trope George Puttenham terms "the Figure of transporte,"[44] becomes for Pound one with the great poem of transportation. "The *Odyssey* high water mark for the adventure story," Pound writes in *Guide to Kulchur*, a "world of irresponsible gods, a very high society without recognizable morals, the individual responsible to himself" (*GK* 38). Or if not Odysseus, then the Jew, the "historical" manifestation of the Odyssean "ethos of a nomadic era" (*SP* 66). Odysseus is skilled in a rhetoric of metaphorical evasion; the Jews are characterized as a people invested in making the "word mean something it does NOT say."[45] Odysseus' delight in "twisty thoughts" is one with his journey of accumulation and appropriation; the linguistic imprecision of the Jews is continuous with the practice of usury, chrematistics in its most extreme form, money released from the referential constraints of human production and need. "Jewgreek is Greekjew" for Pound as well as Joyce. For Pound, however, the "Jewgreek" propagates an aberrant economy, an "improper" linguistic and economic mode of organization.

"Improper" because it is given to what Jean-Joseph Goux terms "la signification *bancaire*," which divorces "la fonction d'échange" from "la fonction de thésaurisation" in the manner formalized by structural linguistics. With Saussure the "naive" concept of language-as-naming, "la fonction de thésaurisation," gives way to the "abstract" concept of language-as-system, "la fonction d'échange"; the syntagmatic relations that bind word to word within a closed semiotic system gain priority over the paradigmatic relations that bind word to referent in a transitive system. Or, to move from the linguistic to the economic, a monetary system based on the circulation of gold as a general equivalent gives way to "unconvertable paper," a mode of economic circulation in which "money is reduced to a 'token' without any intrinsic value, whose convertability or translatability is increasingly hypothetical."[46] Goux associates "la signification bancaire" with the abstract or nonreferential accomplishments of the high modernists—Mallarmé, Valéry, Gide—whereas Pound discerns the contaminating presence of usury, his own version of "la signification bancaire," in virtually all Reformation and post-Reformation art. (Pound defines usury as a "charge for the use of purchasing power, levied without regard to production; often without regard to the possibilities of production" [Canto XLV]. A less mystified vocabulary would speak of fictitious capital formulation, or capital that has a nominal money value and paper existence, but which is without backing in terms of real productive activity or physical assets as collateral. Pound's terminology is archaic at best, yet his polemic is not without force. Capitalism does evince a tendency to subordinate productivity to the operations of capital and the hegemony of banking practices.) Goux and Pound diverge on the question of historical periodization, but they agree on the historicity of all signifying systems, including those, like Saussurean linguistics, that are invested in eliding their own historicity. Pound understood that any attempt to transform the logic of the self-enclosed or self-generating into the inevitable order of things, into the structural truth of things, only perpetuates the status quo. But because he believed the West to be so deeply invested in the business of usury, to move outside the logic of the self-enclosed was to escape the gravitational pull of the Occident altogether.

Hence Pound's Confucianism: in the *Cantos* Confucius comes to function as a proponent of proper names and places in opposition to the Odyssean and Hebraic ethos of the portative, the polytropic. "There is no more important technical term in Confucian philosophy," Pound writes, "than *chih*, the hitching post, position, place one is in and works from" (*Con* 232). If there is a rival term, it is *cheng ming*, the "principle of the rectification of names." A Confucian economy of proper names and places, a poetics of settlement, stands opposed to the occidental ethos of the portative, the culture of metaphor. *Cathay* was a translation—or, as Eliot says, an "invention"—for the sake of the West. The Chinese Cantos, however, gives the Chinese "character," by which Pound means both ideogram and ethos, unappropriated, untranslated, although the attitude of mind that does not translate does provide rough English paraphrases. (Unappropriated as ideogram because the Chinese character, as opposed to what Fenollosa calls the "feeble cohesive force of western phonetic symbols," retains a vital connection to the world of natural objects. As "a vivid shorthand picture of the operations of nature," the ideogram does not involve the circulation of names alienated from the objects they name.[47] Unappropriated as ethos because a Confucian economy, as opposed to the western ethic of unlimited accumulation, retains a vital connection to the world of human productivity and need.) Usury, chrematistics, is redeemed by simple use. Wealth is created not in the manner in which the sky god of Genesis creates the world—money should not talk—but in relation to human labor, the cultivation of land, the production of goods. The western and distinctly ethnocentric thematization of *translatio* as *translatio imperii* or *translatio studii*—the "heliotropic" progress of culture from its eastern origins to its western fulfillment—is precisely the ethos of translation that Pound eschews. Here the poet travels eastward, as it were, whereas in *Cathay* he mistakenly has a character, who nowhere exists in the original, travel westward. Like Dryden, the early Pound conceived of translation as an occasion for cultural imperialism, as an opportunity to appropriate so many museum pieces of "Splendour and Magnificence." "Epilogue" speaks of a poetic *nostos,* an Odyssean homecoming replete with the appropriated goods of others: "I bring you the spoils, my nation, / I, who went out in exile, / Am returned to thee with gifts."[48] It is telling that Pound chose not to include the poem in *Personae,* his definitive collection of shorter poems.

It would require but little ingenuity to show how Pound's eastern sojourn effects a radical transformation of the practice of translation in the *Cantos.* In the Adams Cantos, which follows immediately after the Chinese Cantos, virtually all of Pound's twenty-five hundred lines have a recognizable and single source, identifiable by page and line number in the *Works* of John Adams.[49] Most of the material in the Chinese Cantos, moreover, is derived from Seraphim Couvreur's translation of the *Li-ki* and Joseph de Mailla's *Histoire générale de la Chine.* A poem that begins with a translation which is without recourse to an original or single source undergoes a radical transformation of its understanding of translation. And what is radical here is the transitive nature of the project, the attempt to transmit semantic content. Pound writes the Chinese Cantos not in an effort to supply the West with "things of Magnificence and Splendour"—we have, in any case, chinoiserie enough—but in the belief that the dissemination of Confucian wisdom could prevent war. Pound is manifestly not interested in "transforming" his source materials; indeed, the most frequent criticism directed against the Chinese and Adams Cantos is their "unpoetic" fidelity to their sources. (Again, it is difficult to know how "transformation," the term Derrida prefers to "translation," can be more than a description, rather than a disruption, of the conventional relation of poets to their sources.) True, the Chinese Cantos, like Canto I, is mostly a translation of translations, primarily the work of eighteenth-century French Jesuits. The title page of de Mailla's *Histoire* identifies the work as a translation of the *Tong-kien-kang-mu* (ca. 1190), which is a digest of the *Comprehensive Mirror for Aid in Government* (ca. 1090), which in turn is a digest of extant dynastic histories. Pound's stated preference, however, was for sources that included the original, and if the *Histoire*, the most extensively used of the digests, did not, no text available to Pound did. This is not to suggest that Pound's choice of texts was innocent of ideological determinants. He held the *Histoire* to be an accurate rendering of the Chinese, a translation of the principle of *cheng ming* into "termes propres" (Canto LX), the linguistic precision that is the essence of Confucianism and the foundation of the just state. It is not accidental, moreover, that the *Historie* (published 1777–85) is an eighteenth-century text. The positive construction of China sent back to Europe by the Jesuits was generally well received by philosophes and those in search of alternative models for European development. It was not until the nineteenth century that China fully emerged in the European imagination as a decadent, ahistorical (read: noncapitalist) society passively awaiting western domination.[50]

But it is not my purpose here to recommend Pound's refusal of *translatio* as cultural imperialism or to advocate the wisdom of his critique of the culture of metaphor. The agrarian world of classical China is hardly a viable model of alternative development for the industrial West, and any commitment to the principle of *cheng ming* needs to recall the very real violence that attended its imposition and administration in China.[51] The poetics of the proper name, as Barthes insists, is also a politics:

> In the Stalinist world, in which *definition*, that is to say the separation between Good and Evil, becomes the sole content of all language, there are no more words without values attached to them, so that finally the function of writing is to cut out one stage of a process: there is no more lapse of time between naming and judging, and the closed character of language is perfected, since in the last analysis it is a value which is given as an explanation of another value.[52]

The "Name Decrees" issued by Hitler's Ministry of the Interior suffered no lapse of time between naming and judging: Jews were restricted to the use of Old Testament names, the better to subject them to a variety of other punitive measures. (Esra, a form of Pound's own "Christian" name, was among those deemed appropriate for Jews.)[53] The imbrication of the poetic and the political could not be more brutally obvious, but even if one were to concede their theoretical separability, Pound's sinophilia remains open to critique. Here, for example, is Andrew Parker:

> The ideogram . . . has always belonged to the structure of *writing*: if Pound believed Chinese to be "the ideal language of the world" in terms

of its supposed ability to circumvent the arbitrariness specific to phonetic writing, it yet must be recognized that *no* writing (whether phonetic or nonphonetic) has ever remained "intact and untouched" by such arbitrariness. Pound's very distinction between "abstract phonetic writing" and "motivated nonphonetic writing" consequently must be revised, for not only have "largely nonphonetic scripts like Chinese and Japanese included phonetic elements very early" (that is to say, "from the very beginning"), but we must always acknowledge that *"there is no purely phonetic writing"* (by reason of the necessary spacing of signs, punctuation, intervals, the differences indispensable for the functioning of graphemes, etc).[54]

Parker's highly Derridean critique of Pound is intent on transforming an opposition between "arbitrariness" and "motivation" into a relation of co-implication, in which each is the condition of the other's possibility. Phonetic writing is not the sole preserve of the arbitrary, as Pound contends, but the *"différance* of its equally rhetorical other," the "largely nonphonetic" scripts of China and Japan. Difference becomes what Derrida terms the "'differed' within the systematic ordering [*l'économie*] of the same," a nonbinary relation of nonidentity and nondifference. The argument intends to break with the ethnocentricism of western humanism, which effectively reduces the Orient, again in Derrida's formulation, to a "sort of European hallucination," to the pure difference that is the non-Occident.[55] But whatever its intentions, "co-implication" is not readily distinguishable from co-option. Barthes argues that "any classical humanism postulates that in scratching the history of men a little, the relativity of their institutions or the superficial diversity of their skins, . . . one very quickly reaches the solid rock of a universal human nature."[56] In the Derridean version of this humanism, one has only to scratch the languages of men and women a little, the relativity of their historical development or the superficial diversity of their structures, and one very quickly reaches the non-solid non-bedrock of universal *différance.* No matter that Chinese has no word for "metaphor," that in Chinese literary tradition a poem is normally presumed to be nonfictional;[57] superficial differences belie the (non)presence of a global and globalizing *différance.* In *Of Grammatology* Derrida celebrates Pound's refusal of western phonocentricism and all that it subtends: "This is the meaning of the work of Fenollosa whose influence upon Ezra Pound and his poetics is well known: this irreducibly graphic poetics was, with that of Mallarmé, the first break in the most entrenched Western tradition. The fascination that the Chinese ideogram exercised on Pound's writing may thus be given all its historical significance."[58] But the "all" of Derrida's formulation promises more than it delivers: "the historical significance" of any "structure of writing" is not exhausted by its formal, phenomenal, or structural properties. Printing was invented in China probably a half century before its first appearance in Europe, yet it had none of the revolutionary impact that it was to have in the West. And for the most obvious of reasons: behind the occidental culture of print stand capitalist printers and printing houses—"print-capitalism," as Benedict Anderson styles it.[59] The ideogram does in fact participate in the arbitrariness of western phonetic writing, yet its production, dissemination, and consumption belong to an altogether different socioeconomic order, and any attempt to assimilate the one to the other risks perpetuating the humanist enterprise by another name. With Derrida a universal "human nature" becomes a universal grammatology. But not with Pound. The interest lies in the opposition, in the difference.

Pound is not unique, of course, in juxtaposing an occidental proclivity for alien or alias names, a culture of metaphor, against an oriental dedication to *cheng ming*. Herbert Schneidau, for example, celebrates a biblical West that, in opposition to both its mythological past and oriental "other," claims no divine authority for its insitutions, no indwelling of the sacred in the secular:

> "Christianity attacks human life at so deep a level that it disallows all existing culture." The point is of the essence for a religion which could not find God in the Law or the Temple even though he had ordained them. Yet this negative knowledge is no Christian innovation: the prophets too find a gap between God and the institutions set up in his name, and turn against his cult.

Unlike, say, the *Aeneid*, the Bible insists that humankind is answerable not to culture but to a transcendent Being from whose perspective all worldly activity is vanity. For Schneidau this explains the "critical attitude" that is allegedly unique to the West, which in turn accounts for its "rapid evolution," as opposed to those other cultures—such as the "eternal" Orient, the static obverse of the Faustian West—that Schneidau, following Lévi-Strauss, terms "cold." Schneidau does concede that "the Bible can be used as a culture-supporting myth," but with the qualification that "the insidious effect of the Yahwist vision makes the support problematic at best."[60]

This is to assume, however, that the problematic is always experienced as a problem; it is to ignore what D. A. Miller characterizes as the "whole range of practices whereby our culture has become increasingly adept in taking benefit of doubt."[61] "Sacred discontent," for instance, issues in little more than the compulsion to continuous labor that is at the heart of biblical Protestantism. In fact, Max Weber contends,

> the *summum bonum* of this ethic, the earning of more and more money, combined with the strict avoidance of all spontaneous enjoyment of life, is above all completely devoid of any eudaemonistic, not to say hedonistic, admixture. It is thought of so purely as an end in itself, that from the point of view of the happiness of, or utility to, the single individual, it appears entirely transcendental and absolutely irrational.[62]

But if useless to the individual, an ethos of perpetual acquisition, underwritten by an ontology of "sacred discontent," is indispensable to an economic order that labors only to keep on going. Capitalism guarantees the pursuit of happiness. The actual goal is as transcendental in its own way as Augustine's City of God.

It is in this context that Pound's insistence that work be "measured and gauged toward human needs" reverberates with its full utopian force. Work has a goal but is not itself a goal; work is done inside a system but is not itself coincident with that system (an opinion he would come to modify in conformity with the fascist fetishization of work). The denigration of worldly activity in the name of a Being whose very transcendence and ineffability promote incessant activity is an intolerable paradox. Production should do more than sustain the order of production:

> Tempus tacendi, tempus loquendi.
> Never inside the country to raise the standards of living
> but always abroad to increase the profits of usurers,
> dixit Lenin,
> and gun sales lead to more gun sales
>   they do not clutter the market for gunnery
>   there is no saturation
> Pisa, in the 23rd year of the effort in sight of the tower
> and Till was hung yesterday
> for murder and rape with trimmings   plus Cholkis
>   plus mythology, thought he was Zeus ram or another one.
>   (Canto LXXIV)

The absence of any teleology save that of self-perpetuation is itself the teleology latent in the economic logic of capitalism. Guns do not, cannot, "saturate" the market—there is no "clutter"—only because the market is structurally immune to saturation. Gun sales lead to more gun sales and war leads to more war. In *Jefferson and/or Mussolini* Pound argues for the uniqueness of the arms industry: "[T]he selling of guns and powders differs from ALL other industries in that the more you sell the greater the demand for it."[63] It is unique, however, only in the degree of its explicitness. The selling of munitions makes murderously clear the internal finality of an economic order that seeks only to perpetuate itself.

An economic order that Pound opposes to mythic consciousness, to the renewed paganism, the redemption from "clutter," that is the promise of Mussolini:

> Mussolini found himself in the cluttered rubbish and cluttered splendour of the dozen or more strata of human effort: history, the romanesque cluttered over with barocco, every possible sort of refinement, dust-covered, sub-divided, passive, sceptical, lazy, caressed by milleniar sun. Rome, Byzantium, Homeric Greece still in Sicily, *belle au bois dormante*. . . . (*JM* 66)

As Jupiter the bull to Europa, so Mussolini the bull or "boss" to Europe. Redemption depends on what a 1912 poem calls "The Return," the recovery of mythic consciousness that is also the resurrection of the flesh:

> ah, see the tentative
> Movements, and the slow feet,

> The trouble in the pace and the uncertain
> Wavering!
>
> *(P 74)*

The return is tentative because the pagan gods have long been exiled, or long reduced to little more than mythological *vestigia,* under the Judeo-Christian dispensation. Yet return they must—to embodiment, to the world—if worldly activity is to regain a properly worldly center of gravity. The project fails on the level of the political—"maggots" come to "eat / the dead bullock" (Canto LXXIV) or *bos,* the slaughtered body of Mussolini— yet continuity with the divine remains unbroken:

> I surrender neither the empire nor the temples plural
> nor the constitution nor yet the city of Dioce
> each one in his god's name.
>
> (Canto LXXIV)

By insisting on vestigial traces of polytheism in the very text that would reduce his own pantheon to *vestigia,* Pound turns the authority of the Bible against itself: Micah 4:5, "For all the peoples walk each in the name of its god", becomes an argument for "temples plural." Pound does considerable violence to the text in quoting so selectively, yet when he does gesture toward theological orthodoxy, it is only to suggest the cultural disaster born of it:

> all of which leads to the death-cells
> each in the name of its god
> or longevity because as says Aristotle
> philosophy is not for young men
> their *Katholou* can not be sufficiently derived from
>   their *hekasta*
> their generalities cannot be born from a sufficient phalanx of particulars.
>
> (Canto LXXIV)

The alternatives could not be starker: "each in the name of its god" leads either to "temples plural" or the "death-cells," either to cultural renewal or genocide. The choice is between a "god"—or what Kenneth Burke calls a "god term," such as "generality"—who is discontinuous with the lived particulars of human experience and gods who exist in an unbroken continuum with the mundane.[64] The former, the presiding deity of the death camps, is the male sky god of Judeo-Christian tradition; the latter are the multiple gods, male and female, that inhere in the dream of the city of Dioce. Redemption depends on a recuperated physicality, a non-failed literalism. Mythological *vestigia* must become literal footsteps.

This is because Pound's poetry goes in fear of the abstraction he construed as our distinctly Jewish and, to a lesser extent, Protestant inheritance. (Pound tended to exempt Catholicism, particularly of the medieval variety, from his general censure of occidental abstraction, largely because he held it to be a religion of embodiment and modified polytheism, at least partially continuous with its pagan past.) The Jewish taste for abstraction degrades myth into allegory, and when the world is rendered allegorical, gods no longer walk in men's gardens (*LE* 431). In the standard literary histories Plutarch is credited with being the first to recover the failed literalism of pagan poetry in the mode of allegorical interpretation; in Pound's demonology it is some "unpleasing Semite or Parsee or Syrian" (*LE* 431). Pound's paganism, his distinctly nonbiblical insistence on the continuity of the human and the divine, is discontinuous with the western fetishization of discontent and alienation; his refusal of the ideology of *translatio imperii* and *translation studii* is discontinuous with the ethnocentricism of western humanism. But not the anti-Semitism: it is fully of the culture it alleges to redeem. I address this anti-Semitism and its relation to Pound's fascism in the third section of this chapter. First, however, the Pisan Cantos, for if the lyric interlude is unique in the context of the larger poem that contains it, it too is fully of the culture it makes no pretense to redeem.

Carceral Poetics

Pound's investment in a poetics of tropological stability, of fixed addresses and proper names, survives the fall of Mussolini and the collapse of the fascist dream:

> "definition can not be shut down under a box lid"
> but if the gelatine be effaced whereon is the record?
> "wherein is no responsible person
>   having a front name, a hind name and an address"
> "not a right but a duty"
>   those words still stand uncancelled,
> "Presente!"
>
> (Canto LXXVIII)

The words that still stand defiantly "uncancelled" are Mussolini's, elsewhere given by Pound as "We are tired of a government in which there is no responsible person having a hind name, a front name and an address" (*SP* 261). Il Duce is the promise of a Confucianism of the here and now, of the principle of *cheng ming* introduced into the life of historical action, yet the words that "still stand uncancelled" paradoxically stand unidentified, unattributed. (There is in fact no person here bearing "a front name, a hind name and an address.") In one sense the poem would seem to embody or enact its thematic burden in the manner deemed obligatory by New Critical aesthetics. The "historical blackout" against which it inveighs—the universal conspiracy to destroy, suppress, or subvert vital documents and voices—is the historical blackout it guards against.[65] In another sense, however, the poem seems discontinuous with its thematic burden, as if the fall of Mussolini were somehow poetically as well as politically disabling. The Pound of the internment at Pisa continues to believe "in the resurrection of Italy," but with the crucial qualification that it is "now in the mind indestructible" (Canto LXXIV). Like Kung, who said nothing of the "other-worldly," Mussolini pursued not "an ideal republic situated in a platonic paradise but an arrangement possible in the year VIII or IX of the Era Fascisti" (*JM* 57). Given the fall of the dictator and the collapse of the fascist dream, however, the poetically plangent stands surrogate for the politically possible.

So an arrrangement once thought possible at a specific place and time becomes the "city of Dioce whose terraces are the colour of stars" (Canto LXXIV). Here it is not an airy nothingness that is given a local habitation and a name, but a local habitation and a name that are translated into an airy nothingness, a thoroughly poeticized vision of the fascist city of man. Such a city belongs not to a Confucian poetic of the transitive or pragmatic, but to the founding gesture of western metaphysics, which, Derrida notwithstanding, may well be the privileging of *translatio,* of metaphor: "I understand. . . . You mean the city whose establishment we have described, the city whose home is in the ideal, for I think that it can be found nowhere on earth."[66] The city that emerges at the conclusion of book 9 of the *Republic* is ultimately a figure for the city, the prototype of Pound's city of Dioce ("in the mind indestructible"), a utopian vision of literally nowhere or no place. At Salò by the Lago di Garda a powerless Mussolini read the *Republic,* having become, like Pound, the unacknowledged legislator of an imaginary world.[67] The world is recalcitrant; words console.

Words console, but the historical world cannot be spoken into existence. True, the "Ouan Jin" of Canto LXXIV, like the sky god of Genesis, speaks or names "many things" into being, but what is perceived as "good" in the biblical text is so much "clutter" in Pound's:

> and Rouse found they spoke of Elias
> in telling the tales of Odysseus   Ο὘ ΤΙΣ
>   Ο὘ ΤΙΣ
> "I am noman, my name is noman"
> but Wanjina is, shall we say, Ouan Jin
> or the man with an education
> and whose mouth was removed by his father
>   because he made too many *things*
> whereby cluttered the bushman's baggage
> vide the expedition of Frobenius' pupils about 1938
>   to Auss'ralia
> Ouan Jin spoke and thereby created the named
>   thereby making clutter
> the bane of men moving
> and so his mouth was removed
> as you will find it removed in his pictures.
>   (Canto LXXIV)

Ouan Jin is but one name in a complex montage of myths and names: the stories repeated by Rouse of extant oral narratives of the voyages of Odysseus, now traveling under the name "Elias," which is itself a near anagram of "alias"; the story of Odysseus proper, "no man" or "no one" as he calls himself in his confrontation with Polyphemus; and the story of Wanjina, the Australian fertility god whom Pound renames "Ouan Jin." Elias/ Odysseus, "Jewgreek" or "Greekjew," dissolves into Ouan Jin/Wanjina, which is entirely appropriate: Odysseus Polytropos, the man of many turns or tropes, characteristically resists fixed identity. "I am become a name" says Tennyson's Ulysses, to which Pound's Ouan Jin might have added many names, any name, against which Pound invokes the example of the Paraclete: "in principio verbum / paraclete or the verbum perfectum: sinceritas" (Canto LXXIV). The Paraclete, the promise of a man standing beside his word or name (*para,* beside; *kalein,* the named), of continuity between a speaking subject and a spoken utterance, is not an operable presence or category in the world of the *Odyssey.*[68] With one exception: Odysseus reveals his proper name to Polyphemus, which, in binding his actions to his person, allows the Cyclops to call down a curse upon his head. But Odysseus is rarely so unwily, and like his Homeric counterpart Ouan Jin inhabits a world that is without "responsible persons having a front name, a hind name and a fixed address." He "made too many *things /* whereby cluttered the bushman's baggage": this is the world of "clutter" from which Mussolini promises a violent redemption.

The *verbum perfectum,* the word that is made perfect in the coincidence of a speaking subject and a spoken utterance, finds pragmatic realization in the conditions under which fascist discourse is produced and disseminated.[69] "It seems to me," the poet-broadcaster wrote to Cornelio di Marzio in December 1941, "that my speeches on the radio must continue IN MY OWN NAME, and with my voice, and not anonymously. . . . I can't write anonymous letters!!! . . . Either one fights, or one does not."[70] The Pound of Radio Rome saw himself as a man "standing beside" his name and voice, and he held freedom of the airwaves to be the prerequisite of all free speech, particularly in a world in which newspapers were under the control of the usocrats. Free speech "without free radio speech is as zero" (Canto LXXIV); a legal right without the economic means to exercise it is effectively no right at all. (One can easily imagine Pound's response to the contemporary form the liberal myth of free speech or discourse has assumed: "free writing," the free play of signifiers in a free textual universe. Free, that is, from the archaic tyranny of a transcendental signified, but still bound to the material conditions that govern the production and dissemination of discourse in the bourgeois West.) Pound could speak "freely," in both senses of the word, on Radio Rome. Such was proof positive that Fascist Italy was free.

A purely literary understanding of *sinceritas* would no doubt cite the Pisan Cantos, not the radio broadcasts, as its central example. Lyric is conventionally held to be the mode of the "authentic" self, and the poem is indeed lyric: "The enormous tragedy of the dream in the peasant's bent / shoulders" (Canto LXXIV). By radically decontextualizing the peasant, these, the opening lines of the Pisan Cantos, register tragedy as a quasi-eternal or natural fact. Unlike western poetics, which tends to follow Aristotle in privileging the tragic, Chinese poetics is innocent of the genre. But here Pound breaks with the pragmatics of *cheng ming* and Confucianism, as if the lyric beauty of the lines were itself compensation for their content. In turning to poetry as "a possible friend and comforter," as an antidote to the historical world, the Lady Valentine of *Mauberley* merely perpetuates the historical nightmare; an art that consoles for the horrors of a "botched civilization" necessarily functions as an agent of it:

> There died a myriad,
> And of the best, among them,
> For an old bitch gone in the teeth,
> For a botched civilization.
>
> *(P 191)*

There died a myriad "For two gross of broken statues, / For a few thousand battered books" (*P* 191)—for, not despite, cultural accomplishments and goods. But whereas the Lady Valentine pursues aesthetic consolation, *Mauberley* demands cultural transformation. The poem is generally taken to be Pound's farewell (or good riddance) to his own earlier aesthetic and aestheticizing self, but what *Mauberley* would banish, the Pisan Cantos effectively recuperates. The lyric interlude defers to the Lady Valentine's aesthetic.

Mauberley begins with the burial of a poet who sought "to resuscitate" the dead:

> For three years, out of key with his time,
> He strove to resuscitate the dead art
> Of poetry; to maintain "the sublime"
> In the old sense. Wrong from the start—
>
> *(P 187)*

If the "he" of this opening ode, "E.P. Ode Pour L'Election De Son Sepulchre," can be identified with Pound's earlier self, "'the sublime' / In the old sense" might better read "the lyric / In the old sense." From the start much of the work was in the lyric mode, heavily influenced by troubadour tradition and Provençal poetry. The movement from lyric (or pastoral) to epic is the most conventional of paradigms for the poetic career, but the return to (or of) the lyric voice in the Pisan Cantos makes of Pound a revenant, a ghost of his former self who, like Andreas Divus in Canto I, refuses to "lie quiet." Because the "E.P." of *Mauberley* is given to "the obscure reveries / Of the inward gaze," he is characterized as "out of key with his time." But if out of key historically, "E.P." is continuous with the literary tradition of which he is literally the dead end: the poetics of late romanticism is given to the lyricization of epic, in the manner of the *Prelude*, or to the lyric proper.

Mauberley rejects the poetics of the inward gaze even as it remains sympathetic to it:

> Beneath the sagging roof
> The stylist has taken shelter,
> Unpaid, uncelebrated,
> At last from the world's welter
> Nature receives him.
>
> (*P* 195)

The "stylist" occupies the paradigmatic position of the romantic artist, sequestered from the "world's welter," committed to a stylistic purity that is an implicit rebuke to the world which leaves it "unpaid, uncelebrated." Poetic marginality is an honorable stance, yet it presupposes a distinctly liberal dichotomy between the self and society, and Pound labors to tell the tale of the tribe, to promote and disseminate the corporate values of the postliberal state.[71] (Hence, both the poetic wake for "E.P" and one of the most significant caesuras within the *Cantos:* the abandonment of the figure of Odysseus, "the individual responsible to himself," in favor of a Confucian poetics of settlement and social responsibility.) Poetry is not a "possible friend and comforter / In the case of revolution" but the active agent of it—Massimo Bacigalupo characterizes the *Cantos* as "the sacred poem of the Nazi-Fascist millennium."[72] Poetry becomes a museum piece sequestered from "the world's welter" only after fascism fails in its historical ambitions.

The "sacred poem of the Nazi-Fascist millennium" is by definition transitive and so opposed to the *écart* of metaphor, the withdrawal or deviation from direct reference which Gérard Genette characterizes as "la figure comme écart entre le signe et le sens, somme espace intérieur du langage," and which lyric poetry, particularly of the romantic variety, tends to render external or literal.[73] Coleridge's "This Lime-Tree Bower My Prison," for example, begins with the experience of deprivation—an accident confines the speaker, unlike his friends, to the bower—only to redeem literal confinement as spiritual and poetic liberation:

> A delight
> Comes sudden on my heart, and I am glad
> As I myself were there! Nor in this bower,
> This little lime-tree bower, have I not mark'd
> Much that has sooth'd me.[74]

The agoraphobic strategy of the poem enacts an understanding of metaphor in which the suspension of ordinary descriptive reference is but an initial bracketing, the negative condition of an indirect reference built on the ruins of the direct.[75] The suspension is intended as provisional, and the speaker claims vicarious participation in the world beyond the embowered self. Yet the entire poem is haunted by the carceral possibilities latent in its title, which also inform the canonical definition of the lyric: "That song has always seemed to us like the lament of a prisoner in a solitary cell, ourselves listening, unseen in the next." John Stuart Mill deleted the sentence when he republished "What Is Poetry?," but its carceral thematics persist: "[E]loquence is *heard*, poetry is *over*heard. Eloquence supposes an audience; the peculiarity of poetry appears to us to lie in the poet's utter unconsciousness of a listener. Poetry is feeling confessing itself to itself, in moments of solitude."[76] The Pisan Cantos was written literally in solitary confinement, in carceral seclusion in a wire cage. The lyric cry did have an immediate audience of one—the prison camp censor—yet the poem is generally celebrated as "feeling confessing itself to itself," as physical constriction transformed into spiritual and poetic freedom.

Celebrated, in fact, as a return to the poetic "in the old sense." Lewis Hyde argues that the incarcerated Pound "was shoved toward an inner life again, out of his mechanical opinions, and the poems return to poetry for a while."[77] "Poetry" is synonymous with the lyric, or, as Mill contends, the lyric is "more eminently and peculiarly poetry than any other [kind]."[78] Hyde's argument is comforting—Pound's fascism and anti-Semitism are dismissed as but a mechanical operation of the spirit—yet it hardly corresponds to the facts, either poetic or biographical:

> Long portions of the *Cantos*—particularly those written in the decade 1935–45—are rhetorical in Yeats's sense. The voice is full of opinion without erotic heat, like an old pensioner chewing his disappointed politics in a barbershop. The history cantos, in particular—all the material about China and the long portrait of John Adams—are deadly dull, never informed with the fire, complexity, or surprise that are the mark of living images. . . . Working out of "good will" alone, the poem becomes mired in time, argument, and explanation, forgetting the atemporal mystery it set out to protect. (229–30)

Long portions of the *Cantos* are indeed "deadly dull," including much of "the material about China and the long portrait of John Adams." But it is difficult to know how a "disappointed politics," especially in the earlier part of the decade 1935–45, which witnessed the growth and consolidation of European fascism, can account for the want of fire and complexity in a poem dedicated to effecting a fascist revolution. It may be, however, that Hyde is objecting not to a disappointed politics but to a politics insufficiently disappointed, and hence to a poetic too directly involved in the "mire" of history. Like the Lady of Shalott, Pound "willfully" abandons an embowered or enclosed space, the *écart* of metaphor, and, like his Victorian precursor, he comes to grief. He is redeemed only when he is shoved back into "inner space," when Tennyson's faerie castle becomes a wire cage.

All this assumes, however, that "feeling confessing itself to itself, in moments of solitude," has the power to redeem. The Pisan Cantos is frequently read as a "confession" in an almost literal sense, and hence as a form of self-indictment. Pound "was forced to walk backwards," Hyde maintains, "out of pride into sympathy" (230). And from sympathy comes lyric beauty: "The ant's a centaur in his dragon world. / Pull down thy vanity." But "pride" is not the most damning of charges that can be

brought against Pound—unless this is a tribunal in the theological sense—
and tragic recognition is not the only possible reading of the poem:

> The ant's a centaur in his dragon world.
> Pull down thy vanity, it is not man
> Made courage, or made order, or made grace,
> ·
>   Pull down thy vanity
> Thou art a beaten dog beneath the hail,
> a swollen magpie in a fitful sun,
> Half black half white
> Nor knowst'ou wing from tail
> Pull down thy vanity
>   How mean thy hates
> Fostered in falsity,
>   Pull down thy vanity,
> Rathe to destroy, niggard in charity,
> Pull down thy vanity,
>   I say pull down.
>   (Canto LXXXI)

The addressee of this passage is generally taken to be Pound himself; a
poetic mode that is defined as "feeling confessing itself to itself, in soli-
tude," can logically have no other. Yet as Peter D'Epiro suggests, the
passage can also be read in the most naively referential fashion. "Half black
half white" is fully legible only in relation to the U.S. forces—Jerome
McGann notes the racist pun in "niggard of charity"[79]—and so to the
"vanity" of those who imprison, not the subject who is imprisoned. The
passage thus becomes simple, if beautiful, invective. What is not vanity,
Pound maintains, is "To have gathered from the air a live tradition":

> But to have done instead of not doing
>   this is not vanity
> To have, with decency, knocked
> That a Blunt should open
>   To have gathered from the air a live tradition
> or from a fine old eye the unconquered flame
> This is not vanity.
>   Here error is all in the not done,
> all in the diffidence that faltered. . . .
>   (Canto LXXXI)

What is not vanity is, among other things, the hateful broadcasts ("To have
gathered from the air") Pound delivered for the fascist cause on Radio
Rome; the "error" in the "not done" may include the broadcasts that he
failed to deliver, despite his apparent willingness or desire to do so, for
Hitler. In any case, Pound remains, even amidst the wreckage of Europe, a
man standing by his word, and his "confession" is dominated by sins of
omission rather than commission. Hence the irony that was soon to over-

take him: Pound was judged not legally responsible for his words, not mentally competent to stand trial for treason.

The Pisan Cantos confesses to nothing, or nothing more damning than "the diffidence that faltered," yet the poem does acknowledge its distance from any future acts of commission. Physical constriction is translated into poetic freedom, and this wire cage my prison becomes, as it were, a lime-tree bower:

> That from the gates of death,
>> that from the gates of death: Whitman or Lovelace
>>> found on the jo-house seat at that
> in a cheap edition! [and thanks to Professor Speare]
> hast'ou swum in a sea of air strip
>> through an aeon of nothingness,
> when the raft broke and the waters went over me.
>
> (Canto LXXX)

As the nymph's magic veil to Odysseus (he is given it when the breakup of his raft threatens disaster) so M. E. Speare's 1940 *Pocket Book of English and American Verse* to Pound (he discovered it on the seat of a camp latrine): the literary representation of a rescue or a redemption becomes the re-demption that is the literary. The "ego scriptor" of the Pisan Cantos writes "As a lone ant from a broken ant-hill / from the wreckage of Europe" (Canto LXXVI), but the poem itself is never fully of the historical catastro-phe it records:

> Tudor indeed is gone and every rose,
> Blood-red, blanch-white that in the sunset glows
> Cries: "Blood, Blood, Blood!" against the gothic stone
> Of England, as the Howard or Boleyn knows.
>
> (Canto LXXX)

Because the regular quatrain, one of several in this canto, is in no way characteristic of the *Cantos* in general, its introduction here is all the more telling. Poetic form is transformative of, and hence consolation for, a history of "Blood, Blood, Blood!"

The poem that returns to the aestheticism abandoned in *Mauberley* is met with the approbation *Mauberley* finds suspect:

> Doubtful, somewhat, of the value
> Of well-gowned approbation
> Of literary effort
> But never of The Lady Valentine's vocation.
>
> (P 196)

The Pisan Cantos was awarded the Bollingen Prize in poetry in 1949, which is about as "well-gowned" as "approbation / Of literary effort" gets. (The awarding committee included Conrad Aiken, W. H. Auden, T. S. Eliot, Robert Lowell, Katherine Anne Porter, Allen Tate, and Robert

Penn Warren.) The committee, no doubt anticipating the furor the grant-
ing of the award to a fascist and anti-Semite would occasion, attempted to
school the public in the rudiments of New Critical aesthetics. "To permit
other considerations than that of poetic achievement to sway the decision,"
the official justification ran, "would destroy the significance of the award
and would in principle deny the validity of that objective perception of
value on which civilized society must rest."[80] But to its credit the public
proved recalcitrant, and the granting of the award to a fascist sympathizer
provoked an outcry that is almost unimaginable today (unimaginable be-
cause the poetic is now virtually synonymous with the politically irrele-
vant). Given his personal circumstances, Pound had reason to be grateful
for the award. Given the cultural and historical ambitions of his poem,
however, he had reason to question his good fortune. Hence, yet another
of the ironies to which his career was given: the Pisan Cantos is celebrated
in conformity with aesthetic criteria that the larger poem utterly rejects.

Little has changed. The lyric interlude continues to be received as what
Christine Froula calls

> the crux, the trial and the touchstone, of Pound's lifework. In them,
> suddenly, the "poem including history" *becomes* history. The documentary
> poetics of the Malatesta Cantos, of the Sienese, Chinese, and American
> history cantos, trains itself upon the here-and-now as the sixty-year-old
> poet, caught by his own errors in the nets of history, with waves of
> worldwide catastrophe crashing over him, struggles to survive. In that
> struggle, the surviving and the witnessing become one inseparable act.[81]

The elegiac tone of this passage is in keeping with the poem that occasions
it, yet the Pisan Cantos "becomes history" only because history itself be-
comes an object of aesthetic consumption. The "form of the poem and
main progress is [*sic*] conditioned by its own inner shape," the poet-
prisoner told the camp censor, "but the life of the D.T.C. [Disciplinary
Training Centre] passing OUTSIDE the scheme cannot but impinge, or
break into the main flow."[82] Pound acknowledges, and the poem registers,
an "outside" to the carceral bower:

> Le Paradis n'est pas artificiel
> but spezzato apparently
> it exists only in fragments unexpected excellent sausage,
> the smell of mint, for example.
> (Canto LXXIV)

The Virgilian *labores,* the debt or duty that a poet owes to culture, gives
way to a lyric celebration of the natural, the world "passing" outside the
D.T.C. The "main progress of the poem" is determined not by the histori-
cal revolution it hopes to effect or the worldwide catastrophe that over-
takes it but by its own "inner shape" or natural "flow." Like Spinoza,
Pound maintained that "the more perfect a thing is the more it acts and the
less it suffers."[83] That is, the more perfect a thing is, the more it is given to

the epic virtue of praxis rather than to the lyric plangencies of pathos. For the Pound of the Pisan Cantos, however,

> nothing matters but the quality
> of the affection—
> in the end—that has carved the trace in the mind
> dove sta memoria. . . .
> (Canto LXXVI)

The praxis that had been previously rendered elegiac—"error is all in the not done, / all in the diffidence that faltered"—is here subsumed into lyric pathos. The "quality of the affection," which is recollected in a moment of carceral tranquillity, redeems all. No new historical or documentary material is introduced, and if the poem acknowledges a world external to its carceral self, it is primarily focused on its own internal operations. The Pisan Cantos "contained nothing in the nature of cypher or intended obscurity" Pound assured the camp censor. "They did however contain allusions and references to matter in the seventy-one cantos already published."[84] Difficulties and obscurities are construed as formal, as the inevitable result of a long poem turning back on itself. (The Pisan Cantos is long by modern standards—longer by far, for example, than *The Waste Land*— yet it is easily read in a moment of punctal withdrawal from the actual. Epic implies length, and length, as Poe reminds the modern world, contaminates the autonomy of literary interests.) The "crux, the trial and the touchstone" of the life work is thus open to the critique Pound himself directs against *The Waste Land*: "These fragments you have shelved (shored)" (Canto VIII). Amid the "ruin" of the modern world, Eliot takes refuge in the library. "From the wreckage of Europe" Pound does much the same. Like the poems in Speare's *Anthology,* the Pisan Cantos comes to occupy the privatized, ontologically discrete space of the library, the anthology, the book.

And so the tale of the tribe, the collective voice of history, becomes a private cry from a solitary cell, the voice of the poet who bears the name "no one" or "no man": "ΟΫ ΤΙΣ, ΟΫ ΤΙ? Odysseus / the name of my family" (Canto LXXIV). Pound returns to the persona of Odysseus, but an Odysseus now assimilated to the conventional namelessness of lyric utterance, the innominate condition of a self understood as prior or posterior to the social.[85] A "man's 'name' is his reference," Pound argues in *ABC of Reading.* "He has, after a time, credit" (25). "As to the *form* of *The Cantos,*" he writes in 1939, "All I can say or pray is: *wait* till it's there. I mean wait till I get 'em written" (*L* 323). Pound asks that a line of fiduciary credit be extended to his signature or proper name, which also happens to be a monetary unit. The reader's current investment of time and faith, which in 1939 may seem imprudent, will pay dividends at some unspecified date in the future.[86] By the time of the Pisan Cantos, however, the disaster of the historical investment becomes the redemption of the poetic: the name

"Ezra Pound" gains a new credit or currency in its very effacement, in the retreat into the namelessness of lyric utterance. "Dove sta memoria" the poet writes, and Pound is indeed remembered for "the quality of the affection," the very real beauty of his privatized cri de coeur. He "was out of step / with his time," it would seem, only when he insisted that poetry might make something happen.

The Elpenor of Canto I enjoins Odysseus to bury his body in proper ritual fashion:

> "I slept in Circe's ingle.
> "Going down the long ladder unguarded,
> "I fell against the buttress,
> "Shattered the nape-nerve, the soul sought Avernus.
> "But thou, O King, I bid remember me, unwept, unburied,
> "Heap up mine arms, be tomb by sea-bord, and inscribed:
> *"A man of no fortune, and with a name to come."*

The criticism of Odysseus, the hero responsible only to himself or to the fortunes of his own name, is implicit. Canto XX renders it explicit:

> "What gain with Odysseus,
> "They that died in the whirlpool
> "And after many vain labours,
> "Living by stolen meat, chained to the rowingbench,
> "That he should have a great fame
>   "And lie by night with the goddess?
> "Their names are not written in bronze
>   "Nor their rowing sticks set with Elpenor's;
> "Nor have they mound by sea-bord."

Odysseus' men share in his great labors but not his "great fame"; unlike Elpenor, they are denied the posthumous fame of ritual remembrance, the conventional reward for heroic existence. Odysseus' namelessness is strategic and self-interested; the innominate condition of his men betrays, or oxymoronically represents, their exclusion from the space of representation. The Homeric word for "fate, fortune, lot or doom" derives from *moira,* "part, portion, share," especially "a proper share"; it carries with it the suggestion of a just distribution of goods, which Pound held to be a central economic problem.[87] In the *Odyssey,* however, the collective distribution of goods, including access to the space of representation, gives way to something resembling or anticipating the purely private accumulation of wealth. The tale of Odysseus Polytropos is manifestly not the tale of the tribe, not the narrative of *isomoria,* equal fate and equal shares. It is Virgil who conceives of the heroic in communal terms—no hero has ever been less "responsible to himself" than Aeneas—and thus Virgil who commands Pound's loyalties. Pound casts his lot with the poet of imperial Rome, however, only to meet his own Carthage in the Pisan Cantos. Like Dido's city, the lyric interlude is a retreat from the historical into the private and

aesthetic. The poem reiterates the plight of Elpenor—"a man of no for-
tune, and with a name to come"—but in no way redresses it. The Pisan
Cantos makes or redeems only Pound's private fortune as a poet, and that
fortune is amassed at the cost of a collective destiny or *isomoria*.

One can only be grateful, of course, that Pound was finally limited to
dreaming his republic, given the horror to which he lent the authority of
his name. Yet the horror of the specific political investments cannot be
conflated—*pace* Lewis Hyde—with a politicized poetic itself. To insist on
the axiomatic: there never has been a poetic that transcends the political or
the historical. Indeed, poetry is perhaps never so fully political, or so
politically useful to the powers that be, as when it stands in a compensatory
relation to the actual. But this is to assume that the Pisan Cantos is discon-
tinuous with the otherwise transitive project of the larger poem, and
although this has been an operable assumption of my own argument to this
point, I want to conclude by advancing a seemingly contradictory thesis.
Pound's fascism is best understand not as a reactionary response to an
ethos of metaphoric displacement but as a commitment to metaphor, at
one with his failure to read the culture of metaphor other than meta-
phorically.

"Jewspapers"

Not that this should give any comfort whatsoever, but Pound was only
reluctantly a fascist. Or, better, Pound was only reluctantly political in any
sense of the term. Consider the question posed by his 1933 article "Murder
by Capital": "What drives, or what can drive a man interested almost
exclusively in the arts, into social theory or into a study of the 'gross
material aspects' . . . of the present?" Pound's answer, already implicit in
the formulation of the question, is the atrocities that have been perpetrated
against art. "I have blood lust," he continues, "because of what I have seen
done to, and attempted against, the arts in my time" (*SP* 228–29). In the
name of art the poet abandons the realm of artistic autonomy, and only to
reconstruct the "gross material aspects" of the age in the image and inter-
ests of art. Aestheticism is not abandoned but rendered militant, intro-
duced, to return to Benjamin's formulation, into the heart of political life
itself.

Benjamin is frequently claimed as a poststructuralist before the fact, but
the argument of the concluding moments of "The Work of Art in the Age
of Mechanical Reproduction" might be expected to trouble the current
theoretical regime, which recognizes no meaningful distinction between
the operations of power and their discursive manifestations. Certainly
poststructuralism can lay claim to a subversive politics, which it routinely
does, only if power can be said to inhere in its rhetorical legitimacy, which
poststructuralism, no less routinely, exposes as illegitimate.[88] But as Ben-
jamin suggests, the blurring of the distinction, the effacing of the differ-
ence, may be itself a strategy of power. Fascism substitutes a compensatory

right to expression for the exercise of real economic power; it succeeds to the extent that it recovers anticapitalist fervor for capitalist property relations. The initial Fasci di Combattimento, the so-called fascists of the first hour, advocated a program of democratic, semisocialist reform, which included the suppression of joint stock companies; the confiscation of unproductive capital, excess war profits, and church properties; the turning over of land to peasants for associative cultivation; and the creation of a national system of industrial management by syndicates of workers and technicians. The founding Twenty-Five Points of Hitler's National Socialist German Workers' party recommended partial collectivism in opposition to the interests of big business, large landholders, financial institutions, and major corporations, the strict regulation or nationalization of which was to be harmonized with small-scale individual ownership.[89] Neither program was ever instituted, although Italian Fascism remained theoretically committed to the ideal of collectivism, and the Twenty-Five Points of the German Workers' party were never officially repudiated. Neither is what we now tend to characterize, however vaguely, as "fascist." The obvious question thus arises: Why?

Fascism is a response to a specific economic order. Like marxism, it is predicated on the notion (here I am quoting Pound) that capitalism has shown itself "as little else than the idea that unprincipled thieves and antisocial groups should be allowed to gnaw into . . . the right to share out the fruits of a common co-operative labour" (*SP* 298). But fascism is not marxism, although much tends to be made of the possibility that Pound's critique of capitalism might well have taken a progressive turn. Between 1930 and 1934 Pound was engaged in a sustained dialogue with the U.S. left: the poet who actively labored in the cause of the fascist city of man was also a regular contributor to radical and/or left-leaning journals.[90] (The young Mussolini was himself the editor of *Avanti!*, the Socialist party newspaper.) "Gents who make guns like to sell 'em," Pound writes in *Jefferson and/or Mussolini;* "such is the present state of the world, in the bourgeois demo-liberal anti-Marxian anti-fascist anti-Leninist system" (72). Speculation on the form Pound's opposition to the "bourgeois demo-liberal" establishment might have taken is, of course, comforting. In substituting an alleged purity of motives for what thus becomes but the misguided nature of the politics, it rehearses the redemptive gesture— "nothing matters but the quality/of the affection"—that is at the heart of the Pisan Cantos. Yet some sense of alternative historical possibilities is necessary, at least if fascism is not to be reduced to the ahistorical condition of a generalized pathology. "Whoever is not willing to talk about capitalism," Max Horkheimer cautions, "should remain silent about fascism as well,"[91] but fascism also defines itself against the other great international movement of the early twentieth century which its anticapitalist fervor might well have become: communism. And on this, the choice of right over left, Pound is perfectly explicit. He complains that "no party programme ever contains enough of his [the artist's] programme to give him the least satisfaction" (*SP* 215), but the artist's interests are clearly decisive: "I don't believe any estimate of Mussolini will be valid unless it *starts* from his passion for construction. Treat him as artifex and all details fall into place. Take him as anything but the artist and you will get muddled with contradictions" (*JM* 33–34). Pound cast his lot with Mussolini because he believed the dictator to be engaged in a project analogous to his own.

Mussolini as *artifex* or Hitler as artist—Pound's advice on how to "take" the former is also Goebbels's on how to "take" the latter:

> Politics, too, is perhaps an art, if not the highest and most all-embracing art there is. Art and artists are not only there to unite; their far more important task is to create a form, to expel the ill trends and make room for the healthy to develop. As a German politician I therefore cannot recognize the dividing line you [Wilhelm Furtwängler] hold to be the only one, namely that between good and bad art. Art must not only be good, it must also be conditioned by the exigencies of the people or, rather, only an art that draws on the *Volkstum* as a whole may ultimately be regarded as good and mean something for the people to whom it is directed.[92]

The individual art object is to be judged in terms of the larger aesthetic project that Goebbels elsewhere terms "the plastic art of the State,"[93] which is directed toward the exigencies of a people who want nothing better or more than to express themselves. Liberal democracies allow for the "free" expression and dissemination of individual opinions; in "the plastic art of the state," the communal or the community is itself the living artwork, and the people are at once the collective creator and the realized content of the work. Mussolini declared that fascist theater must become a "teatro per ventimila," theater for twenty thousand.[94] Liberal culture, at least in its early modern phase, presupposes the dominance of the private and privatizing experience of the novel; the older, communal energies of the theater survive, but only as marginal or elitist forms of cultural experience. *Homo fascistus,* however, knows himself "ecstatically," not oppositionally, in relation to the world; hence both the expansion of the theater proper, or an aesthetic of size, mass, and volume, and the general aestheticization of life, the highly choreographed parades, rallies, and the like. The fascist ideal of the *Gesamtkunstwerk* is not, then, reducible to its explicitly aesthetic manifestations—say, the Festspiel at Bayreuth. For if the Festspiel was to be for Germany what the Greater Dionysia was for Greece—"the place where a people, gathered together in their State, provide themselves with a representation of what they are and what grounds them as such"[95]—then all of Nazi Germany, all of fascist Europe, was a Festspiel.

But this is not the only sense, and certainly not the most obvious sense, in which fascism can be understood in terms of its representational technologies and strategies. "A representative body wherein each kind of worker is represented by a man of his own trade," Pound argues, "cannot fall into the same *kind* of senility as one wherein he is represented by a professional politician."⁹⁶ "If America went corporate," he speculates on Radio Rome, "I would be MORE represented in the confederation of artists and professional men than I would be as a citizen of Montgomery county" (*EPS* 324). Fascist Italy did little to challenge the class structure. It did, however, provide for the direct representation of specific class and/or economic interests. In 1928 the National Council of Corporations, which in theory regulated the Italian economy, changed its system of representation from the political to the occupational, which Pound held to be more representative than the old model parliaments. And as with fascist assemblies, so too with fascist discourse: "AN AWAKENED INTELLIGENCE" animates the nation, Pound rejoices, "and a new LANGUAGE" informs "the debates in the Chambers" (*JM* 73). "What drives, or what can drive a man interested almost exclusively in the arts, into social theory or into a study of the 'gross material aspects' . . . of the present?": a revolution in and access to representation.

But a revolution that strategically misrepresents the nature of the capitalism it thus fails to challenge, a revolution that figures economic injustice as racial villainy, the better to divert anticapitalist sentiment from its proper target. Peter Nicholls notes that the appeal of C. H. Douglas and the economics of social credit is easily explicable in terms of its reduction of all economic injustice to a single cause, lack of sufficient purchasing power on the part of the consumer, which can be remedied through modifications in, rather than any fundamental challenge to, the logic of capitalism. Social creditism allows for the expression of popular resentment against capitalist practices—the compulsion to continuous labor, the creation of artificial scarcity and demand, the concentration of economic power—without striking at the heart of capitalist property relations themselves.⁹⁷ For "a man interested preeminently in the arts," moreover, it has the added advantage of providing for a fully coherent, if undermotivated, *narrative* of economic injustice. "There is a turning point in the poem toward the middle," Pound explained in a BBC interview. "Up to that point it is a sort of detective story, and one is looking for the crime."⁹⁸ Pound's epic is something of an economic whodunit, and his formal challenge as a poet, if not his obligation as an economist, is to provide an aesthetically satisfying explanation.

But here social creditism proved wanting, for there is no strong sense in Douglas that any particular class of persons is "criminally" responsible for economic injustice. Rather, injustice is held to be structurally indigenous to the system, the profiteering of any given individuals or classes of individuals (and Douglas's own anti-Semitism) notwithstanding. Structural injustice is not, however, amenable to conventional narrative elaboration; like structural terrorism or genocide, as opposed to individual acts of political violence, it belies the narrative tendency to locate agency in human volition or consciousness. A fully satisfying detective story presupposes an identifiable criminal replete with criminal motives—"Murder by Capital," but what motivates the act? "In Italy, as elsewhere," Pound cautions, "crime fiction has served to distract attention from the great underlying crime, the crime of the usocratic system itself" (*SP* 341). Pound himself, however, remains caught within the mystifying conventions he warns against. Structural injustice is refigured as racial villainy and "la significa-tion bancaire" is given a local habitation and a name. The great criminal of the *Cantos* emerges as the international banking system under the control of an international conspiracy of Jews.

If the Jew tends to figure prominently in the construction of ameliora-tive narratives of capitalist injustice, it is because the Jew proved indispens-able in the transition to a capitalist economy, in mediating the contradic-tion between the emerging needs of business and government for a new system of credit and the old moral and legal prohibitions against usury. Lester Little argues that the Jews did not fully acquire their alterior status in the Christian West until the twelfth century. The era that witnessed the rise of the profit economy and the growth of major urban centers "set up" the Jew, in both senses of the term, in finance, thereby positing as vil-lainously "alien" or "other" its own structural necessity.[99] Not that Chris-tians allowed theological niceties to interfere with their economic interests. Luther opposed usury in conscience only, not in effect, and Calvin oblig-ingly brought conscience into line: "[I]f all usury is condemned, tighter fetters are imposed on the conscience than the Lord himself would wish."[100] Henceforth theology would be theology, business would be business, and never the twain would meet. Pound rages against this divi-sion of knowledge and labor as evidence of a "REJEWdiazed religion" (*EPS* 411), but it is little more than the full coming into being of the bourgeois settlement. For it is on this tacit but nevertheless rigid separation of spheres—what is right "in theory" need not apply "in practice"—that the modern world is founded.[101] Or, to reverse the perspective, what is implic-itly accepted "in practice" can be effectively denied "in theory." Long after usury became the norm in the bourgeois West, it continued to be identified as a specifically Jewish practice or aberration. Hence the paradox, which proved murderous: the Jew came to function as the referent for an eco-nomic order whose very lack of referentiality—usury presupposes a closed semiotic system, an economic order in which money breeds money with-out reference to goods produced or work done—was experienced as un-just.

Capitalism as a closed semiotic system best characterizes the latter de-cades of the nineteenth and the early decades of the twentieth centuries, which witnessed a quantitative economic transformation, "the passage from liberal (or industrial or competitive) capitalism to the capitalism of monopolies and huge trusts," a transition that roughly corresponded to the decline of gold money, economic signs that are convertible or translatable into material wealth, and its replacement by bank notes, signs whose con-vertibility, translatability, or referentiality is purely hypothetical.[102] The creator of financial empires—the Gatsby-like individual whose immense wealth bears no immediate or discernible relation to entrepreneurial activity—dominates the age. Or, rather, the economic logic of the age subordinates industrial enterprise to the hitherto unprecedented power of financial institutions and the hegemony of banking practices. David Harvey notes that the depression that originated in Britain in 1846–47, the first full-fledged crisis of capitalist overaccumulation, "seriously challenged received ideas as to the meaning and role of money in social life." Earlier, relatively localized crises had been attributable to specific and immediate causes (natural calamities, geopolitical struggle, and the like). The depression of 1846–47, however, was both general (because of the internationalism of money power it quickly came to engulf the entirety of the capitalist world) and structural (it registered an overt antagonism between "the financial system, the whole structure of credit moneys and 'fictitious capitals,'" and its monetary base, "gold and other tangible commodities that give a clear physical meaning to money"). After 1850 stock and capital markets were systematically organized and opened to generalized participation under legal rules of incorporation and market contract, but the tension between credit and specie money was far from resolved. The years 1890–1929 again witnessed an unprecedented growth—rivaled only by our own historical moment—in the power of finance capital, or an unprecedented concentration of power in financial institutions. The Rothschilds, who function in the *Cantos* as the very embodiment of "la signification bancaire" (although it is of the essence of the latter to resist embodiment), came to dominate the economic life of Europe.[103] Capitalism entered the phase that Rudolph Hilferding, who was the first to theorize the transition, termed "finance" or "monopoly" capitalism, which Lenin subsequently deemed "the economic quintessence of imperialism."[104] Capitalism made itself new, but not Pound. He remained caught within the old myths, the story of the Jews and capitalism.

Fictitious capital as opposed to "real property": Pound is the poet of the latter, in Sartre's sense of the term:

> The anti-Semite has a fundamental incomprehension of the various forms of modern property: money, securities, etc. They are abstractions . . . a sign of wealth, not a concrete possession. The anti-Semite can conceive only of a type of primitive ownership of land based on a veritable magical rapport, in which the thing possessed and its possessor are united by a bond of mystical participation; he is the poet of real property. . . .[105]

Against the abstraction that is modern wealth, Pound advocates the operations of the Monte dei Paschi, the Sienese bank—"damn good bank" (Canto XLII)—that was literally grounded in a type of collective "ownership of land," the pastures of Siena that sustained the Sienese flocks. To own deposits or shares in the bank was to own *luoghi* or "places" on the mountainside; the "Monte" as bank or money was coincident with the *monte* as mount or land. Because the bank paid its depositors or shareholders at the same rate at which it lent money—minus half a percent, which went for overhead—it was effectively nonprofit. "'The foundation, Siena, has been to keep bridle on usury'" (Canto XLIV): the circulation of money grounded in "real property" stands as the redeemed counterpart to the dissemination of fictitious capital, mere economic "signs."

Gold is not "real property"; like most populists Pound viewed the gold standard as a fetishization of the sign. Because it does not "germinate like grain" (*SP* 349), because it bears no "organic" relation to the rhythms of "natural increase," it can only misrepresent the reality of wealth, which is derived from nature alone. Better, Pound argued, Silvio Gesell's *Schwundgeld*, "scrip money" or "perishable currency," which resists the conflation of economic signs—money "is NOT in itself abundance"—and true value, which is derived "from labour and nature" alone (*SP* 294). Unlike the self-generating or self-proliferating nature of banking capital, scrip money is a form of "counter-usury," a tax on the nonproductive deployment of capital, an economy in which a dollar becomes systematically less valuable the longer it is retained.[106] Ideally, currency should be "no more durable than potatoes, crops, or fabrics" (*SP* 336); it should last "only as long as things last in the material world" (*SP* 349). The "various degrees of durability" of goods—transient, durable, permanent— "could conceivably (but very cumbrously) be *each* represented by money that should melt at parallel rate" (*SP* 277). Capitalist money is arbitrary in Saussure's sense of the term: its specific materialities bear no necessary relation to true wealth. Or, as Coleridge might say, capitalist money does not participate in the nature of the reality it renders intelligible. (Although the term "capitalist money" has become something of an anachronism. "Compared to the ever more vaporous hierarchy of exchange, money, itself, has been devalued as *too weighty*. . . . Now, *the use of money* has become the most evident indicator of poverty, or at least illegitimacy [street peddlers, drug dealers, dispensers of bribes, and so on]. The signs of solvency have become increasingly invisible.")[107] But if *Schwundgeld* suggests a romantic aesthetic, it is the romantic symbol introduced into the life of historic action.[108] "Call things by their proper names—in the market" (Canto XXXIV): the poetics of *le mot juste* is also an economics.

A just or true representation of wealth participates in the nature of the reality it renders intelligible. It follows that misrepresentations will involve a certain blockage or mediation. Pound calls this "usury":

> Stonecutter is kept from his stone
> weaver is kept from his loom
> WITH USURA
> wool comes not to market
> sheep bringeth no gain with usura
>
> . . . .
>   Pietro Lombardo
> came not by usura
> Duccio came not by usura
> nor Pier della Francesca; Zuan Bellin' not by usura
> nor was "La Calunnia" painted.
>
> . . . .

> Usura slayeth the child in the womb
> It stayeth the young man's courting
> It hath brought palsey to bed, lyeth
> between the young bride and her bridegroom.
>   (Canto XLV)

"USURA" is said to mediate or "come between" otherwise transitive rela-
tions: economic, artistic, and sexual. But in fact "USURA" comes between
only the poet and the economic order he purports to critique. "With
USURA" the experience of alienation, the condition of being in capitalist
society, is misnamed, falsely specified as a villainous conspiracy from with-
out rather than a structural necessity from within. Consider Pound's rage
at the (alleged) Charter of the Bank of England—it enjoys *"benefit of
interest on all / the moneys which it, the bank, creates out of nothing"* (Canto
XLVI)—which might at first seem reasonable enough. There is something
appealing, if naive and nostalgic, in the call for an economic order mea-
sured and gauged by human requirements, in a poetic given to the politics
of need rather than the metaphysics of desire. But the economic critique is
translated into, subsumed by, the anti-Semitism that substitutes for it.
Pound "reads" economic creation ex nihilo, the ostensible privilege of the
Bank of England, not as a phase in the historical development of capitalism
but in relation to the sky god of Genesis, whose creation of the world ex
nihilo betrays the ahistorical essence of all things Judaic. The "first great
HOAX" was the "substitution of kike god . . . for universal god," from
which all subsequent hoaxes and abuses follow.[109] So usury becomes "Jew-
sury" (*EPS* 254), and the Jew as a figure for figuration or mediation comes
between Pound and any plausible reading of the "gross material aspects" of
the age. Pound reads the nonreferential or autoreferential status of the
linguistic sign, moreover, not as an aesthetic analogue of "unconvertable
paper," the closed semiotics of capitalist money, but as the ahistorical
essence of all things Judaic. The Jews are a people without interest in verbal
precision, indeed, a people with a vested interest in making the "word
mean something it does *NOT* say" (*EPS* 284). So "Jewsury" finds its explic-
itly aesthetic analogue in the poetics of "Jewspapers" (*SP* 299). "It is, of
course, useless to engage in antisemitism," Pound cautions, "leaving intact
the *Hebraic monetary system* which is a most tremendous instrument of
usury" (*SP* 351). But history suggests otherwise. Anti-Semitism proves
highly useful in recovering anticapitalist sentiment for capitalist property
relations that are thus left "intact."

Hence the anomaly: Pound's idolization of Mussolini and his admira-
tion for Hitler cannot be explained in terms of either man's commitment to
or implementation of his own economic theories. Pound was opposed, for
example, to deficit financing, yet Hitler created his immense war machine
through deficit spending. But if the economic realities of fascism cannot
account for Pound's commitment to it, its reduction of structural injustice
to racial villainy can. (Mussolini's Italy was considerably less racist than
Hitler's Germany, but then Pound was considerably more racist than Mus-

solini's Italy.)[110] "Why curse Adolph," Pound asks; "why not get down to bedrock? . . . As always jewish outlaw and crook leads the sheriff's posse back to the ghetto."[111] The narrative of economic crime and punishment is recast as a western, but it is otherwise much the same story: in a world in which structural injustice is figured as "crooks" and crooks as Jews, the task of the sheriff's posse or the führer's goons is all the easier. In a 1933 article for *New English Weekly* Pound blithely decrees that "[t]he class struggle is *foutu*": "Marx did not anchor history to one spot. He perceived a reality. The class war is no longer with us. There is a fight on. Yes. And it has been on for some time; not between one class and another, but between humanity at large and one of the most ignoble oligarchies the world has yet suffered."[112] In his first speech to the Chamber of Deputies (June 21, 1921), Mussolini explicitly denies that "all of human history can be explained by economic determinism." A kinder, gentler capitalism is the order of the day: "We assert . . . that the real history of capitalism is only now beginning, because capitalism is not just a system of oppression; it also represents a choice of values, a co-ordination of hierarchies, a more amply developed sense of individual responsibility."[113] In 1934 Mussolini decrees "the end of liberal capitalism" and a final resolution to the problem of production.[114] Neither "the beginning of the real history of capitalism" nor "the end of liberal capitalism" challenges the relations of production or control over the means of production. Class antagonism is superseded by, or is revealed always to have been an allegory of, the more fundamental antagonism, the master narrative: the fight between humanity at large and the Jews. Anti-Semitism was not much in evidence in Fascist Italy—given fascist standards of anti-Semitism—until its waning hours, and then only under the threat of Nazi guns. But in this Italy was the exception and Pound and Hitler extreme versions of the norm. As Arno Mayer argues: "Nearly everywhere . . . in non-Communist Europe, and particularly in eastern and central Europe, a mixture of traditional Judeophobia and new political anti-Semitism informed the ideology and program of the inchoate right. Above all, its fascist vanguard used anti-Jewish appeals in preying not only on the resentments of the endangered lower middle classes caught in the maelstrom of modernization but also on the fears of superannuated elites in the upper classes desperate to maintain their overprivileged positions."[115] Class conflict is strategically redirected and recontained: solidarity in the face of the Jewish threat.

Now it would be possible, perhaps even comforting, to stop here. Fascism, if not anti-Semitism, could be abandoned to the dustbin of history, and along with it the modernism against which we, in these postmodernist times, define ourselves. But if nothing else, the Jew as a figure for figuration is still very much with us—too much with us, I want to suggest in conclusion. Not that its "repeat," as Pound would say, in the discourse of poststructuralism, particularly the work of Jacques Derrida, is to be taken as evidence of an abiding anti-Semitism. On the contrary, Judaism has been described as the "unofficial religion" of poststructuralism:

> As posed by deconstruction . . . "excess" would be a property of all
> written texts, a product of the inability of any form of discourse to master
> fully its own rhetorical status. If this "excess" by which writing is distin-
> guished can be understood (provisionally) as "an experience of the infi-
> nitely other"—that is, as an encounter with textual elements which re-
> main irreducibly peripheral with respect to a presiding (authorial)
> consciousness—we might then infer that Judaism conveys a rhetorically
> similar experience, for it forms an analogous, unassimilable "excess" on
> the margins of the dominant (Christian) culture.[116]

In its attempt to recover the hitherto marginalized, be it in respect to a
"presiding (authorial) consciousness" or a "dominant (Christian) culture,"
poststructuralism intends a subversive politics. And it is a welcome an-
tidote to the relentlessly Christian and Christianizing proclivities of much
literary theory. But intentionality, as poststructuralism itself acknowl-
edges, does not govern accomplishment, and despite its best intentions,
poststructuralism unwittingly rehearses an equation that, as Benjamin says
in a different context, allows for "a processing of data in the fascist sense":
the identification of the Jew with figuration or mediation, with the closed
semiotics, the infinitely deferred finalities, of capitalist economies.[117]

In "Edmond Jabès and the Question of the Book," Derrida argues that
"the situation of the Jew [is] exemplary of the situation of the poet, the
man of speech and of writing."[118] As in Heidegger's essay on Hölderlin, in
which the poet is said to be *Zwischenbereich,* caught between the "No-more
of the gods who have fled and the Not-yet of the god that is coming,"[119]
the poet and the Jew, both a people of the book, are celebrated as exiles
adrift in the nonteleological play of language. To write or speak is to
assume the (non)position of the Wandering Jew, to be forever exiled from
meaning, from presence, in a region of linguistic unlikeness. "The situation
of the Jew" is nothing less than—and so, by the same token, nothing more
specific than—the condition of (non)being in language. The diaspora is
translated into a figure for the irreducibility of the figurative itself, and an
existential violence directed against a people is translated into a highly
suspect celebration of language as the same.

Derrida negotiates a relation between language and a historically specific
mode of being in the world, but only at the cost of positing exile, aliena-
tion, as the ontology of both, which may well be characteristic of post-
structuralist appropriations of Judaism in general. Jeffrey Mehlman points
out that Paul de Man's essay on Walter Benjamin and translation, which
scrupulously documents the errors of both Benjamin's English and French
translators, curiously fails to register the most telling error of all: the
growth of languages "bis ans messianistische Ende ihrer Geschichte" is
rendered by Harry Zohn as "until the end of their time."[120] The omission
of the word "messianic" is consistent with de Man's general understanding
of Benjamin, whom he is eager to redeem from Gershom Scholem's sup-
posed misappropriation: "Benjamin [is] closer to certain elements in
Nietzsche than he is to a messianic tradition which he spent his entire life

holding at bay. The man who bears a strong responsibility in this unhappy misinterpretation of Benjamin is Scholem, who deliberately tried to make Benjamin say the opposite of what he said for ends of his own."[121] De Man's critique of Scholem recalls Pound's critique of the Jews—they are a people intent on making "the word mean something it does NOT say"—but it is de Man who seems most intent on holding the messianic at bay. At the very least, the failure to register Zohn's omission of the word "messianic" suggests a Benjamin rehabilitated for ends that are de Man's own. If, then, Judaism is the unofficial religion of poststructuralism, it is a Judaism evacuated of historical specificity and messianic longing, a Judaism recast in the image and interests of the poststructuralist fetishization of the non-teleological.

Derrida's "White Mythology," for example, speaks of usury as "systematically," rather than historically or culturally, "tied to the metaphoric perspective," and so to writing and Judaism:

> The value of *usure* also has to be subjected to interpretation. It seems to have a systematic tie to the metaphorical perspective. It will be rediscovered wherever the theme of metaphor is privileged. . . . This characteristic—the concept of *usure*—belongs not to a narrow historico-theoretical configuration, but more surely to the concept of metaphor itself, and to the long metaphysical sequence that it determines or that determines it.[122]

Despite the critique implied by its prefix, "post-structuralism" remains faithful to the systematic bias of its precursor, even as it argues against the possibility of a systematic metalanguage that would account for textual phenomena. It is no doubt true, as Andrew Parker contends, that "rhetoric and usury have long been linked as synonymous terms designating the production of interdicted (linguistic or economic) values."[123] A long link is not, however, a systematic or structural tie, and it has been some time since "usury" (read: the operations of international finance capital) has been an interdicted "value" or practice in the bourgeois West. (Indeed, what poststructuralism is pleased to call "unassimilable excess" on the margins of the dominant culture curiously resembles the norm.) *Judaism, writing,* and *usury* are not structurally synonymous terms, the poststructuralist elision of the differences notwithstanding: "The difficulty of being Jewish . . . is the same as the difficulty of writing, for Judaism and writing are but the same waiting, the same hope, the same depletion [une même usure]."[124] To the extent that "the same depletion" exhausts the meaning of "une même usure," Judaism is again evacuated of messianic fervor. Entropy, not teleological longing, defines "the difficulty of being Jewish." But to the extent that "une même usure," like the platonic *pharmakon,* also includes its antithetical sense—"excess" or "usury"—Judaism is again assimilated to the logic of capitalism. In Derrida's formulation (or Parker's paraphrase thereof), usury and metaphor belong to the same tropological series in which each functions analogously as an inscription that deflects any transitive relation between a sign and its intended signified. And as each is "the same as" the difficulty of being Jewish, whatever that might mean, poststructuralism rehearses the logic of Ezra Pound. The Jew is metaphor is usury; the Jew is "Jewspapers" is "Jewsury." All are highly valorized terms in the poststructuralist lexicon and demonized ones in Pound's; but the equation that Derrida would render "systematic" or "structural" has its own history, which includes the uses made of it by Ezra Pound. The existential violence in which the equation originated and is-sued needs, then, to be acknowledged, as does the danger inherent in any celebration of the supposed synonymity of its terms. Poststructuralism risks perpetuating, precisely under the guise of the systematic or structural, a thoroughly contingent (not to say specious) identification of a people with the operations of a specific economic order.

Poststructuralist readings of Pound tend to discern in his "hostility toward Judaism . . . an oblique confirmation of his own irreducible 'Jewishness'—evidence for which can be deduced from [his] 'proper' name."[125] It is fascism itself, however, that seeks to make such deductions possible—recall the "Name Decrees" issued by Hitler's Ministry of the Interior—and anti-Semitism is, to say the least, problematic evidence of an "irreducible Jewishness." Robert Casillo, following Parker, maintains that "Pound's effort to write against writing, as against the Jews and their 'poison,' is defeated by the return within his own text and life of that otherness and difference, Jewish and otherwise, which he seeks to re-press."[126] Pound himself, however, was perfectly capable of railing against "Jewsury" in the name of Judaism; like his biblical counterpart, this Ezra also had "plans to rebuild the temple in Jerusalem."[127] Casillo is speaking of the subversive force of the rhetoric, not the conscious identifications of the poet, but here too he is easily matched by Pound:

> Rome rose through the idiom of Caesar, Ovid, and Tacitus, she declined in a welter of rhetoric, the diplomat's "language to conceal thought," and so forth. (*ABC* 33)

> Italy went to rot, destroyed by rhetoric, destroyed by the periodic sen-tence and the flowing paragraph, as the Roman Empire had been de-stroyed before her. For when words cease to cling close to things, king-doms fall, empires wane and diminish. Rome went because it was no longer the fashion to hit the nail on the head.[128]

Pound assumes, in the obligatory poststructuralist fashion, that power inheres in its rhetorical formulations, that it is somehow bound to its rhetorical legitimacy. Poststructuralism celebrates, and Pound bemoans, the subversive effect of rhetoric, but this is little more than a distinction without a difference: both projects remain bound to the level of expres-sion. There is a sense, then, in which Pound's "animus against writing (his own)" is insufficiently developed. The willingness to explain all, including the rise and fall of the Roman Empire, in terms of writing or rhetoric betrays the aestheticizing habits of a man interested preeminently in the arts. And so Pound's economics never progressed beyond a concern with monetary representation and distribution: the question of production having been decreed solved by Mussolini, Pound gave himself over to monetarist gadgetry, the aesthetics of money, the poetics of real property. The much-repeated polemic against metaphor, the catachrestic "habit of defining things always in terms of something else," belies, in fact, a generalized capitulation to it.[129] All was explicable in terms of the tropological fantasy of a Jewish conspiracy, the "race prejudice" that he came to regret as a "suburban prejudice."[130] Much has been made of this palinode, but even here the aestheticism may be asserting itself. To repudiate a prejudice as "suburban" is to reject a vulgarity, not a massive political, ethical, and human failing.

3

T. S. ELIOT
The Poetics of Failure

Eliot's reputation, like Harry's homecoming in *The Family Reunion,* is troubled by the Eumenides, the vengeful ghosts of Milton and Shelley. Northrop Frye, an enemy only to Eliot's cultural polemic, suggests that this need not be so:

> Since the nineteen-twenties, critics have become increasingly aware of the continuity of the English Romantic tradition and of Eliot's place in it. . . . One cannot both accept a tradition and decide what it is to be. For appreciating the real place of Eliot's drama, and perhaps his poetry too, in English literature, the amnesty proposed in "Little Gidding" ["These things have served their purpose: let them be"] does not go far enough. The greatness of his achievement will finally be understood, not in the context of the tradition he chose, but in the context of the tradition that chose him.[1]

Frye's argument recalls Eliot's own "mature" contention that "literary politics" are but tactical games,[2] yet there is a sense in which this expanded amnesty is predicated on an understanding of the relation of the literary to the social which is distinctly (or at least characteristically) non-Eliotic. The cultural polemic "must be considered," Frye concedes, "but [it] can also be clearly separated from Eliot's permanent achievement, leaving that achievement intact" (6). Eliot's reputation could only profit from the separation, but Eliot himself utterly denies its validity:

> I cannot see that poetry can ever be separated from something which I should call belief, and to which I cannot see any reason for refusing the

name of belief, unless we are to reshuffle names altogether. It should hardly be needful to say that it will not inevitably be orthodox Christian belief, although that possibility can be entertained, since Christianity will probably continue to modify itself, as in the past, into something that can be believed. . . . The majority of people live below the level of belief or doubt. It takes application, and a kind of genius, to believe anything. . . . We await . . . the great genius who shall triumphantly succeed in believing *something*.[3]

The separation of the "greatness" of the poem from the beliefs of the poet—and it is telling that Eliot speaks of "beliefs," not politics—presupposes a historical dispensation in which belief in "anything" is merely a secondary or public adjunct "to the content of a real 'private' life, which alone is authentic and genuine."[4] Frye's judgment is accurate: much of the polemic is deplorable. But not, I want to suggest, its refusal of the New Critical aesthetic that would separate the "authentic" accomplishment from the deplorable polemic. There is, as Eliot well knew, something "unpleasant" about T. S. Eliot:

> With his features of clerical cut,
> And his brow so grim
> And his mouth so prim
> And his conversation, so nicely
> Restricted to What Precisely
> And If and Perhaps and But.
> How unpleasant to meet Mr Eliot![5]

But if it is "unpleasant" to meet Mr. Eliot—and perhaps never more so than in these postmodern times—it is no less salutary for that. We have become altogether too adept at separating the suspect political burden from the genuine accomplishment. If nothing else, the deplorable polemic is an exemplary reminder that deplorable polemics cannot be so blithely dismissed.

Raymond Williams acknowledges as much, even as he too takes issue with Eliot's social and cultural agenda:

> I believe his criticism of certain orthodox ideas of "culture" to be valuable, and I think that he has left the ordinary social-democratic case without many relevant answers. As a conservative thinker, he has succeeded in exposing the limitations of an orthodox "liberalism" which has been all too generally and too complacently accepted.[6]

Eliot attributes to orthodox Christianity the ability "to modify itself, as in the past, into something that can be believed," but the observation might be better (or also) applied to orthodox liberalism. Certainly poststructuralism recovers for literature the "frankly ontological distance" from "worldly discourses" that is at the heart of the liberal celebration of culture.[7] True, the current theoretical regime, unlike the New Critical formalism it displaces, does not simply amputate the suspect political content from the "genuine" accomplishment. Rather, it decrees that content "internally distanciated." It never was there, at least not in any coherent or compelling fashion; surgical intervention would be redundant. This is a "modified" liberalism, but a liberalism nevertheless. For under a theoretical dispensation in which "literary language . . . can never mean what it says because it never means anything except the fact that it is saying something that it does not mean,"[8] we can again cozy up to culture—or take up our positions as the middle men and women in the culture industry—secure in the knowledge "that art is on our side against the paradigms of organized [read: fascist] thought."[9]

But to return to the reevaluation of Eliot's place in literary tradition: the literary stock exchange, to borrow a metaphor from Frye, is volatile, and the poet of *The Waste Land,* once the wealthiest and most influential of all possible investors, now finds his stock devalued in favor of the very poets he helped bring to the verge of bankruptcy.[10] Harold Bloom, perhaps the most powerful of the anti-Eliot brokers, has done much to revive the fortunes of all that is Protestant and liberal in opposition to Eliot's Anglo-Catholic canon, but only to follow Eliot in investing everything in myths of decline. The "anxiety of influence" may seem different in kind from the "dissociation of sensibility," but Milton remains the caesura in literary history, the sublime disaster for all subsequent poets, and literary history again participates in a secularized version of the biblical Fall. There is a distinction, if not a difference: for Eliot, Milton is the Fall; for Bloom, after Milton everyone falls.[11] But the broad structural contours of the two arguments are otherwise indistinguishable.

Falls, as Coleridge might say, from the object world: gone is the poetry of Shakespeare, the man who "became all things," and in its place "all things and modes of action shape themselves anew" in the being of Milton. In Foucault's periodization, this "modernism" begins sometime in the seventeenth century, when

> the written word ceases to be included among the signs and forms of truth; language is no longer one of the figurations of the world, or a signature stamped upon things since the beginning of time. . . . It is the task of words to translate the truth if they can; but they no longer have the right to be considered a mark of it. Language has withdrawn from the midst of beings themselves. . . .[12]

Coleridge understood the passage from Shakespeare to Milton to be this withdrawal of language from the midst of things, as he knew his contemporaries to be latter-day casualties of a decisive rupture between "the written word" and "the signs and forms of truth." But whereas Coleridge, like Bloom, declares himself "gratified" by the Miltonic sublime—Milton is himself compensation for the object world he displaces[13]—Eliot is opposed to all valorizations of personality over and above "objective correlatives": "Poetry is not a turning loose of emotion, but an escape from emotion; it is not the expression of personality, but an escape from personality. But, of course, only those who have personality and emotions know what it means to want to escape from these things."[14] Bloom responds to the post-Miltonic "withdrawal of language from the midst of beings" by heroicizing the struggles of poetic subjectivity, Eliot by evacuating that subjectivity of all plenitude. The Miltonic apotheosis of the ego begets only the infernal triad of Whiggery, romanticism, and humanism, against which Eliot defines himself as "classicist in literature, royalist in politics, and anglo-catholic in religion."[15] Eliot and company lost the civil war they instigated—the romanticism-classicism debate—yet there is a sense in which the term "classicist" remains helpful, if only in the manner specified by Foucault:

> [I]t is the Name that organizes all Classical discourse; to speak or to write is not to say things or to express oneself, it is not a matter of playing with language, it is to make one's way towards the sovereign act of nomina-tion, to move, through language, towards the place where things and words are conjoined in their common essence, and which makes it possi-ble to give them a name. (117)

If a classicist does not "play" with language in Foucault's sense of the term, he or she can at least be playful with proper names. "Old Possum" vari-ously signed his name in the pages of *The Egoist* as the Rev. Charles James Grimble of the Vicarage, Leays (he thought it a sensible policy to let people "know about foreign ways and to keep their minds open"); Charles Augustus Conybeare of the Carleton Club, Liverpool (he wanted to know where the writers of philosophical articles in *The Egoist* obtained their ideas); and Muriel A. Schwarz of 60 Alexandria Gardens, Hampstead, N.W. (she thought an article by Wyndham Lewis had cast a slur on "the cheery philosophy of our brave boys in the trenches").[16] But Eliot is characteristically a poet of "invisibility," as Hugh Kenner styles it; he is given to anonymity, not aliases or alibis.[17] And if he takes a certain delight in playing with names, he also cautions that naming "isn't just one of your holiday games" (*CP* 209). Romanticism emanates from and returns to the ego; to speak or to write is to express oneself, which means that romanti-cism "leads its disciples only back upon themselves" (*SW* 31). "Language in a healthy state," however, "presents the object, is so close to the object that the two are identified." In the poetry of Swinburne

> they are identified . . . solely because the object has ceased to exist, because the meaning is merely the hallucination of meaning, because language, uprooted, has adapted itself to an independent life of atmo-spheric nourishment. In Swinburne . . . we see the word "weary" flour-ishing in this way independent of the particular and actual weariness of flesh or spirit. (*SE* 327)

Weariness should be made of sterner stuff.

It is the Name that organizes all classical discourse, but Eliot's classicism is not Pound's *cheng ming* by another name: Eliot is at once less and more radical than his compatriot. Less radical because for all practical purposes the social polemic does not endeavor to transform its culture. *Notes To-*

wards the Definition of Culture, for instance, has little more to offer by way
of practical recommendations than this: "[I]t would appear to be for the
best that the great majority of human beings should go on living in the
place in which they were born."[18] Eliot's desire for topographical stability
is continuous with Pound's politics of fixed addresses, of proper names and
places, but it cannot be equated with an active commitment to founding
the fascist city of man. True, Eliot is innocent only of his friend's passion
for translating ideas into action, not the ideas themselves; he has no invest-
ment in justifying earthly activity in earthly terms. (I am referring to the
postconversion Eliot. My formulation suggests a certain teleology, but as I
argue later—indeed, as I argue in much of this chapter—Eliot's critique of
the liberal settlement need not have issued in his archaicizing Anglo-
Catholicism.) Pound advocates a properly terrestrial fulfillment; Eliot
commits himself to what *Four Quartets* calls "an occupation for the saint"
(*CP* 190), an ethos of Christian love. And it is in this (very limited) sense
that Eliot is the more radical of the two. Pound accepts the "modern"
primacy of the economic, even as he labors to return the West to a pre-
modern state of economic development. Eliot attempts to revive, both as a
category of thought and an experience of the world, the primacy of the
theological, the mode in which the premodern (for Eliot the prelapsarian,
pre-Miltonic) West knew itself and conducted its struggles.

Not that Eliot forgets "the profit and loss" (*CP* 71) in the manner of his
own Phlebas the Phoenician; he registers his objections to an economic
order "imperfectly adapted to every purpose except making money" on any
number of occasions. The British policy of appeasement toward Nazi Ger-
many, for example, which culminated in the 1938 pact between Chamber-
lain and Hitler, elicits from Eliot a memorable denunciation of the logic of
international banking capital:

> We could not match conviction with conviction, we had no ideas with
> which we could either meet or oppose the ideas opposed to us. Was our
> society, which had always been so assured of its superiority and rectitude,
> so confident of its unexamined premises, assembled round anything
> more permanent than a congeries of banks, insurance companies and
> industries, and had it any beliefs more essential than a belief in compound
> interest and the maintenance of dividends?[19]

Eliot's sojourn in the Foreign Department at Lloyds between 1917 and
1925 was very much a schooling in the operations of "banks, insurance
companies and industries"; in 1920, he was "put in charge of settling all
pre-War debts between the Bank and Germans."[20] Experience taught Eliot
that the appeasement of Nazi Germany was perfectly consistent with the
operations of an economic order governed by "a belief in compound inter-
est," yet there is a sense in which Eliot's economics became expert beyond
experience. Conventional wisdom holds that "national prosperity and the
greatest happiness of the greatest number depend entirely on the difference
between good and bad economic theories." All sound thinking is, how-

ever, rooted "in the domain of ethics—in the end, the domain of the-
ology":[21] "[T]he division between those who accept, and those who deny,
Christian revelation, I take to be the most profound division between
human beings. It does not merely go deeper than divisions of class or race;
it is different in kind and cannot be measured by the same scale."[22] Eliot
reduces economics to a subdiscipline of a Judeophobic—and, for all practi-
cal purposes, anti-Semitic—theology.

It is in this context that the more extravagant of Eliot's pronouncements
are best placed. In declaring himself a "royalist in politics" or in characteriz-
ing the divine right of kings as a "noble faith," for example, Eliot is not
simply taking up sides in a seventeenth-century struggle, although the
romance of the Cavalier cause is not lost on the "classicist." Rather, he is
attempting to return faith to its preindividualistic, preliberal status, to
those prelapsarian days in which belief was something other (or more)
than the privatized, subjective experience of the believing subject.[23] In a
paper on comparative anthropology written for Josiah Royce's graduate
seminar at Harvard, Eliot argues that any legitimate study of "primitive"
religious ritual must attempt to recover the meaning it has for its partici-
pants, which is by definition collective, determined by the praxis of the
group, not the consciousness of any individual.[24] And what the youthful
Eliot advocated as the only historically responsible approach to precapital-
ist religious ritual the mature Eliot came to advance as the only viable
alternative to capitalist fragmentation: the community of the faithful, the
earthly adumbration of the City of God. A society that has no "beliefs more
essential than compound interest and the maintenance of dividends" is
powerless to meet the threat of a Hitler, who has himself beliefs more
demonic. The pressing necessity is to return belief to its properly theologi-
cal grounding, in which cause Eliot wrote, in response to the betrayal of
Munich, *The Idea of a Christian Society.*

Eliot acknowledges "two and only two finally tenable" (that is, non-
liberal) "hypotheses about life: the Catholic and the materialistic" (*SE*
514), for only the Catholic and the marxist hypotheses fulfull the ety-
mological promise of *religio,* a binding together. Not that marxism, in the
familiar phrase, is "just another religion." Marxism labors to overcome, not
simply think its way back before, the liberal dichotomy of self and society.
(In the vocabulary of *After Strange Gods,* marxism is "blasphemy" and
liberalism a "heresy" in relation to the "orthodoxy" that is Anglo-
Catholicism. Blasphemy is a negative affirmation of the truth it seeks to
deny; heresy is simply wrong. Eliot has considerably more respect for the
"blasphemer" Joyce than the "heretic" Lawrence.) "Man is man because he
can recognize supernatural realities, not because he can invent them" (*SE*
485). Man is a creature, not a creator; he or she is not a "poet" in the
etymological sense of the term. Such is the Catholic hypothesis. Man is
man because he or she makes material realities, if only on the basis of the
circumstances history provides. Such is the materialist hypothesis.

It is telling, in this context, that *The Waste Land* is dedicated to "il miglior fabbro," "the better maker," and that Eliot retroactively dismisses as unintended (if not downright silly) the "social criticism" his critics discerned in it: "Various critics have done me the honour to interpret the poem in terms of criticism of the contemporary world, have considered it, indeed, as an important bit of social criticism. To me it was only the relief of a personal and wholly insignificant grouse against life; it is just a piece of rhythmical grumbling."[25] If ever the social order were to provide for genuine collective experience, the "Catholic hypothesis" might give way to the "materialist." But Eliot generally guards against any conflation of the spiritually existential and the socially hypothetical. *Four Quartets,* for example, presents as an accomplished fact the state of affairs—the exhaustion of the utopian imagination—it labors to effect:

> We cannot think of a time that is oceanless
> Or of an ocean not littered with wastage
> Or of a future that is not liable
> Like the past, to have no destination.
>
> (CP 186)

It is "the function of art," Eliot writes in "Poetry and Drama," "to bring us to a condition of serenity, stillness, and reconciliation; and then leave us, as Virgil left Dante, to proceed toward a region where that guide can avail us no farther" (*OPP* 87). The analogy conflates the authority of Virgil or pagan poetry with that of poetry itself; Eliot seems to forget that the *Paradiso,* the realm in which Dante's guide is of no avail, is also poetry, not divine writ. But then Dante is the exception that proves virtually all of Eliot's rules, and any blurring of the distinction between culture and religion, poetry and revelation, is to be resisted.

The epigraph to *Notes Towards the Definition of Culture* is a definition of the word *definition,* an attempt to delimit semantic possibilities: "DEFINITION: 1. The setting of bounds; limitation (rare)—1483" (*Oxford English Dictionary*). As Maud Ellmann puts it, "to define is to confine, to put things in their places," which is the burden of Eliot's social polemic in general: the danger that is topographical mobility is also the danger that is tropological slippage or displacement.[26] In *After Strange Gods,* Eliot regrets the opportunities for movement the modern world affords: "We must always remember that—in spite of every means of transport that can be devised—the local community must always be the most permanent, and that the concept of the nation is by no means fixed and invariable" (20–21). The fetishization of land recalls Pound, as does the demonology that attends it: "Reasons of race and religion combine to make any large number of free-thinking Jews undesirable" (*ASG* 20). Culture presupposes a sense of place, and the Jew is identified with topographical mobility:

> My house is a decayed house,
> And the jew squats on the window sill, the owner,
> Spawned in some estaminet of Antwerp,
> Blistered in Brussels, patched and peeled in London.
>
> (CP 37)

The notorious lower-case "jew" of "Gerontion," which remained so in all editions until 1963, denotes a world that is "'owned' by the only proliferating element in it, the international money-power,"[27] "la signification bancaire," which is destructive of all sense of place:

> Mr. Eugenides, the Smyrna merchant
> Unshaven, with a pocket full of currants
> C.i.f. London: documents at sight,
> Asked me in demotic French
> To luncheon at the Canon Street Hotel
> Followed by a weekend at the Metropole.
> (*CP* 68)

The pun on "currants"/"current" binds Mr. Eugenides to Phlebas the Phoenician ("A current under sea / Picked his bones" [*CP* 71]) and "Phoenician" functions as a "euphemism" for "Jewish."[28] For "the Jewish economist," as Eliot terms Marx,[29] the influence of capital is at once liberating and destructive. For Eliot it is simply destructive. The great civilizing force is land, the "life of significant soil" (*CP* 190), which the capitalist expansion of needs, or the capitalist transformation of specific needs into unlimited desire, threatens to destroy.

After Strange Gods concedes "that the whole current of economic determinism is against" its celebration of neoagrarian values: "[I]t does not matter so much at present whether any measures put forward are practical, as whether the aim is a good aim, and the alternatives intolerable" (18). But on the contrary, the lack of practical efficacy matters intensely, for Eliot refuses to ask of culture what only religion can provide. Pound advances a critique of the culture *of* metaphor, Eliot a critique of culture *as* metaphor, which means in practice the culture of Matthew Arnold. "[L]iterature, or Culture, tended with Arnold to usurp the place of Religion" (*SE* 434), and from this initial act of usurpation or metaphorical displacement is born humanism, ersatz religion, "aesthetic religion" (*SE* 440). Quintilian argues that metaphorical "substitution" should stop short of usurpation: "Metaphor should always either occupy a place already vacant for it or if it comes into that of another [it] should be worth more than that which it expels" (*Institutio Oratoria* 8.6). Or if usurpation there must be, the less "worthy" is not to displace the more. But the culture of a Matthew Arnold comes to occupy a place that was not vacant, and the less worthy does usurp the more. Pater's aestheticism is a diminished substitute for Arnold's humanism, and Arnold's humanism is a diminished substitute for religion. "Only when religion has been partly retired and confined," Eliot complains, only "when an Arnold can sternly remind us that Culture is wider than Religion, do we get 'religious art' and in due course 'aesthetic religion'" (*SE* 440). The denigration of "religious art" might seem curious—this is, after all, the author of *Choruses from the Rock* and *Murder in the Cathedral*—yet the adjective is, or should be, strictly redundant. It presupposes the

special case, the unique phenomenon; but when "religion is in a flourish-
ing state, when the whole mind of society is moderately healthy and in
order, there is an easy and natural association between religion and art" (*SE*
440), and hence no need for the adjective. A culture in which religion is
"retired" or "confined," like an economics in which theology is not domi-
nant, is capable of nothing.

"The point of view which I am struggling to attack," Eliot writes in
"Tradition and the Individual Talent," "is perhaps related to the meta-
physical theory of the substantial unity of the soul" (*SE* 19). Exclusively
related, it might be added, for the "struggle" is conducted only on the level
of the "soul" or subject. The Cartesian *cogito* or the Fichtian "I am I" is
emptied of its plentitude, but the solidity of the object world is never
subjected to an analogous demystification. The critique of subjectivism
issues in little more than diametrical opposition to it, which, as Pierre
Bourdieu contends,

> is not genuinely to *break* with it, but to fall into the fetishism of social laws
> to which objectivism consigns itself when in establishing between struc-
> ture and practice the relation of the virtual to the actual, of the score to the
> performance, of essence to existence, it merely substitutes for the creative
> man of subjectivism a man subjected to the dead laws of a natural his-
> tory.[30]

Gone is the poetry of Shakespeare, "the man who became all things," and
in its place "all things and modes of action shape themselves anew in the
person of Milton." But in Eliot the object world returns with a vengeance,
as if to mock whatever control the subject would exercise over it. Like
Marx, Eliot insists that individuals are governed by objective structures
that are determining in relation to them; unlike Marx, however, Eliot
empties the subject of all agency. The relation between "structure and
practice," or tradition and individual talent, is the relation of the "virtual to
the actual, of the score to the performance." The "score" is not a good in
itself, for Eliot would have us know things as they are, know that they can
never be otherwise, and know that they will never suffice. Raymond
Williams observes that in the first half of the twentieth century culture was
required to perform the role of a transcendental arbiter of values, despite its
own manifest hostility to any notion of the transcendental.[31] But Eliot
makes no such paradoxical demands: "[M]an is man because he can recog-
nize supernatural realities, not because he can invent them."

It is this antiutopianism, this undervaluation of cultural labor, that I
explore here. I begin with what I take to be Eliot's playful *Ars Poetica*, "The
Naming of Cats," the first poem in *Old Possum's Book of Practical Cats*,
perhaps the most underread volume in the most widely read oeuvre of the
century. This might seem to place Eliot's individual talent within a tradi-
tion that extends back to Adam in Eden, yet there is a sense in which the
poem revises its biblical prototype. "The Naming of Cats" is concerned
with the recognition, not the giving, of names. The Adamic scene of

nomination is an *imitatio* of the divine act of creation, but Eliot is unwilling to grant humankind the status of even a secondary or derivative "creator." Rather than naming his cats, Eliot reproduces the names "that the family use daily" (*CP* 209), which is to reproduce the world as it has been conventionally produced. The individual subject (or cat) is interpellated within the familial, the better to render identity unthinkable outside its confines. As in structural linguistics, to which both "The Naming of Cats" and "Tradition and the Individual Talent" bear a family resemblance, the self is its structural determination. The name that is truly proper—the "Effanineffable / Deep and inscrutable singular Name" (*CP* 209)—forever eludes human discovery. There is no escape from culture, yet culture can never be the site of an authentic identity.

I next turn to "Prufrock" and "Gerontion," dramatic monologues in which the eponymous heroes resist, albeit in different ways, their generic dispensations. Prufrock cannot achieve the lyricism of internalized self-possession, yet he refuses interpellation within the dramatic; Gerontion labors to place himself within the conventions of the dramatic monologue, only to succumb to lyric effusion. Suspended between two worlds—or, as Eliot says of Tiresias, "throbbing between two lives" (*CP* 68)—the self can define itself neither lyrically, in terms of "the substantial unity of the soul," nor dramatically, in terms of its being or function in the world.

I conclude with *The Waste Land,* which is something of an exception in the oeuvre, and *Four Quartets*. The poet who feels obliged to tell his critics that is not what he meant at all—*The Waste Land* is not "an important bit of social criticism"—is evidently worried that his poem has provided alternative possibilities, new social and cultural "scripts." And with reason: *The Waste Land* unwittingly negotiates a relation between structural determination and individual agency that is closer in spirit to the "materialist" than the "Catholic" hypothesis. *Four Quartets,* however, corrects the imbalance. Human agency falls victim to the fetishization of language as the determining "script," and the deconstructive force of the rhetoric evacuates the utopian imagination of all efficacy.

"*The name that the family use daily*"

"A cat," Eliot tells us in "The Naming of Cats," "must have THREE DIFFERENT NAMES":

> First of all, there's the name that the family use daily,
>   Such as Peter, Augustus, Alonzo or James,
>   Such as Victor or Jonathan, George or Bill Bailey—
>   All of them sensible everyday names.
>
> (*CP* 209)

The "name that the family use daily" is presumably the one given at birth, which is at once proper and common, unique and "everyday." Hobbes argues that a "proper name is singular to only one thing,"[32] yet the "sensible everyday names" of "The Naming of Cats" are explicitly contrasted to the name "that's particular," the name "that never belong[s] to more than one cat" (*CP* 209). "Bill Bailey" is not *the* Bill Bailey, but *a* Bill Bailey, someone or something in the order of things conventionally classified as Bill Baileys. Proper names are commonly thought to be semantically empty; they refer but do not mean. Yet if nothing else, names mean, or are one of the means whereby, the subject is initially placed, put in its place, in relation to the social, which our culture tends to manage through the reproduction of family names. "The Naming of Cats" is rather more casual about this process than my observations would suggest, but then an ostensible casualness defines the ideological efficacy of the proper name. What Lacan calls the *caption* of subjectivity—the conditions under which the subject gains access to the social through the agency of language—is never acknowledged for what it is. I experience my proper name not as a "capture" or subjection but as the index of my free and unique subjectivity.[33] "What's the use of their having names?" the Gnat asks Alice of Wonderland fame. "No use to *them*," she replies, "but it's useful to the people that name them."[34]

If a proper name were "singular to only one thing," it would be opposed to "sensible everyday names" or common nouns. The word *name* itself, however, is a common noun, which Eliot's habit of transforming it into a proper noun only emphasizes:

> Love is the unfamiliar Name.
> (*CP* 196)

> His ineffable effable
> Effanineffable
> Deep and inscrutable singular Name.
> (*CP* 209)

Because a proper name already presupposes a classification, and hence a system of differences, there never can be a unique appellation reserved for the presence of a unique subjectivity. As Derrida argues, the proper name is never in fact proper:

> To name, to give names . . . is the originary violence of language which consists in inscribing within a difference, in classifying, in suspending the vocative absolute. To think the unique *within* the system, to inscribe it there, such is the gesture of the arche-writing: arche-violence, loss of the proper, of absolute proximity, of self-presence. . . .[35]

"The Naming of Cats" thinks the "unique" with a family system or structure, which it thus serves to reproduce. "The Ad-dressing of Cats," the companion piece to "The Naming of Cats," thinks the "unique" within a closed semiotic system, which it serves to reproduce:

> *How would you ad-dress a Cat?*

> So first, your memory I'll jog,
> And say: A CAT IS NOT A DOG.
> (*CP* 234)

The first thing that can be said about a cat is that it is not a dog, which Saussure maintains is the most precise thing that can ever be said about any linguistic sign:

> In all . . . cases what we find, instead of *ideas* given in advance, are *values* emanating from a linguistic system. If we say that these values correspond to certain concepts, it must be understood that the concepts in question are purely differential. That is to say they are concepts defined not positively, in terms of their content, but negatively by contrast with other items in the same system. What characterizes each most exactly is being whatever the others are not.[36]

The term *cat* or *dog* functions not in relation to a prediscursive entity given in advance but diacritically, in terms of a structure of value-laden oppositions that are produced within language itself. Hence, cats are constructed linguistically. But the name that the family uses daily or imposes at birth— "gives," the conventional locution, is a mystification—also positions the subject within the family, within the "value" that is the familial. Hence, cats are constructed culturally.

"The Naming of Cats" suggests the argument of Saussure's *Course in General Linguistics,* but Eliot stops short of Saussure's contention that in language "there are only differences, *and no positive terms*" (118). "A CAT IS NOT A DOG" is the first of three modes of address, and the second would seem to define positively what the first delimits relationally: "Again I must remind you that / A Dog's a Dog—A CAT'S A CAT (*CP* 235). Likewise, "the name that the family use daily" is but the first of three names in "The Naming of Cats," and the second name never belongs to more than one cat:

> But I tell you, a cat needs a name that's particular,
>   A name that's peculiar, and more dignified,
> Else how can he keep up his tail perpendicular,
>   Or spread out his whiskers, or cherish his pride?
> Of names of this kind, I can give you a quorum,
>   Such as Munkustrap, Quaxo, or Coricopat,
> Such as Bombalurina, or else Jellylorum—
>   Names that never belong to more than one cat.
>   (*CP* 209)

But the "particular" or "peculiar" is not the fully proper, and unlike, say, Gertrude Stein's "A rose is a rose is a rose," the double tautology of "A Dog's a Dog—A CAT'S A CAT" is precisely that, a double or differential tautology. The diacritical relation subtends the positive formulations.

Differential relations can, of course, produce the illusion of identity as plenitude or internalized self-possession, which, as Marx suggests, issues in a form of identity fetishism:

> In a sort of way, it is with man as with commodities. Since he comes into the world neither with a looking glass in his hand, nor as a Fichtian philosopher, to whom "I am I" is sufficient, man first sees and recognises

himself in other men. Peter only establishes his own identity as a man by comparing himself with Paul as being of like kind. And thereby Paul, just as he stands in his Pauline personality, becomes to Peter the type of the genus homo.[37]

Peter establishes his identity differentially in relation to Paul; in the construction of social identity, as in structural linguistics, there are only differences without positive terms. Yet if the reality is what Marx terms "reflexive determination," Peter nevertheless knows Paul in the alleged fullness of his Pauline personality; differential relations do not necessarily impinge on the experiential coherence and stability of the *cogito*. Paul Hirst writes:

> The subject is a locus prior to and appropriative of all its attributes. This concept of subject as an *epistemological-ontological point* is given its classic formulation by Descartes in the *Discourse on Method*. The subject is the prior (already presupposed) point of inspection-possession, identifying (and thereby annexing) experiences and attributes as its own. Possession stems from *identification* ("I think therefore I am"): the subject is *possessor of itself,* capable of constituting itself in the moment of identifying thoughts as *its own* (proper—proprietal to it).[38]

The Cartesian metaphysic presupposes the detachment of the *cogito* from the material world; the subject is prior to all things, which it is therefore free to appropriate as its own. The word *proper* is from the Latin *proprius,* the particular, the unique, that which belongs only to the self, and the celebration of the self as the unproblematic possessor of itself easily comes to serve as a metaphysical apology for proprietal relations in general. It is not accidental that Locke, who maintains that "all (except proper) Names are general," is the author of an influential defense of private property.[39] But Eliot refuses Locke's exception—not even proper names are truly proper—and thus the ideology of the subject implicit in it. The self, as Michael Claverton learns in *The Elder Statesman,* is never coincident with itself:

LORD CLAVERTON: Perhaps you intend to change your name to Gomez?
GOMEZ: Oh no, Dick, there are plenty of other good names.
MONICA: Michael, Michael, you can't abandon your family
And your very self—it's a kind of suicide. (*CP* 576)

Like T[homas] S[tearns] Eliot, Michael Claverton's "very self" is his family name: *le nom propre* guarantees individual identity only because it is *not* a unique appellation reserved for the presence of a unique individual. *Four Quartets* includes the words of Thomas Elyot ("In daunsinge, signifying matrimonie"); like the two "L. Blooms" of *Ulysses,* the two "Thomas Eli[y]ots" of *Four Quartets* argue a world in which the proper name is not personal property. Yet if Eliot evacuates the *cogito* of its illusory plenitude, he never subjects the object world, or the mode in which that world is appropriated and manipulated by human subjects, to an analogous operation. The "diametric opposition to subjectivism," to return to Bourdieu's formulation, merely issues in a fetishization of "dead laws."

Not that Eliot is committed, at least on the level of ontology or metaphysics, to the objectivity of the object world:

> [A name] denotes an object which is not itself, and yet, when we ask just what this object is which is denoted, we have nothing to point to but the name.
>
> We . . . have an object which is constituted by the denoting, though what we denote has an existence as an object only because it is also not an object.[40] . . .

Because the object is constituted in the very act of naming it, there never can be an actual object of perception; there is no signified-in-itself, no foundation for language, as de Man argues, other than its own power to posit:

> Poetic language can do nothing but originate anew over and over again; it is always constitutive, able to posit regardless of presence but, by the same token, unable to give a foundation to what it posits except as an intent of consciousness. The word is always a free presence to the mind, the means by which the permanence of natural entities can be put into question and thus negated.[41]

De Man and Eliot might seem the strangest of bedfellows, yet the argument of "Intentional Structure of the Romantic Image" is broadly consistent with that of *Knowledge and Experience in the Philosophy of F. H. Bradley*. Or the two would be consistent were Eliot's dissertation restricted to what it terms a "metaphysically . . . real world" (*KE* 52). But it is not in fact so restricted. The metaphysically real is set over and against the "practical world," and in the latter metaphysical quandaries find an essentially practical solution (*KE* 52). Naming, as Althusser insists, does have a foundation for what it posits more substantial than an intent of consciousness:

> [I]deology "acts" or "functions" in such a way that it "recruits" subjects among the individuals (it recruits them all) or "transforms" the individuals into subjects (it transforms them all) by that very precise operation that I have called *interpellation* or hailing, and which can be imagined along the lines of the most commonplace police (or other) hailing: "Hey you there!"[42]

Interpellation posits or constructs a "subject" even as it negates the concrete individual, the biological self. In de Man's formulation language is the "means by which the permanence of natural entities can be put into question and thus negated." But if the subject is an effect of language in a "metaphysically real world," it nevertheless experiences itself as both a unique subjectivity and an objective reality in the practical world. All bourgeois institutions—familial, legal, academic—function to sustain the fiction of the individual that is itself the invention of the bourgeoisie. (It is in this sense that the *caption* of subjectivity is never experienced for what is, that the conventional locution is "to give" rather than "to impose" a name.)

For all practical purposes, what is without foundation in a "metaphysically real" world achieves the status of a concrete historical reality.

If ideology thus "acts" or "functions" to reproduce subjects subjected to an ideological order, who in turn reproduce the order that produced them, ideology *is* the systematic reproduction of the "real" and not simply a mystified relation to it:

> Men make their own history, but they do not make it just as they please; they do not make it under circumstances chosen by themselves, but under circumstances directly found, given and transmitted from the past. The tradition of all the dead generations weighs like a nightmare on the brain of the living. And just when they seem engaged in revolutionising themselves and things, in creating something entirely new, precisely in such epochs of revolutionary crisis they anxiously conjure up the spirits of the past to their service and borrow from them names, battle slogans and costumes in order to present the new scene of world history in this time-honoured disguise and this borrowed language.[43]

Men make their own history much in the manner in which Eliot says individual talent makes literature:

> No poet, no artist of any art, has his complete meaning alone. His significance, his appreciation is the appreciation of his relation to the dead poets and artists. You cannot value him alone; you must set him, for contrast and comparison, among the dead. I mean this as a principle of aesthetic, not merely historical, criticism. The necessity that he shall conform, that he shall cohere, is not onesided; what happens when a new work of art is created is something that happens simultaneously to all the works of art which preceded it. The existing monuments form an ideal order among themselves, which is modified by the introduction of the new (the really new) work of art among them. The existing order is complete before the new work arrives; for order to persist after the supervention of novelty, the *whole* existing order must be, if ever so slightly, altered; and so the relations, proportions, values of each work of art toward the whole are readjusted; and this is conformity between the old and new. (*SE* 15)

Individuals make literature "under circumstances directly found, transmitted, and given from the past," but therein lies the extent of Eliot's affinities with Marx. Eliot's concerns are structural, not genetic. Like the *Course in General Linguistics*, "Tradition and the Individual Talent" reduces all concrete human utterances to the manifestation of possibilities already latent in an "ideal" structural paradigm. Structure is "complete" before the "supervention of novelty"; signification, in Saussure's formulation, is "imposed rather than freely chosen. . . . No individual is able, even if he wished, to modify in any way a choice already established in the language. Nor can the linguistic community exercise its authority to change even a single word. The community, as much as the individual, is bound to its language" (71). Nothing in the central thesis of the *Course* requires this radical denial of human agency: the sign is arbitrary only in relation to its signified, not its cultural context. Indeed, if anything seems arbitrary here it is the insistence that signification is fixed with respect to the linguistic community that uses it. The structural bias of "Tradition and the Individual Talent" is less rigid than that of the *Course*—if the new is proleptically governed by the old, the old is retroactively modified by the new— yet it too works toward the "conformity" that is the assimilation of the new to the structural determinants of an "ideal" order. The perspective is, of course, easily reversed: *langue* or tradition could be construed as an extrapolation from, a hypostasis of, the totality of concrete human utterances. But this would be to return ostensibly "ideal" orders to their basis in concrete human productivity, to entertain the possibility of a future that is not in "conformity" with the past.

Humankind is enjoined to recognize, not invent, spiritual realities, and so "The Naming of Cats" is finally about the recognition, not the giving, of names:

> But above all and beyond there's still one name left over,
> And that is the name that you never will guess;
> The name that no human research can discover—
> But THE CAT HIMSELF KNOWS, and will never confess.
> When you notice a cat in profound meditation,
> The reason, I tell you, is always the same:
> His mind is engaged in a rapt contemplation
> Of the thought, of the thought, of the thought of his name:
> His ineffable effable
> Effanineffable
> Deep and inscrutable singular Name.
>
> (*CP* 209)

The name that is "deep and inscrutable," the only truly proper name, eludes human discovery; the poet, no less than the cat, stands in rapt contemplation before the mystery of the "Effanineffable." "The Naming of Cats" brings us to the point where it can avail us no further, but the poem as guide is not therefore inefficacious. The "Effanineffable," the poetic adumbration of the truly proper, pivots on the infix "in." Read in the etymological sense of inwardness, the word suggests the word within a word; read in the etymological sense of negativity, the word suggests the word within a word unable to speak a word. Eliot's poetry honors both meanings, but in a strictly hierarchical fashion. The Word toward which all words strive renders ironic the pretensions of the aesthetic, even as words have the contingent authority of an instrumental good.

Romanticism moves too precipitously toward the "deep and inscrutable": "What is permanent and good in Romanticism is curiosity . . . a curiosity which recognizes that any life, if accurately and profoundly penetrated, is interesting and always strange. Romanticism is a short cut to the strangeness without the reality, and it leads its disciples only back upon themselves" (31). Romanticism both returns its disciples to themselves and propels them forward through a world that is without density or specificity. Albert Cook associates the romantic propensity for "retrospection and prospection" with an understanding of the self that is lacking "moorings in a particular place and class"; the elision of the object world leaves the subject free, if in imagination only, to roam through unlimited time and space.[44] Eliot insists, however, on what he calls "the reality," not in an effort to reconcile us to it but to release us from "practical desire" (*CP* 173), from any attempt to imagine a future different in kind from the nightmare of the past. The world cannot be other than what it is, yet things as they are can never suffice.

Eliot is necessarily opposed, then, to any poetic that privileges the imaginatively hypothetical—Shelley is his prime example—over and above the spiritually existential: "It [poetry] awakens and enlarges the mind itself by rendering it the receptacle of a thousand unapprehended combinations of thought. Poetry lifts the veil from the hidden beauty of the world, and makes familiar objects as if they were not familiar."[45] Shelley's distinctly structuralist contention that language is "combinatory," relational rather than referential, informs his critique of the conventional romantic metaphor of the aeolian harp: "But there is a principle within the human being, and perhaps all sentient beings, which acts otherwise than in the lyre, and produces not melody alone but harmony, by an internal adjustment of sounds or motions thus excited to the impression which excite them."[46] Unlike Wordsworth, for whom the "best poetry" is born of contact with the "best objects"—which potentially reduces language to that "primitive purity, and shortness," so much desired by the Royal Society, "when men delivr'd so many *things,* almost in an equal number of *words*"[47]—Shelley emphasizes the "internal adjustments of sounds or motions." These are said to reflect the operations of consciousness rather than the determinants of the medium, a stance that disqualifies Shelley from full membership in the structuralist brotherhood.[48] But this is perhaps all to his credit. A structuralist poetic that makes the mind "a receptacle for a thousand unapprehended combinations of thought" does not simply manifest a possibility latent in an "ideal order," Shelley's Platonism notwithstanding. Prospective rather than contemplative, the *Defense of Poetry* is given to the imaginatively possible, which is also the socially desirable: "The most unfailing herald, companion and follower of the awakening of a great people to work a beneficial change in opinion or institution, is poetry." Eliot quotes this passage from the *Defense*—he christens it "the first appearance of the kinetic or revolutionary theory of poetry"—and worries the relation it posits between poetry and revolutionary activity.[49] He concludes, much to his relief, that it is both vague and false; yet "worries" is precisely the word that catches his relation to "kinetic" theories of poetry. Pound attempts to forge a poetic of the transitive, of direct social and political intervention. Eliot privileges stillness. He is thus opposed to any poetic that maintains or exacerbates the tension between the socially actual and desirable, between what is and what might be. This includes his own "Prufrock."

Cartesian Poetics

"Let us go," begins "The Love Song of J. Alfred Prufrock," although the going is unmotivated by any good or goal that inheres in a destination:

> Let us go then, you and I,
> When the evening is spread out against the sky
> Like a patient etherised upon a table;
> Let us go, through certain half-deserted streets,
> The muttering retreats
> Of restless nights in one-night cheap hotels
> And sawdust restaurants with oyster-shells:
> Streets that follow like a tedious argument
> Of insidious intent
> To lead you to an overwhelming question . . .
> Oh, do not ask, "What is it?"
> Let us go and make our visit.
>
> (CP 13)

"Allons!" begins section 13 of Whitman's "Song of the Open Road," "allons" to what is as endless

> . . . as it was beginningless,
> To undergo much, tramps of days, rests of nights,
> To merge all in the travel they tend to, and the days and nights they
>   tend to,
> Again to merge them in the start of superior journeys,
> To see nothing anywhere but what you may reach it and pass it,
> To conceive no time, however distant, but what you may reach it and
>   pass it.[50]

Eliot's poem rehearses the "Allons!" of Whitman's, but only to transform its comforting "rests of nights" into the disturbing "restless nights," its injunction "to conceive no time" into the neurosis of a repeated assurance that "there will be time." In a world that is "endless as it was beginningless," in which all things exist only to be reached and surpassed, the subject is without moorings in specific time and place. A complex play of retrospection and prospection structures both "The Song of the Open Road" and "Prufrock," although in the latter retrospection ("For I have known them all already") renders prospection ("There will be time") meaningless, and all is subsumed into the plangencies of the past conditional ("I should have been"). Faring forward is not a good or goal in itself, for faring forward is the condition of desire, not love:

> Desire itself is movement
> Not in itself desirable;
> Love is itself unmoving,
> Only the cause and end of movement.
>
> (CP 175)

Eliot's true love song is spoken not by the Prufrock who fares forward but by the Simeon who awaits, like Becket in *Murder in the Cathedral*, a revelation that can never be actively or willfully pursued.

Song is traditionally associated with lyric, but "Prufrock," by common consensus, is a dramatic monologue, although one that concludes with a virtual parody of the canonical definition of lyric: "I have heard the mermaids singing, each to each. / I do not think that they will sing to me" (*CP* 16). "Eloquence is *heard*, poetry is *over*heard. Eloquence supposes an audience; the peculiarity of poetry appears to us to lie in the poet's utter unconsciousness of a listener."[51] The mermaids who sing "each to each" are overheard, and if they are not unconscious of, they are at least indifferent to, their auditor or audience of one. Mill maintains that a certain "unconsciousness" is the peculiarity of poetry in general, but the peculiarity of the dramatic monologue is its awareness of its auditor, conventionally a silent one. Consider the epigraph to "Prufrock":

> S'io credessi che mia risposta fosse
> a persona che mai tornasse al mondo,
> questa fiamma staria senza più scosse.
> Ma per ciò che giammai di questo fondo
> non tornò vivo alcun, s'i'odo il vero,
> senza tema d'infamia ti rispondo.
>
> (*CP* 13)

If Guido da Montefeltro thought his response were addressed to one who might repeat it, he could not without fear of infamy answer Dante. But because Guido believes his auditor to be a resident of (rather than a tourist in) hell, Dante hears directly what otherwise could not or would not be revealed. "Prufrock" begins, then, with an "eloquence" that can be "heard" only because it is thought to be of no pracitcal use to anyone; it concludes with a "song" that is "overheard," but which is unconscious of, or indifferent to, its human auditor. The poem plays with the conventions of lyric and dramatic monologue but negotiates no compromise between the two. Prufrock cannot attain the lyricism of internalized self-possession, yet he resists interpellation within the dramatic; the self is neither coincident with itself nor meaningfully engaged with anything external to it.

F. H. Bradley dismisses the former, the *cogito,* as a "delusion of theory":

> I am myself by sharing with others, by including in my essence relations to them, the relations of the social state. If I wish to realize my true being, I must therefore realize something beyond my being as a mere this or that. . . . In short, man is a social being; he is real only because he is social, and can realize himself only because it is as social that he realizes himself. The mere individual is a delusion of theory; and the attempt to realize it in practice is the starvation and mutilation of human nature, with total sterility or the production of monsters.[52]

The attempt to realize in practice this delusion of theory is the ambition of "Waldo," as Eliot's "Cousin Nancy" terms Emerson, one of the two "guardians of the faith" (*CP* 30), the liberal cult of self-reliance: "Society is a joint-stock company, in which the members agree, for the better securing of his bread to each shareholder, to surrender the liberty and culture of the eater. The virtue in most request is conformity. . . . It loves not realities and creators, but names and customs. Whoso would be a man must be a nonconformist."[53] It is difficult to know how one can be a nonconformist while laboring under the injunction to become one, but the eponymous Cousin Nancy of Eliot's poem is untroubled by the apparent contradiction:

> Miss Nancy Ellicott smoked
> And danced all the modern dances;
> And her aunts were not quite sure how they felt about it,
> But they knew that it was modern.
>
> (*CP* 30)

Individualism is here but the fashionable conformity that seeks to shock the good bourgeoisie—this is manifestly not what *The Waste Land* calls "the awful daring of a moment's surrender" (*CP* 74). The self-reliance that purports to challenge the logic of the social as "joint-stock company" is actually the mode of subjectivity nurtured in and required by it. For all practical purposes Emerson is a company man: "It is easy in the world to live after the world's opinion; it is easy in solitude to live after our own; but the great man is he who in the midst of the crowd keeps with perfect sweetness the independence of solitude."[54] This serene self-possession "in the midst of the crowd" makes complicity with the social—what could be easier?—an index of greatness. In *The Waste Land,* however, the happy meeting of public and private becomes a crowd flowing over London Bridge, in which each man fixes "his eyes before his feet" (*CP* 62), the demonic form of the community of individual solitudes. And in "Prufrock" there is no meeting of lyric solitude and "the world's opinion."

Herbert Tucker characterizes the Browning monologue as the plot of lyricism resisted:

> [I]n Browning the lyrical flight from narrative, temporality, and identity appears through a characteristic, and characterizing, resistance to its allure. Browning's Ulysses, had he invented one, would speak while bound to the mast of a ship bound elsewhere; his life would take its bearing from what he heard the Sirens sing, and their music would remain an unheard melody suffusing his monologue without rising to the surface of utterance. Such a plot of lyricism resisted would mark his poem as a dramatic monologue. . . .[55]

The voices of the "sea-girls" are an unheard or unrepresented melody in "Prufrock," but unlike the Browning monologue or Pound's epic (the Pisan Cantos excepted), the poem is less the plot of lyricism resisted than of lyricism desired. Not lyricism attained in the manner of Tennyson's "Ulysses" or "Tithonis," which run the contextualizing devices of the dramatic monologue in reverse in order to facilitate a lyric drive:[56] "Prufrock" does not fully accommodate the lyric impulses of its eponymous hero. The poem remains faithful, however, only to the letter of its generic dispensation. The typical Browning monologue is structured as an agon between competing discourses, "an historical, narrative, metonymic text and a symbolic, lyrical, and metaphoric text that adjoins it and jockeys with it for authority."[57] "Prufrock" evinces much the same struggle, but lyricism denied is not lyricism resisted, and the dramatic discourse does not emerge unscathed from the struggle.

Prufrock bears a proper name, which is sufficient to distinguish his song from the innominate condition of lyric utterance, but he is not thereby a character or speaker in Browning's sense of the term. The name is little more than the rubric under which the poem organizes its rhetorical effects, what "La Figlia Che Piange" calls a "gesture and a pose" (*CP* 34).[58] And if the "I" is only minimally contextualized, the "you" that accompanies it on its journey of "insidious intent" (*CP* 13) is virtually a pronominal sign of an empty or absent subjectivity. Readers of the poem, including T. S. Eliot, have posited a variety of identities—Prufrock's "divided self"; "Dante or some analogue of Dante's"; "an unidentified male companion"[59]—but the poem itself refuses to specify, which is thoroughly characteristic of it. Precisely when, for example, is the "then" of the opening line? After the epigraph from Dante, and so in conformity with the conditions under which Guido speaks? Or before the "when" of the second line, and hence in relation to an evening that has yet to arrive? The very different poetic medium of *Four Quartets* openly acknowledges the semantic emptiness of the conventional markers of spatiotemporal perspective: "I can only say, *there* we have been: but I cannot say where" (*CP* 173). Dramatic monologues, however, promise a local habitation as well as a name, which "Prufrock" introduces only to elide: "Streets that follow like a tedious argument / Of insidious intent" dissolves landscape into wordscape. W. K. Wimsatt argues that it is "nearly possible, tantalizingly plausible, to suppose a basic story of a little man [why little?] approaching a tea party at which there is a woman to whom he might . . . propose marriage." He posits this "basic story," however, only to dismiss it as "almost hallucinatory."[60] If, then, the "symbolic, lyrical, and metaphoric" discourse never fully emerges, neither does the poem's "historical, narrative, and metonymic" self.

Like the roses of "Burnt Norton," which have "the look of flowers that are looked at" (*CP* 172), Prufrock sees himself as seen by others. In effect, he experiences his generic dispensation as a kind of curse:

> And indeed there will be time
> To wonder, "Do I dare?" and, "Do I Dare?"
> Time to turn back and descend the stair,

> With a bald spot in the middle of my hair—
> (They will say: "How his hair is growing thin!")
> My morning coat, my collar mounting firmly to the chin,
> My necktie rich and modest, but asserted by a simple pin—
> (They will say: "But how his arms and legs are thin!")
>
> (*CP* 14)

Prufrock "fixes" himself as he is "fixed" by others:

> And I have known the eyes already, known them all—
> The eyes that fix you in a formulated phrase,
> And when I am formulated, sprawling on a pin,
> When I am pinned and wriggling on the wall,
> Then how should I begin
> To spit out all the butt-ends of my days and ways?
> And how should I presume?
>
> (*CP* 14–15)

Prufrock does "presume." He posits a thoroughly subjective freedom, a self that is never coincident with any of its public gestures or poses:

> There will be time, there will be time
> To prepare a face to meet the faces that you meet;
> There will be time to murder and create,
> And time for all the works and days of hands
> That lift and drop a question on your plate;
> Time for you and time for me,
> And time yet for a hundred indecisions,
> And for a hundred visions and revisions,
> Before the taking of a toast and tea.
>
> (*CP* 14)

But it is a freedom indistinguishable from compulsion. Prufrock can do nothing but revise, forever modifying the decision, forever revising the vision, he has never in fact made or had. The "true" self takes up residence in the "soul" even as it prepares a face to meet the faces that it meets. Such is Prufrock's response to the degraded spectacle of the world as theater.

If Prufrock is not Prince Hamlet, as he asserts—although it is a curious assertion: no one has suggested that he is—he is nevertheless the prince's epigone. And the prince enters the play that bears his name only to reject any role that a man might play, any positionality, social or familial, that the world as stage affords him, that the world as stage imposes on him:

> Seemes Maddam, nay it is, I know not seems,
> Tis not alone my incky cloake good mother
> Nor customary suites of solembe blacke
> Nor windie suspiration of forst breath
> No, nor the fruitfull riuer in the eye,
> Nor the deiected hauior of the visage
> Together with all formes, moodes, and shewes of griefe
> That can denote me truely, these indeed seeme,

> For they are actions that a man might play
> But I haue that within which passeth showe
> These but the trappings and the suites of woe.[61]

In the gap that opens up between the inner life of the subject, experiencing itself as "that within which passeth showe," and an inauthentic exterior, the tawdry spectacle of the world's "seemings," there "begins to insist, however prematurely, the figure that is to dominate and organize bourgeois culture."[62] Northrop Frye speaks of the ordered society in Shakespeare's plays as "ecstatic" in Heidegger's sense of the term: "[I]ts members are outside themselves, at work in the world, and their being is their function."[63] But Claudius' Denmark is manifestly not ordered, which, according to the "B" of Eliot's "Dialogue on Dramatic Poetry," is more or less the norm, or the non-norm, in Shakespeare's world in general:

> Restoration comedy is a comedy of social manners. It presupposes the existence of a society, therefore of social and moral laws. (It owes much to Jonson, but little to Shakespeare—anyway, Shakespeare was too great to have much influence.) It laughs at the members of society who transgress its laws. The tragedy of Shakespeare goes much deeper and yet it tells us only that weakness of character leads to disaster. There is no background of social order such as you perceive behind Corneille and Sophocles. (*SE* 53)

The praise is highly ambivalent. Shakespeare's plays are "deeper" than their Restoration counterparts—Hamlet would thoroughly applaud the criterion of depth—yet they tell us "only that weakness of character leads to disaster." The source of the ambivalence, or the proof that Shakespeare's age "moved in a steady current, with back-eddies certainly, towards anarchy and chaos" (*SE* 54), is the priority given to character, the relative freedom character enjoys in determining its own fate. "His story requires Romans or kings," Johnson says of Shakespeare, "but he thinks only on men." The formulation, as Paul Fry observes, reverses Aristotle by redeploying Aristotelian terms: "Whereas for Aristotle the mere accidents of character reside in his idiosyncratic nature, for Johnson they are constituted by his role or office—by his assigned place, in short, in the plot."[64] Likewise, the well-rounded, three-dimensional characters of novelistic fame follow Hamlet's lead in defining themselves not "ecstatically," but oppositionally, in relation to the world, however much it may be with them.[65] Ian Watt argues the novel is the first genre to establish the connection between proper names and "fully individualized entities"; more recently Michael Ragussis has suggested that fiction, unlike philosophy, seeks to name individuals without classifying them.[66] The proper name understood as a unique appellation reserved for the presence of a unique individual is appropriate to a genre in which "man" is prior to his "role" or "office." It is anathema, however, to Eliot's attempt to recover genuine collective experience for the modern world. Eliot dismisses *Hamlet* as an "artistic failure" (*SE* 143), but his antipathy can be generalized to all that the play uncannily anticipates: the displacement of theater by the novel as a defining cultural experience.[67] The ascendancy of the latter in bourgeois culture is bound to its "superior efficacy in producing and providing for privatized subjects,"[68] in promoting "the metaphysical theory of the substantial unity of the soul." It follows that Eliot's turn to drama is motivated by its superior efficacy in producing and providing for collective experience. Eliot's career resolves, as it were, the tension latent in his first major poem.

It is a tension that informs "Prufrock" on the level of language as well as genre. The semantic is sacrificed to the plangent, and we fare forward on the strength of rhythm and rhyme alone:

> In the room the women come and go
> Talking of Michelangelo.
>
> (*CP* 14)

The caesura preceding the preposition heightens the drama of syntactic disclosure, yet the object of the preposition or the subject of the conversation suggests little more than auditory necessity, the open "o" of "Michelangelo" reiterating the open "o" of "go," "Oh, do not ask," and the poem's initial injunction. "I grow old," Prufrock bemoans, ". . . I grow old . . . / I shall wear the bottom of my trousers rolled" (*CP* 16). Even fashion for the fastidious, it would seem, is dictated by the auditory exigencies of the vowel sound "o."

Roman Jakobson argues that the "poetic function projects the principle of equivalence from the axis of selection into the axis of combination," which he illustrates with the example of rhyme, an obvious instance of the priority of structural similarity over syntagmatic continuity. Or as Leopold Bloom engagingly puts it: "That is how poets write, the similar sounds."[69] But if "Prufrock" foregrounds the palpability of its auditory self, it does so at the expense of its semantic integrity; the effect is that we "hear the sound of the sound rather than the meaning of the meaning."[70] "You do not want the syllables to stand steady," Augustine cautions,

> you want them to fly away, so that others may succeed to them and you may hear the whole statement. So it is always with all things out of which some one being is constituted, and the parts out of which it is fashioned do not all exist at once. All things together bring us more delight, if they can all be sensed at once, than do their single parts.[71]

As the syllable to the word, so the word to the sentence, the sentence to the narrative, and the narrative to the meaning—words to the Word, although a crucial synapse divides the two. "There will be time," Prufrock assures himself, or whomever, "time for you and time for me." But if all time is squandered in syllables that dilate in the mouth, if narrative time future is perpetually forestalled in phonetic time present, then all narrative time is unredeemable. Emily Dickinson's "Perished Patterns" ("The Perished Patterns murmur— / But His Perturbless Plan / Proceed") phonetically protest, and by their protest defer, the temporal articulation of a teleological "Authority." But for both the Bishops of Hippo—Augustine of Hippo and the poet of "The Hippopotamus"—disclosure is properly a drama of succession, and deferral can only be a narrative version of the sin of *tarditas,* a slowness in turning toward God. "Let us go. . . ."

The repeated assertion that "there will be time" can, of course, be read as a means of playing for time, of sustaining the life of desire by strategically distancing or deferring any possible object of desire.[72] "In the end one loves one's desire and not what is desired": Nietzsche's formulation is ontological, but it best characterizes the operations of desire in their distinctly modern form.[73] Eliot takes the name "Prufrock," which figures only in his title, from an advertisement that appeared for "Prufrock-Littau, furniture wholesalers" in St. Louis at the turn of the century; the "sea-girls" who sing "each to each" at the conclusion of the poem may owe something to the ubiquitous "seaside girls" who appeared in advertisements at much the same time.[74] Prufrock's desire, which is always in excess of any possible fulfillment, or suspended on the threshold of a future fulfillment, is compatible with an economic order in which advertising was soon to become the definitive activity, if not art. In such a context desire can never come to rest on an adequate object; there is always something other, different, better, more. Pound imagines an economic system measured and gauged according to human needs. The world of "Prufrock" is predicated on the exercise of unlimited desire.

Jay Gatsby, a distinctly non-Eliotic character, invests all in a disastrous object of desire and suffers two distinctly Eliotic hells: the pain of love unsatisfied and the greater pain of love satisfied. Yet there is a sense in which the novel, if not its titular hero, survives the investment by virtue of the rhetorical fortissimo of its concluding moments. That the dream falters on an object incommensurate with Gatsby's capacity for wonder is finally unimportant; the heightened sensitivity to the rhythmical promises of life carries the novel beyond the wreckage. The object of desire disappears, or daily retreats from view. Rhetorical plangency requires only the promise of a future that remains future. Gatsby says of Daisy:

> "Her voice is full of money." . . .
> That was it. I'd never understood before. It was full of money—that was the inexhaustible charm that rose and fell in it, the jingle of it, the cymbals' song of it. . . . High in a white palace the king's daughter, the golden girl. . . .

Daisy's voice resembles nothing so much as Fitzgerald's prose: "It eluded us then, but that's no matter—tomorrow we will run faster, stretch out our arms farther. . . . And one fine morning—."[75] This, too, is full of the mobility, "the lack of particularity," the "infinitely removed finality" of money.[76]

Full, that is, of the music of "Prufrock," which Hugh Kenner, who shares something of Eliot's aversion to the rhythms of pathos, the music of the desiring self, terms "the pretensions toward which rhythmical speech incorrigibly reaches."[77] "Toward which" is the crucial phrase here, for if Eliot "awaits the great genius who shall triumphantly succeed in believing *something*," the rhythms of pathos (Whitman's "tends to") remain forever "toward," caught in an autotelic world of perpetual propulsion. The women who "come and go" do not speak "of" Michelangelo but "in" Michelangelo, or in the phonetic patterning in which the liquid "o" predominates. There are, then, any number of "other good names," the lesson of *The Elder Statesman* notwithstanding—"Marlon Brando" might do as well (a suggestion I owe to some anonymous graffiti). But if "Prufrock" is given to auditory mazes, "Gerontion" is dominated by the syntactical rather than the plangent, the semantic rather than the metrical. The earlier injunction suffers a sea change, and what was once compelling action or propulsion ("Let us go") emerges as an obligation to "think now." The minor Ion, perhaps the poem's most conspicuous metrical feature— ". . . iñ ă drỳ moñth . . . aẗ tȟe hòt gaẗes . . . iñ tȟe waȓm raìn . . . Aňd tȟe jèw squàts . . . Iň dĕpràved Mày . . . iň tȟe nèxt ròom . . . ŏf ă drỳ braìn"—throws a heavy burden on its stressed syllables, and the semantic content rises to the occasion. "Prufrock" gives us the plangencies of an American song of a no longer open road, "Gerontion" the tortuous syntax and semantics of European history.

Indeed, there is a sense in which "Gerontion"—ambiguously both the name of a poem and a character—is only tortuous syntax and semantics, a self that can know itself only in labyrinthine discourse. Descartes writes: "I shall now close my eyes, I shall stop my ears, I shall call away all my senses, I shall efface even from my thoughts all images of corporeal things."[78] Gerontion echoes: "I have lost my sight, smell, hearing, taste and touch: / How should I use them for your closer contact?" (*CP* 38). Gerontion echoes Descartes's formulation, but in the mode of loss rather than desire. The Hamlet who would have his too solid flesh melt, thaw, and resolve itself into a dew begs release from physical embodiment, the most fundamental condition of dramatic existence. So too Prufrock: the man who would be "a pair of ragged claws / Scuttling across the floors of silent seas" (*CP* 15) desires the Cartesian evacuation of "sight, smell, hearing, taste and touch." For Hamlet and Prufrock bodilessness is a consummation devoutly to be wished for; with Gerontion it is an achieved fact. But then Hamlet and Prufrock refuse their generic dispensations, whereas Gerontion seeks to place himself within its conventions:

> I was neither at the hot gates
> Nor fought in the warm rain
> Nor knee deep in the salt marsh, heaving a cutlass,
> Bitten by flies, fought.
> My house is a decayed house,
> And the jew squats on the window sill, the owner,
> Spawned in some estaminet of Antwerp,
> Blistered in Brussels, patched and peeled in London.
>   (*CP* 37)

Gerontion cannot define himself "ecstatically"; he is not outside himself, at work in the world, and his being is not his function. But if not "ecstatically" he nevertheless defines himself by his inability to define himself so. The *cogito* is by definition the thing that thinks; it doubts the existence of everything except its own thinkingness, including even that of its own body. "Gerontion" is dominated by the Cartesian injunction—"Think now . . . Think now . . . Think . . . Think at last . . . Think at last"—but thought exercises itself on a distinctly non-Cartesian subject:

> After such knowledge, what forgiveness? Think now
> History has many cunning passages, contrived corridors
> And issues, deceives with whispering ambitions,
> Guides us by vanities. Think now
> She gives when our attention is distracted
> And what she gives, gives with such supple confusions
> That the giving famishes the craving. Gives too late
> What's not believed in, or if still believed,
> In memory only, reconsidered passion. Gives too soon
> Into weak hands, what's thought can be dispensed with
> Till the refusal propagates a fear.
>
> (*CP* 38)

The "cunning" passages are distinctly vaginal, and their negotiation is manifestly not the work of a man who effaces from his thought "all images of corporeal things." Thought attempts to know not its own thinkingness but its historical genesis, the "before" of this disastrous knowledge; thought attempts to recover in the contemplation of its own historicity the physicality it has lost. But no consummation ensues. History either "gives too late" what is but a "reconsidered passion" or gives "too soon" what is refused. The "knowledge" that admits of no forgiveness is neither intellectual nor carnal but the Cartesian fissure between the two. "After such knowledge" suggests, of course, a fall into self-consciousness that predates the Cartesian settlement, the very origins of secular history, the expulsion from Eden, "after" which humankind knows both its nakedness and its utter separateness of self. Yet if this too represents a separation of body from soul, the spectacular physicality of, say, Celia's martyrdom in *The Cocktail Party*—she is "crucified / Very near an ant-hill" (*CP* 434)— exposes it as the pseudoseparation that it is.[79] The triumph of the *cogito* or "the metaphysical theory of the substantial unity of the soul"—or, for that matter, its contemporary analogue, the triumph of the self-division or non-selfsameness of the self—presupposes a historical dispensation in which textuality, not the body, is the privileged locus of (non)identity.

Dramatic monologues, to rehearse the textbook formulation, are predicated on the fiction of a speaking subject and a silent auditor, an intersubjective relation. The *cogito,* however, can know itself only in relation to itself; it necessarily takes up residence in the private and privatizing realm of textuality. Gerontion's initial act of self-fashioning virtually rehearses the words of a life already rendered textual, A. C. Benson's *Life of Edward*

FitzGerald, and the boy to whom he supposedly speaks is literally a reading subject. The thing that thinks is perforce the thing that reads and writes; the "I" enjoys a transitive relation only to its own non-selfsameness. In a variation of the familiar Hegelian paradox—"the hand that inflicts the wound is also the hand that heals it"—Gerontion attempts to think his way back before the Cartesian conflation of thinking and being. But to no avail:

> What will the spider do,
> Suspend its operations, will the weevil
> Delay? De Bailhache, Fresca, Mrs. Cammel, whirled
> Beyond the circuit of the shuddering Bear
> In fractured atoms. Gull against the wind, in the windy straits
> Of Belle Isle, or running on the Horn.
> White feathers in the snow, the Gulf claims,
> And an old man driven by the Trades
> To a sleepy corner.
>   Tenants of the house,
> Thoughts of a dry brain in a dry season.
>
>   (*CP* 38–39)

The highly Jacobean verse of "Gerontion" characteristically risks a form of semantic and syntactic overload, yet the poem concludes with a "pat image" ("Thoughts of a dry brain in a dry season") at the furthest remove from the earlier syntactic and semantic density.[80] The plangencies of Tennyson's "Ulysses" intrude—"It may be that the gulfs will wash us down; / It may be that we shall touch the Happy Isles"—and the poem succumbs to lyric effusion. "I would meet you upon this honestly," Gerontion claims, and he initially seems honest enough. "I was neither at the hot gates / Nor fought in the warm rain" suggests a negative attempt to meet the demands of the dramatic monologue, and hence to make contact with something exterior to the self. But the *cogito* finally disgorges its tenants, the thoughts of a dry brain in a dry season, which are revealed as internal to the *cogito.* The poem suspends its syntactic and semantic operations, and we are swept away in the "windy straits," the auditory determinants, of Tennysonian plangencies. Like "Prufrock," "Gerontion" ends with a form of death by water, which is also death by lyric.

"Dante is telling a story. Tennyson is only stating an elegiac mood" (*SE* 336): this is Eliot's version of the conflict between incompatible incarnations of the figure of Ulysses, although here the warring parties are Dante and Tennyson, not Dante and Homer. Tennyson haunts Eliot's imagination, but it is Dante, in Eliot as well as Pound, who emerges triumphant. "Mood" cannot find adequate representation unless bound to "story"; the "artistic failure" that is *Hamlet* lies in the incompatibility between the protagonist's "emotions" and the "story" that neither generates nor accounts for them (*SE* 145). Eliot expresses his preference in formal terms— Dante's dramatic narrative is superior to Tennyson's lyricized monologue—but it is determined by an abiding ideological investment. Consciousness is not prior to the social, the historical.

"Gerontion" concludes with a catalogue of highly idiosyncratic proper names—"De Bailhache, Fresca, Mrs. Cammel"—not unlike "the roll," as Eliot terms it, of Milton's

> . . . Cambula, seat of Cathaian Can
> And Samarchand by Oxus, Temir's throne,
> To Paquin of Sinaean kings, and thence
> To Agra and Lahor of great Mogul
> Down to the golden Chersonese, or where
> The Persian in Ecbatan sate, or since
> In Hispahan, or where the Russian Ksar
> On Mosco, or the Sultan in Bizance,
> Turchestan-born. . . .
>
> (*OPP* 144)

Eliot concedes that this is great fun to read, but that he cannot consider such an "immoderate" use of merely resonant proper names "serious poetry" (*OPP* 144). But if Eliot cannot, others can and do. "From the moment that the proper name is erased in a system," Derrida argues, "there is writing, there is a 'subject' from the moment that this obliteration of the proper is produced."[81] What is obliterated here is the referential force of the proper name; what remains is the resonant materiality of the signifying medium, say, the open "o" of "Michelangelo." But what Derrida's argument does not obliterate is the long tradition, at once philosophical and literary, of the subordination of nominal reference. Sidney's *Apology for Poetry*, for example, is an early and influential attempt to release literature from the "truth" value of proper names:

> [P]oets give names to men they write of, which argueth a conceit of an actual truth, and so, not being true, proves a falsehood. . . . But that is easily answered. Their naming of men is but to make their picture the more lively, and not to build any history; painting men, they cannot leave men nameless. We see we cannot play at chess but that we must give names to our chessmen; and yet, methinks, he were a very partial champion of truth that would say we lied for giving a piece of wood the reverend title of bishop.[82]

It would be possible to plot the movement from Sidney's "conceit of an actual truth" to Derrida's "obliteration of the proper" in some detail. Joel Fineman argues that the history of the philosophy of proper names is "the progressive and increasingly dogmatic subordination . . . of nominal reference . . . first to extension, then to expression, then to intention," and finally to a nominality that denotes only nominality.[83] But this would be to reiterate, albeit with a different focus, the history of humanist translation, and Eliot, if not Derrida, is discontinuous with it. The "Philomel" of "A Game of Chess," for example, is received as little more than a resonant proper name. She attempts to name her violator, to articulate content, only to be lost amidst "withered stumps of time" (*CP* 64), the private gallery world of "A Game of Chess." *The Waste Land* construes this reduction of nominality to pure nominality, to an instance of the "poetic" or the "literary," as a perversion of the poetic function; yet the poem itself resembles nothing so much as the private gallery world it represents: it too is so much bric-à-brac or bricolage. Not long after its publication, the poem, like the poet whose name it so problematically bears, came to denote Culture itself, a "perfect conspiracy of approval" (*SE* 147), as Eliot says of Jonson's reputation. For it may be that *The Waste Land* is involved in a conspiracy vis-à-vis culture of a somewhat different kind:

> "That corpse you planted last year in your garden,
> "Has it begun to sprout? Will it bloom this year?
> "Or has the sudden frost disturbed its bed?"
>
> (*CP* 63)

The Waste Land explicitly asks only if the "corpse"—the corpus, the canon—will bloom again. It unwittingly entertains, however, a far more interesting question: Should it bloom again?

"The corpse you planted"

Pound's relation to the novel is competitive: the *Cantos* seeks to reclaim for poetry the engagement with political, economic, and social realities that had become, since the nineteenth century, the exclusive provenance of the novel.[84] Eliot's relation is dismissive:

> It is here that Mr. Joyce's parallel use of the Odyssey has a great importance. It has the importance of a scientific discovery. No one else has built a novel upon such a foundation before: it has never before been necessary. I am not begging the question in calling *Ulysses* a "novel"; and if you call it an epic it will not matter. If it is not a novel, that is simply because the novel is a form which will no longer serve; it is because the novel, instead of being a form, was simply the expression of an age which had not sufficiently lost all form to feel the need of something stricter.[85]

Eliot continues to be received today as a virtual custodian of tradition, yet here he dismisses with remarkable aplomb what Franco Moretti calls "the most exemplary form of two centuries of European civilization."[86] "[I]nstead of narrative method," Eliot argues, "we may now use," indeed, must use "the mythical method," which consists "in manipulating a continuous parallel between contemporaneity and antiquity. . . . It is simply a way of controlling, of ordering, of giving a shape and a significance to the immense panorama of futility and anarchy which is contemporary history" (270). The contemporary novelist (or the contemporary poet: the essay is occasioned by *Ulysses;* it is about *The Waste Land*) imposes form inorganically from without. Eliot is frequently accused of creating a literature of literature, but the age, "'Ulysses,' Order, and Myth" contends, leaves no alternative to the literary paradigm. The nineteenth-century novelist did

not raid the library only because the nineteenth century had "not suffi-
ciently lost"—to rehearse Eliot's curious locution—all sense of form "to
feel the need of something stricter" (187). The twentieth century has.
Joyce takes up the *Odyssey* and Eliot *The Golden Bough* because the age
requires "something stricter" than anything the age itself can provide.
Moretti again: "The relationship between epoch and culture that had char-
acterized the age of the novel has been overturned: here the epoch is
completely formless, and culture is *only* form, abstract ordering ability."[87]
     So Eliot the theorist argues, although his poem suggests otherwise:

> The Chair she sat in, like a burnished throne,
> Glowed on the marble, where the glass
> Held up by standards wrought with fruited vines
> From which a golden Cupidon peeped out
> (Another hid his eyes behind his wing)
> Doubled the flames of sevenbranched candelabra
> Reflecting light upon the table as
> The glitter of her jewels rose to meet it,
> From satin cases poured in rich profusion.
>
> (*CP* 64)

The syntactic force of the poetry dissipates amid the various reflections and
sensations it catalogs, as it disposes of so much bric-à-brac in the language
of Shakespeare ("The Chair she sat in"), Virgil ("laquearia"), and Milton,
or Spenser as mediated by Milton ("sylvan scene"). The poetry, which is all
texture and affect, mimes the content of a room that is all Culture and
Cultural Ambition. Indeed, poem and room, form and content, come into
focus, to the extent that either admits of specific focus, on the most tradi-
tional of images for poetic activity:

> Above the antique mantel was displayed
> As though a window gave upon the sylvan scene
> The change of Philomel, by the barbarous king
> So rudely forced; yet there the nightingale
> Filled all the desert with inviolable voice
> And still she cried, and still the world pursues,
> "Jug Jug" to dirty ears.
> And other withered stumps of time
> Were told upon the walls; staring forms
> Leaned out, leaning, hushing the room enclosed.
>
> (*CP* 64)

Ut pictura poesis, a speaking picture, poetry as defined by Horace. Form and
content seem indistinguishable, however, only because content has been
sacrificed to form. The painting displayed above the mantel is not in fact a
"speaking picture" but a picture silenced or unheard; content is attempting
to articulate itself, but to no avail. Much of the opening movement of "A
Game of Chess" resembles a private gallery world of antiquities. Much, but
not all. The "staring form" above the "antique mantel" could be Munch's
Scream, although no one, apparently, would notice the difference.

Now the particular "sylvan scene" displayed above the mantel happens to depict Philomel, "by the barbarous king / So rudely forced"—that is, raped and mutilated by Tereus, the king of Thrace. The lurid story is "told upon the walls"—the desert in which Philomel's "inviolable voice" still cries out is *The Waste Land*—but it tells only of its own antiquity, "withered stumps of time." For if culture is only "abstract ordering ability," cultural artifacts cannot articulate content; there can be no meaningful distinction between the "sylvan scene" that is Satan's description of Adam and Eve before the Fall and a "sylvan scene" of rape and mutilation. Philomel's story includes her heroic attempt to transmit content, to name her violator:

> Twit twit twit
> Jug jug jug jug jug jug
> So rudely forc'd.
> Tereu
>
> (*CP* 67–68)

Raped by Tereus (twice in Ovid's version of the myth), her tongue removed to render her incapable of relating the atrocity, Philomel nevertheless weaves her story into a tapestry; she is eventually "changed" into a nightingale and her sister Procne into a swallow (or Procne into a nightingale and Philomel into a swallow: there is some confusion between the Greek and Latin versions of the myth). "'Jug jug' to dirty ears" suggests, of course, a failure of reception, as if the world were waste because it does not attend to the voices of its cultural past. It is precisely Philomel's attempt to tell her story, however, that *The Waste Land* fails to tell. No mention is made of her weaving, as if the poem feared any reminder of the connection between textuality (from the Latin *textus,* "weaving") and Tereus' violent silencing of Philomel. For it is a violence that *The Waste Land* rehearses, both in its truncation or mutilation of Philomel's story and in its assimilation of it to an "antiquity" that it recognizes only as "form." "Philomel" is little more than a resonant proper name, the highbrow equivalent of "that Shakespeherian Rag" (*CP* 65).

Plato argues that Philomel sings not "in lamentation" but in "prophetic vision"; she possesses foreknowledge of the otherworldly blessings to come.[88] A prophetic Philomel would be consistent with the larger structure of *The Waste Land*—all the major symbols and "characters" (for want of a better term) have their origins in Madame Sosostris's wicked pack of cards—yet if Eliot's Philomel is prophetic, she sings not of otherworldly blessings to come but of her foreknowledge, indeed her "foresuffering," of the immense panorama of futility and anarchy that is contemporary history:

> Now Albert's coming back, make yourself a bit smart.
> He'll want to know what you done with that money he gave you
> To get yourself some teeth. He did, I was there.
> You have them all out, Lil, and get a nice set,

He said, I swear, I can't bear to look at you.
And no more can't I, I said, and think of poor Albert,
He's been in the army four years, he wants a good time,
And if you don't give it him, there's others will, I said.
Oh is there, she said. Something o' that, I said.
Then I'll know who to thank, she said, and give me a straight look.
HURRY UP PLEASE ITS TIME
If you don't like it you can get on with it, I said.
Others can pick and choose if you can't.
But if Albert makes off, it won't be for lack of telling.
You ought to be ashamed, I said, to look so antique.

(*CP* 65–66)

Lil looks "so antique" because her story reiterates, in what is virtually a travesty of the form-giving function of "antiquity" with the poem, the tale told above the "antique mantel." The mythological paradigm is displaced toward realism—Philomel's mutilated mouth becomes Lil's bad teeth ("You have them all out"), and the most horrifying of rapes is refigured as legalized, routinized sexual violence ("What you get married for if you don't want children?")—but the persistence of the "antique" paradigm is clear enough. Not that it weighs like a nightmare on the minds of the living. Lil has not read the poem in which she figures, and the inhabitants of *The Waste Land,* unlike the speakers of the monologues, are not much given to self-reflection. The little there is tends to be postcoital:

She turns and looks a moment in the glass,
Hardly aware of her departed lover;
Her brain allows one half-formed thought to pass:
"Well now that's done: and I'm glad it's over."

(*CP* 69)

And:

"My feet are at Moorgate, and my heart
Under my feet. After the event
He wept. He promised 'a new start.'
I made no comment. What should I resent?"

(*CP* 70)

But the "event" is never in fact "done," never "over," for there is a sense in which the poem admits of only one event, endlessly repeated. A poem that deals out its characters from a deck of cards fixes identity in advance, and all possible permutations and combinations are structurally limited from the start.[89] The Tarot deck is "antique," but antiquity does not function as "simply a way of controlling, of ordering, of giving a shape and a significance to the immense panorama of futility and anarchy which is contemporary history." Rather, it absorbs contemporaneity "up," as it were, into itself. In the language of structural linguistics the paradigmatic code precedes and subtends the syntagmatic axis; in the language of "Tradition and the Individual Talent" there is "conformity between the old and the new."

From which issues the futility, anarchy, and sexual violence that is contemporary history. Philomel's story is Lil's life.

"But if Albert makes off," Lil is told, "it won't be for lack of telling" (*CP* 66), which is exactly right: Lil's fate, like Madame Sosostris's clairvoyance, involves the priority of word to deed. "'Ulysses,' Order, and Myth" divorces "antiquity," which it recognizes only as form, from contemporaneity, which it dismisses as utterly formless. The fate of Lil, however, suggests a terrible continuity. To return to Eliot's definition of the function of art only partially quoted earlier:

> For it is ultimately the function of art, in imposing a credible order *upon* ordinary reality [my emphasis], and thereby eliciting some perception of an order *in* reality [Eliot's emphasis], to bring us to a condition of serenity, stillness, and reconciliation; and then leave us, as Virgil left Dante, to proceed toward a region where that guide can avail us no farther. (*OPP* 87)

This is a remarkably demystified characterization of a project that aims to mystify: art can elicit some perception of an order that inheres *in* reality only if it strategically elides the fact that it has already imposed that order *on* reality. Eliot is utterly innocent, for example, of the Cratylic delusion, the archaic notion that names are somehow motivated by their objects or referents. Names "adhere" to objects and individuals, as Thom Gunn puts it; they do not *in*here:

> The local names are concepts: the Ravine
> Pemmican Ridge, North Col, Death Camp. They mean
> The streetless rise, the dazzling abstract drifts
> To which particular names adhere by chance,
> From custom lightly, not from character.[90]

Eliot would speak of "from tradition deeply," not "from custom lightly," and when names adhere deeply enough from tradition they effectively inhere "from character." Michael Claverton's desire to change his name is met with an expression of shock: "Michael, Michael, you can't abandon your family / And your very self—it's kind of suicide." The wish to be newly born outside the confines of bourgeois familism is refigured as "a kind of suicide," which renders the family, "the most important channel of transmission of culture" (*NTDC* 43), the sole preserve of identity. *The Waste Land* engages in a similar strategy. It too posits "a kind of death," the corpse in Stetson's garden, only to argue for its resuscitation. Cultural rejuvenation is rendered unthinkable outside the confines of "antique forms," the traditional corpus or canon.

"To be restored," we are told in "East Coker," "our sickness must grow worse":

> Our only health is the disease
> If we obey the dying nurse
> Whose constant care is not to please

> But to remind of our, and Adam's curse,
> And that, to be restored, our sickness must grow worse.
>
> (*CP* 181)

This is Christian homeopathy, a world in which even "Sin is Behovely," in which all manner of things guarantee that "All shall be well" (*CP* 195). *The Waste Land* is cultural homeopathy.[91] Strictly speaking, the "sickness" cannot grow curatively "worse"—it is, after all, a corpse in Stetson's garden—but it may be that *The Waste Land* exaggerates the rumors of his death, the better to dramatize its own homeopathic powers. For its powers are homeopathic: if the diagnosis is a want of significant form in the modern world—"Son of man / You cannot say, or guess, for you know only / A heap of broken images" (*CP* 61)—the poem homeopathically reproduces the fragmentation it descries:

> *Poi s'ascose nel foco che gli affina*
> *Quando fiam uti chelidon*—O swallow swallow
> *Le Prince d'Aquitaine à la tour abolie*
> These fragments I have shored against my ruins
> Why then Ile fit you. Hieronymo's mad againe.
> Datta. Dayadhvam. Damyata.
>
> (*CP* 75)

"These fragments I have shored against my ruins" conflates disease and antidote. Or almost: "fragments," which suggest a spatial dispersal, are not coincident with "ruins," which suggest temporal effacement. Fragments against ruins is space against time. The condition from which virtually all of the inhabitants of *The Waste Land* suffer—"I can connect / Nothing with nothing" (*CP* 70)—resembles what Jakobson terms a "contiguity disorder," the language impairment that tends to restrict discourse to one-word sentences ("Da") and one-sentence utterances:

> The syntactical rules organizing words into higher units are lost; this loss, called a grammaticism, causes the degeneration of the sentence into a mere "word heap." . . . Word order becomes chaotic; the ties of gram-matical coordination and subordination . . . are dissolved. As might be expected, words endowed with purely grammatical functions, like con-junctions, prepositions, pronouns, and articles disappear first. . . .[92]

Because the poem thematizes the loss of rules organizing "words into higher units" as just that, a loss rather than a liberation, it serves as negative testimony to the legitimacy of those rules. (A "contiguity disorder" can be diagnosed as such only if the individual speech act is referred back or "up" to a paradigmatic code that sits in structural judgment upon it.) "Disorder" so conceived does not, therefore, challenge "order"; like the sin that *Four Quartets* renders "Behovely," it merely confirms the validity of those "rules" or "antique" forms it violates but does not call into question. *He Do the Police in Different Voices:* as the rejected title of the poem suggests, the fragmentation solicits, rather than threatens, the most traditional forms of authority.

All this should be familiar enough, if only because the current apologists for the canon engage in much the same strategy. As D. A. Miller observes, "'Traditional culture' [is] imagined to be in critical condition, perhaps even in extremis," which provides the occasion for prescribing yet another restorative dose of traditional culture.[93] The corpus cannot do anything but "bloom again," as it perpetually finds sustenance in the rumors of its own death. *The Waste Land* consoles us for the conditions of its production, for the necessity of its existence. The poem is written because traditional culture is imagined to be in its death throes, yet the poem itself becomes evidence of the abiding vitality of that culture. The fate of Lil, however, suggests that the corpus is altogether too healthy, or at least too adept at haunting the living. Lil is a revenant; her very name is contained in "Philomel." There can be, then, no question of whether or not the corpse will bloom again. Nothing has died.

The economic and institutional forces that govern the production, dissemination, and consumption of literature in the modern world require the signature of an author. *The Waste Land* is no exception. The poem is dedicated to "il miglio fabbro," but it bears the "signature" T. S. Eliot; indeed, it is the poem that makes Eliot's name.[94] Foucault characterizes this coming into being of the author function as "a privileged moment in the *individualization* of ideas," although Eliot the classicist could hardly experience it as a welcome one.[95] Notes came to be appended to the poem (if one of Eliot's several explanations is to be credited) in order to forestall the charges of plagiarism that had been leveled against the earlier work. Plagiarism can arise as an issue, however, only if the signature, the unique subjectivity of the author-creator, is thought to guarantee the value and authenticity of the art object. As with "fine" wines, so too with literary and academic discourse: *appellation contrôlée.*[96] But again, this is everything that the classicism seeks to guard against. "To write or speak is not to say things or to express oneself"; rather, "it is to make one's way toward the sovereign act of nomination, to move, through language, towards that place where words and things are conjoined in their common essence, and which makes it possible to give them a name." The authorial signature that adheres to *The Waste Land* should remain, must remain, functionally empty.

Yet it cannot, at least according to the logic of "'Ulysses,' Order, and Myth." The nineteenth-century novel is "the expression of an age which had not sufficiently lost all form to feel the need of something stricter"; the novelist reproduces a world that is already the reflection of an order; he or she has only to *describe* (a mystification formalized in the convention that designates certain narrators as omniscient but not ominpotent). The modern writer, however, is obliged to *order*. The mythical method is Eliot's way "of controlling, of ordering, of giving a shape and a significance" to the immense panorama of futility and anarchy that is contemporary history, yet Eliot "gives" order—here, too, "imposes" would be the more accurate term—only to deny responsibility for it. *The Waste Land* pretends to enjoy what "'Ulysses,' Order, and Myth" identifies as a nineteenth-century dispensation. (As Wilde says of Wordsworth, "He found in stones the sermons he had already hidden there.")[97] To impose a credible order *upon* reality, and thereby elicit some perception of an order *in* reality: the poem fails to negotiate the impossible paradox.

Consider the relation *The Waste Land* establishes among what is "foretold," "foresuffered," and "enacted":

> I Tiresias, old man with wrinkled dugs
> Perceived the scene, and foretold the rest—
> I too awaited the expected guest.
>
> *(CP 68)*

> (And I Tiresias have foresuffered all
> Enacted on this same divan or bed;
> I who have sat by Thebes below the wall
> And walked among the lowest of the dead.)
>
> *(CP 69)*

Eliot's note says of this: "Tiresias, although a mere spectator and not indeed a 'character,' is yet the most important personage in the poem, uniting all the rest. . . . What Tiresias *sees,* in fact, is the substance of the poem" (*CP* 78). But Tiresias is manifestly not a "mere spectator": he both "foretells" and "foresuffers" the drama on the divan. The continuity between antiquity and contemporaneity is, if anything, too absolute, and a condition of spectatorial "stillness, serenity, and reconciliation" hardly seems an appropriate response to it. On the contrary, the tawdry ménage à trois argues the need to intervene between what is foretold and what is enacted, to release the present from the tyranny of the past. Like Dante the "copyist" or "scribe" ("quella materia ond' io son fatto scriba"),[98] Eliot would define himself as amanuensis. But the carrying over of tradition, like the mechanical reproduction of words—one of the three is a typist—is not a good in itself. The encounter begins with a description of the body mechanical:

> At the violet hour, when the eyes and back
> Turn upward from the desk, when the human engine waits
> Like a taxi throbbing waiting. . . .
>
> *(CP 68)*

It ends with the same:

> "Well now that's done: and I'm glad it's over."
> When lovely woman stoops to folly and
> Paces about her room again, alone,
> She smooths her hair with automatic hand,
> And puts a record on the gramophone.
>
> *(CP 69)*

The human body assumes the properties of the objects it creates, but which now turn, Frankenstein-like, on their creator.

Eliot asks us to credit Tiresias' sight—what he *"sees, in fact, is the sub-stance of the poem"*—but it is by no means certain that the "substance" of the poem is anything intrinsic to it. (*The Waste Land* is dominated by ghostly voices, not the clear visual images of Dante.) "What the Thunder Said" is revelatory, which suggests that the reader is brought to a condition of "serenity, stillness, and reconciliation" before the poem itself. But the revelation is itself hortatory—"Give, Sympathize, Control"—which implies that the poem finds fulfillment not in spectatorial consumption (or voyeurism, as the case may be), but in the life of historical action beyond its confines. In one version of the Grail quest catalogued in Jessie Weston's *From Ritual to Romance,* it is the quester's own "word," rather than any Word revealed to him, that restores the land:

> All this was done by what he said,
> This land whose streams no water fed,
> Its fountains dry, its fields unplowed,
> His word once more with health endowed.[99]

To the extent that the questing subject can be identified with the reader—the "hypocrite lecteur" (*CP* 63) of "The Burial of the Dead," whose relation to "the heap of broken images" is manifestly not spectatorial—the poem works against a contemplative reception. "Il miglior fabbro," the first reader of the poem, was effectively its coauthor; there is no reason why subsequent readings should not be likewise "writerly" in Barthes's sense of the term. But if anything exposes the poem's problematic relation to the creature/creator dichotomy that governs Eliot's aesthetic it is the attempt to reassert authorial control over it. *The Waste Land* is not "an important bit of social criticism" Eliot scolds his admiring critics, but only "the relief of a personal and wholly insignificant grouse against life; it is just a piece of rhythmical grumbling." Better an immense trivialization than any sugges-tion of social criticism.

But *The Waste Land* is not lyrical grumbling. Like the *Cantos* it is a seminal moment in the delyricization of epic, in the deinternalization of quest romance. It is a radically deindividualizing poem: "Just as the one-eyed merchant, seller of currants, melts into the Phoenician Sailor, and the latter is not wholly distinct from Ferdinand Prince of Naples, so all the women are one woman, and the two sexes meet in Tiresias" (*CP* 78). If the note misrepresents Tiresias' position vis-à-vis the poem, it does specify the corporate nature of identity within it, which is not the internalized self-possession of the Cartesian *cogito*. In a world in which everything depends on the health of the king's body—the purpose of the quest is to restore "the rich king who in distress does lay"[100]—identity is corporate or "ecstatic," predicated on dependent membership within the body politic, which is the king's body in its social form. Identity presupposes not uniqueness but the isomorphisms that G. Ferraro identifies as the essence of mythical thought:

> The semantic function of myth consists essentially in the link which it sets
> up between the different levels, in the multiple parallelisms which it

institutes between the various spheres of human experience. . . . It seems worthwhile to specify the semantic peculiarity of myth in its ability to attest that between different orders (for example, the cosmic order, the cultural, the zoological, meteorological, social . . .) there is a precise isomorphism. . . . Each myth . . . must be considered as a veritable *intercode* destined to permit a reciprocal convertibility between the different levels.[101]

The parallelisms instituted by mythical thought differ from the metaphysical conceits of the dramatic monologues.[102] In the latter "'the most heterogenous ideas are yoked by violence together,'" and the "force of this impeachment lies in the failure of the conjunction, the fact that often the ideas are yoked but not united" (*SE* 283). The failure is appropriate to the historical situation of the monologues, which are written, as it were, from this side of the Cartesian divide:

> Let us go then, you and I,
> When the evening is spread out against the sky
> Like a patient etherised upon a table. . . .
>   (*CP* 13)

The conceit introduces a world in which private and public, inner and outer, are structurally discontinuous. Heterogenous ideas are yoked rather than united; they participate in a distinctly Nietzschean or modern suspicion of the force of the conjunction, of the error of identifying what cannot be identified. The multiple parallelisms of *The Waste Land*, however, seek to recover the world on the far side of the Cartesian divide. Identity is not threatened by isomorphisms between or among spheres; it is incompatible only with a commitment to a uniqueness that is "the same as any other," but which nevertheless prohibits any sense of the collective or communal. Identity presupposes the full force of the conjunction or copula: Tiresias is the one-eyed merchant is Phlebas is Ferdinand; the cosmic is the cultural is the zoological is the social.

The formulation suggests metaphor in its "radical" or copular form—"A is B"[103]—yet mythical thought is opposed to the *phora* of metaphor, "change with respect to location." Because corporate identity presupposes dependent membership within the body politic, alterity of placement can be entertained only as the absurd proposition that one part of the body might substitute for another.[104] Or, to return to Madame Sosostris's table: all the characters in the poem are already contained in her "wicked pack of cards," and all possible permutations and combinations are structurally determined in advance. *Les jeux sont faits.* Unlike Mallarmé's dice, Madame Sosostris's cards do abolish chance and change.

The mythical method is "primitive" in Lévi-Strauss's sense of the term, not so much a bad grace response to historical change as an utter denial of it:

> [A]ll societies are in history and change. . . . [But] societies react to this common condition in very different fashions. Some accept it, with good or ill grace, and its consequences (to themselves and other societies)

assume immense proportions through their attention to it. Others (which we call primitive for this reason) want to deny it and try, with a dexterity we underestimate, to make the states of their development they consider "prior" as permanent as possible.[105]

Yet if *The Waste Land* is indeed a form of this "primitive" refusal of historical change, it is not therefore opposed to the cultural situation it homeopathically reproduces. We take considerable pride in having developed, unlike our oriental "other," a culture of history, but as Horkheimer and Adorno insist, the image is not the actuality:

> Enlightenment dissolves the injustice of the old inequality—unmediated lordship and mastery—but at the same time perpetuates it in universal mediation, in the relation of any one existent to any other. It does what Kierkegaard praises his Protestant ethic for, and what in the Heraclean epic cycle is one of the primal images of mythic power; it excises the incommensurable. Not only are qualities dissolved in thought, but men are brought to actual conformity. The blessing that the market does not enquire after one's birth is paid for by the barterer, in that he models the potentialities that are his by birth on the production of the commodities that can be bought in the market. Men were given their individuality as unique in each case, different to all others, so that it might all the more surely be made the same as any other.[106]

The unmediated lordship and mastery of an older order, the overt inequalities of precapitalist society, are displaced by a new inequality that "excises the incommensurable." The market does not enquire after differences of birth, but only because it subjects all differences to a "universal mediation." In an economic order in which exchange value is the new lord and master, all qualities are reduced to quantitative equivalences. The specificity of objects dissolves into the abstraction of their endless exchangeability, as does the uniqueness of the subject: potentialities developed with an eye to the market are effectively colonized and quantified by it. In effect, the "dialectic of enlightenment" recovers the endless repetition, the thoroughly fixed and static character, of the mythical past it alleges to leave behind:

> Abstraction, the tool of enlightenment, treats its objects as did fate, the notion of which it rejects: it liquidates them. Under the leveling domination of abstraction (which makes everything in nature repeatable), and of industry (for which abstraction ordains repetition), the freedom themselves [*sic*] finally came to form that "herd" which Hegel has declared to be the result of the Enlightenment. (13)

This is very much a culture that denies change and excises difference. Its uniqueness resides solely in the superior dexterity with which it does so.

The Waste Land demands, then, not the sacrifice of a lived individuality—there is nothing there to sacrifice—but the illusion thereof:

> Unreal City,
> Under the brown fog of a winter dawn,
> A crowd flowed over London Bridge, so many,

> I had not thought death had undone so many.
> Sighs, short and infrequent, were exhaled,
> And each man fixed his eyes before his feet.
>
> (CP 62)

A "crowd" of individual solitudes is the parody form of the collective; so many carceral selves is the demonic obverse of the corporate:

> I have heard the key
> Turn in the door once and turn once only
> We think of the key, each in his prison
> Thinking of the key, each confirms a prison.
>
> (CP 74)[107]

The self can be subsumed "up" into the hierarchical fixity of ritual and myth proper or sink lower into the leveling fixity of abstract repetition, the mode in which the body mechanical (re)lives its mythological past. But *The Waste Land* admits of no compromise between the two. The meeting of the typist and the young man carbuncular is intelligible either in terms of the linear axis of abstract repetition, the movement of "mechanical arms" and "human engines," or in terms of the vertical axis of mythic reenactment, the fate "foretold" and "foresuffered" by Tiresias. It is manifestly not the meeting of two personalities, two unique subjects.

In the Preface to *Lyrical Ballads,* Wordsworth attributes the urban thirst for "extraordinary incident" to a compensatory desire for the individuality that urbanization itself obliterates:

> [A] multitude of causes unknown to former times are now acting with a combined force to blunt the discriminating powers of the mind, and unfitting it for all voluntary exertion to reduce it to a state of almost savage torpor. The most effective of these causes are the great national events which are daily taking place, and the encreasing accumulation of men in cities, where the uniformity of their occupations produces a craving for extraordinary incident which the rapid communication of intelligence hourly gratifies.[108]

The historical situation analyzed by *The Waste Land* might seem an exacerbated version of this urban uniformity. Modernism is a poetry of the city in a way that romanticism is not, and in the counter- or postnatural world of *The Waste Land*—"if it rains, a closed car at four" (CP 65)—"torpor" is itself desired. April is "the cruellest month" (CP 61) precisely because it awakens "savage" or archaic desires. For Eliot, however, "the most effective" of the causes that make for uniformity are not simply "great national events" but the internationalism of each and every event; not simply "the encreasing accumulation of men in cities" but the uniformity of all cities, the homogenization of all space. "Jerusalem Athens Alexandria / Vienna London / Unreal" (CP 73).

Pre–World I Europe, as Eliot says in a different context, was "united in the strife" that divided it (CP 195). Innovations in communication and transportation, the vast expansion of trade and foreign investment after

1850, the unlimited mobility of capital and commodities: all served to put the major capitalist powers on the path of globalism, which fundamentally redefined spatiotemporal coordinates. Stephen Kern argues that the compression of the categories of time and space "tightened the skein of internationalism and facilitated international co-operation" even as it "divided nations as they all grabbed for empire and clashed in a series of crises." Hence the terrible irony: global war became possible only when the world was united—albeit in a parody form of community, or in a proximity without community, as if Wordsworth's city now stretched across the entirety of the capitalist world—to a hitherto unprecedented degree.[109] The Heidegger of "the years *l'entre deux guerres*" (*CP* 182) regrets the effacement of difference, the loss of the categories of "here" and "now," which is the modern:

> From a metaphysical point of view, Russia and America are the same; the same dreary technological frenzy, the same unrestricted organization of the average man. At a time when the furthermost corner of the globe has been conquered by technology and opened to economic exploitation; when any incident whatsoever, regardless of where and when it occurs, can be communicated to the rest of the world at any desired speed; . . . when time has ceased to be anything other than velocity, instantaneousness and simultaneity, and time as history has vanished from the life of all peoples . . . then, yes, then, through all this turmoil a question still haunts us like a specter: What for? Whither? What then?[110]

There is either the dreary universalism of "technological frenzy," the global sameness of a world governed by "the profit and the loss," or the redeemed universalism of mythological reenactment.

Or such would be the case if the mythical method were in fact only method, if antiquity functioned simply as a "means of ordering, of giving a shape and a significance" to the immense panorama of futility that is the here and now. Lévi-Strauss notes that mythical thought, in its effort to make a "prior" state of affairs as permanent as possible, calls upon "earlier ends . . . to play the part of means: the signified changes into the signifying and vice versa" (21):

> [T]he characteristic feature of mythical thought, as of "bricolage" on the practical plane, is that it builds up structured sets, not directly with other structured sets but by using the remains and debris of events: in French "des bribes et des morceaux," or odds and ends in English, fossilized evidence of the history of an individual or a society. The relation between the diachronic and the synchronic is therefore in a sense reversed. Mythical thought, that "bricoleur," builds up structures by fitting together events, or rather the remains of events. . . . (21–22)

The Waste Land is frequently read as an instance of bricolage in Lévi-Strauss's sense of the term. The Thames bears "no empty bottles, sandwich papers," or "other testimony of summer nights" (*CP* 67), but the poem itself is built from "des bribes et des morceaux," the fossilized evidence of "prior" cultural states. And true to the pre-posterous reversal of diachronic and synchronic modes characteristic of mythical thought, these earlier "ends"—the poem's various decontextualized quotations and allusions—are called upon to play the part of "means." Culture is evacuated of "signified" content, even as it is granted the power to bestow significance. "Tradition and the Individual Talent" accepts this as an article of faith; "the existing monuments" form an "ideal order among themselves," as if order were an ideal unto itself. But *The Waste Land* puts the faith to the test, and in so doing recovers the content of prior cultural states that are exposed as anything but ideal. The poem originally took for its epigraph a passage from Conrad:

> Did he live his life again in every detail of desire, temptation, and surrender during that supreme moment of complete knowledge? He cried in a whisper at some image, at some vision,—he cried out twice, a cry that was no more than a breath—
>
>   "The horror! the horror!"[111]

"Little Gidding" characterizes this as "the rending pain of re-enactment / Of all that you have done, and been" (*CP* 194); "East Coker" speaks of "a lifetime burning in every moment / And not the lifetime of one man only" (*CP* 182). In *Four Quartets* the pain of reenactment is recollected in tranquillity; in *The Waste Land* it is suffered in the flesh. Lil "lives again" in every significant "detail of desire" the myth of Philomel: "the horror" is the continuity, the refusal of a "prior" state of affairs to remain "prior." Benjamin's ambivalent reflections on the politics of culture—"There is no document of civilization which is not at the same time a document of barbarism. And just as such a document is not free of barbarism, barbarism taints also the manner in which it was transmitted from one owner to another"[112]—might stand as epigraph to *The Waste Land*.

Four Quartets dismisses these terrors as "the usual / Pastimes and drugs":

>   . . . [to] riddle the inevitable
> With playing cards, fiddle with pentagrams
> Or barbituric acids, or dissect
> The recurrent image into pre-conscious terrors—
> To explore the womb, or tomb, or dreams; all these are usual
> Pastimes and drugs, and features of the press. . . .
>
>   (*CP* 189)

To "riddle the inevitable / With playing cards" is the ambition of both Madame Sosostris's table and the poem in which she figures, the validity of which *Four Quartets* retroactively denies:

>   all these are usual
> Pastimes and drugs, and features of the press:
> And always will be, some of them especially
> When there is distress of nations and perplexity

> Whether on the shores of Asia, or in the Edgware Road.
> Men's curiosity searches past and future
> And clings to that dimension.
>
> (CP 189)

In no obvious sense does to "riddle the inevitable / With playing cards" argue an activity that "clings" to the linear dimension of past and future. Rather, it suggests a secular or degraded counterpart to the "occupation" *Four Quartets* opposes to it:

> But to apprehend
> The point of intersection of the timeless
> With time, is an occupation for the saint—
> No occupation either, but something given
> And taken, in a lifetime's death in love,
> Ardour and selflessness and self-surrender.
>
> (CP 189–90)

Tiresias "apprehends" the "intersection of the timeless / With time," and if Eliot's note is to be believed, "what Tiresias *sees,* in fact, is the substance of the poem." Tiresias is himself merely "antique," not timeless, although the poem, in rendering a prior state of affairs as permanent as possible, strategically effaces the difference between the two. The social, the cultural, is posited as the individual's fate or destiny; but in projecting that destiny onto a "wicked pack of cards," the poem would render things as they are effectively intractable. *The Waste Land* finally succeeds, however, only in demystifying its desire to mystify: the world is waste precisely to the extent that the syntagmatic axis articulates a paradigmatic code that precedes and subtends it. Eliot writes poetry, as men and women make history, on the basis of "circumstances directly found, transmitted, and given from the past." The world is made, but not once and for all. It can be remade differently, if only on the basis of the waste material, "des bribes et des morceaux," that history itself provides. Such, in any case, is the premise of the "honor" Eliot rejects: "Various critics have done me the honor to interpret the poem . . . as an important bit of social criticism." The social is not our destiny, and one cannot ask of culture what only religion can provide. *Four Quartets* maintains that a "people without history / Is not redeemed from time" (CP 197). History itself, however, can never be the agent of redemption.

It is only with romanticism, Eliot complains, that the literary act begins to be conceived as a raid on the absolute, and "its result as a revelation; at the moment literature gathered the inheritance of religion and organized itself on the model which it replaced; the writer became the priest; the purpose of all his gestures was to induce the 'descent' of the 'Real Presence' into his Host."[113] It is only with the regression from the "lucidity" of the preromantics, de Man complains, that literature falls victim to the mystification of the symbol:

> On the level of language the asserted superiority of the symbol over
> allegory, so frequent during the nineteenth century, is one of the forms
> taken by this tenacious self-mystification. Wide areas of the European
> literature of the nineteenth and twentieth centuries appear as regressive
> with regards to the truths that come to light in the last quarter of the
> eighteenth century. For the lucidity of the pre-romantic writers does not
> persist. It does not take long for a symbolic conception of metaphorical
> language to establish itself everywhere. . . .[114]

De Man's complaint is theoretical, Eliot's theological. For de Man the
symbol is a mystification; for Eliot it is a black mass, a parody of transub-
stantiation and hence Incarnation. The two are united, however, in their
rejection of the romantic (specifically Coleridgean) faith that "Real Pres-
ence" and representation can coincide. The postconversion Eliot is com-
mitted to the Incarnation as a spiritual truth and a historical fact, and the
Incarnation is a conventional symbol for the commingling of opposites,
the reconciliation of differences, effected by the romantic symbol. "For he
is our peace," we read in Ephesians 2:14, "who has broken down the
middle wall of partition between us." *Four Quartets* celebrates the Word
made Flesh, the conflation of the eternal and the temporal in the God/man
Christ, yet there is no mimesis on the level of form of the union adum-
brated on the level of content. The poem renounces "nostalgia and the
desire to coincide," as de Man puts it, and establishes its language in the
void of temporal difference (207). If, then, one follows de Man in attribut-
ing "theoretical lucidity" to the preromantics, it must also be attributed to
Four Quartets. By the same token, if one discerns in *Four Quartets* an
ideologically suspect devaluation of cultural labor, a deeply antiutopian
impulse, it must also be attributed to the contemporary denigration of the
"symbolic conception of metaphorical language."

Four Quartets celebrates what it cannot articulate:

> At the still point of the turning world. Neither flesh nor fleshless;
> Neither from nor towards; at the still point, there the dance is,
> But neither arrest nor movement. And do not call it fixity,
> Where past and future are gathered. Neither movement from nor towards,
> Neither ascent nor decline.
>
> (CP 173)

There is no possibility of confusion here between representation and real
presence, no possibility that literature will gather the inheritance of reli-
gion and organize itself on the model it displaces. The metaphor of "the
still point" negates both its terms—"Neither flesh nor fleshless," "neither
arrest nor movement"—and so renounces, in the most conspicuous of
fashions, the desire "to coincide." The "still point" can be known only in
the "betweenness" of what it is not, and *Four Quartets* wants "between-
ness" to be known as its defining modality:

> In the middle, not only in the middle of the way
> But all the way, in a dark wood, in a bramble,

> On the edge of a grimpen, where is no secure foothold,
> And menaced by monsters, fancy lights,
> Risking enchantment.
>
> (*CP* 179)

Dante's "selva oscura" is a topos not only for "the middle of the way" but for "all the way," the no-place of a poem "Caught in the form of limitation / Between un-being and being" (*CP* 175). The Name that organizes all classical discourse is also the Name that organizes all Christian history. We fall into the Babel of human languages, the proliferation of alien or alias names, and we shall be redeemed from them: the apocalyptic promise of "a new name written" (Rev. 2:17) recovers Edenic conditions of naming. But if the Bible posits a reconstituted proper name as the fulfillment of temporal process, *Four Quartets* remains caught in the realm of unlikeness:

> I met one walking, loitering and hurried
> As if blown towards me like the metal leaves
> Before the urban dawn wind unresisting.
> And as I fixed upon the down-turned face
> That pointed scrutiny with which we challenge
> The first-met stranger in the waning dusk
> I caught the sudden look of some dead master
> Whom I had known, forgotten, half recalled
> Both one and many; in the brown baked features
> The eyes of a familiar compound ghost
> Both intimate and unidentifiable.
>
> (*CP* 193)

Early drafts of the poem identify the master as "Ser Brunetto," although in the final version the name is withheld. Eliot justified the deletion, which John Hayward queried, as follows:

> The first [reason for change] is that the visionary figure has now become somewhat more definite and will no doubt be identified . . . with Yeats though I do not mean anything so precise as that. . . . Secondly, although the reference to the Canto [*Inferno* 15] is intended to be explicit, I wished the effect of the whole to be Purgatorial which is much more appropriate.[115]

The desired effect is purgatorial, and Eliot honors Dante by refusing to tread where Dante has no fear to go. Poetry "leaves us, as Virgil left Dante, to proceed toward a region where that guide can avail us no farther," which is the exact point at which Dante is called, for the first time in the *Commedia,* by his proper name:

> Ma Virgilio n'avea lasciati scemi
>   di sé, Virgilio dolcissimo patre,
>   Virgilio a cui per mia salute die'mi:
> né quantunque perdeo l'antica matre,
>   valse a le guance nette di rugiada
>   che, lagrimando, non tornasser atre.

> "Dante, perché Virgilio se ne vada,
>   non pianger anco, no piangere ancora;
>   ché pianger ti conven per altra spada."
>   (*Purgatorio* 30.49–57)[116]

The *Cantos,* which labors "to write Paradise," negotiates this threshold. Thrones concludes with an act analogous to Dante's departure from Virgil. *Four Quartets,* however, remains a poem of diaspora:

> We shall not cease from exploration
> And the end of all our exploring
> Will be to arrive where we started
> And know the place for the first time.
>   (*CP* 197)

Even if the *nostos* were realized, it would accomplish little. The verticality of epiphany, not the circularity of experience, redeems "the waste sad time":

> Sudden in a shaft of sunlight
> Even while the dust moves
> There rises the hidden laughter
> Of children in the foliage
> Quick now, here, now, always—
> Ridiculous the waste sad time
> Stretching before and after.
>   (*CP* 176)

But *Four Quartets* is not in fact an agent of epiphany. The poem is content—indeed, much more than content—simply to register the tension between the redeemed and the ridiculous.

Between the conception and the creation falls the shadow, and *Four Quartets* occupies the interspace:

> . . . every attempt
> Is a wholly new start, and a different kind of failure
> Because one has only learnt to get the better of words
> For the thing one no longer has to say, or the way in which
> One is no longer disposed to say it. And so each venture
> Is a new beginning, a raid on the inarticulate
> With shabby equipment always deteriorating
> In the general mess of imprecision of feeling,
> Undisciplined squads of emotion.
>   (*CP* 182)

The saying and what is to be said, the subject of the enounced and the subject of the enunciation, can never correspond, which the poem says and says again:

> You say I am repeating
> Something I have said before. I shall say it again.
> Shall I say it again?
>   (*CP* 181)

So frequent are these thematizations of failure that it is difficult to decide if *Four Quartets* is a celebration of what it cannot articulate or of the fact that it cannot articulate its content adequately.

Matthew Arnold would no doubt have done Eliot the "honor" of thinking *The Waste Land* "an important bit of social criticism." And it is Arnold, Eliot complains, who gets things fundamentally wrong:

> "Poetry is at bottom a criticism of life." At bottom: that is a great way down; the bottom is the bottom. At the bottom of the abyss is what few ever see, and what those cannot bear to look at for long; and it is not "a criticism of life." If we mean life as a whole—not that Arnold ever saw life as a whole—from top to bottom, can anything that we can say of it ultimately, of that awful mystery, be called criticism? We bring back very little from our rare descents, and that is not criticism. (*UPUC* 111)

There is a certain elitism attached to Eliot's negotiations of the abyss, an aristocracy of anguish, which excludes the likes of Arnold, whose concern with the mundane is itself evidence of a deficient capacity for anguish. There is a certain elitism, moreover, attached to de Man's valorization of the poetics of "an authentically temporal predicament," an aristocracy of rigor, as if only the predicament were authentic and any resolution a vulgar mystification. Eliot complains that Arnold "was so conscious of what, for him, poetry was *for,* that he could not altogether see it for what it is" (*UPUC* 118). Eliot himself, however, is so conscious of what, for him, poetry is *not,* what it is incapable of doing, that he could not altogether see what it might positively be *for.*

No one has ever (to my knowledge) considered *Four Quartets* "an important bit of social criticism"; such is the success of the failure of the poem. True, it is sometimes celebrated in quasi-Heideggerian terms as a poem of "temporal hermeneutics," in which process enjoys ontological priority over form, which is more or less what de Man means by allegory.[117] But for all practical purposes, an "authentically temporal predicament" (de Man's term) or a "temporal hermeneutics" (William Spanos's Heideggerian term) only means that poetry has no practical purpose:

> Either you had no purpose
> Or the purpose is beyond the end you figured
> And is altered in fulfillment.
>
> (*CP* 192)

Because human action can never realize its purpose, humankind can fare forward as if faring forward were a good in itself: "Fare forward, travellers! not escaping from the past / Into different lives, or into any future" (*CP* 188). "Let us go," although here the journey that is unmotivated by any goal becomes, like sin, "Behovely." "What is the moral attitude of Dryden's *Mr. Limberham?,*" the "B" of Eliot's "Dialogue on Dramatic Poetry" is asked. His answer: "It retains its respect for the divine by showing the failure of the human" (*SE* 45). I cannot comment on the justice of the observation as it applies to *Mr. Limberham,* but it exactly catches the "moral attitude" of the *Quartets.* Substitute "rigor" or "authenticity" for the "divine," moreover, and it catches the political efficacy of an "authentically temporal predicament."

4

PAUL DE MAN
The Poetics of Collaboration

"The Resistance to Theory," Paul de Man's widely influential 1982 essay, begins by noting the resistance the essay originally encountered. Commissioned by the Committee on Research Activities of the Modern Language Association for its volume *Introduction to Scholarship in Modern Languages and Literatures,* the piece was nevertheless judged inappropriate by the editors, who declined to print it. De Man characterizes the decision, in the version of the essay since published in the volume that shares its name, as "altogether justified, as well as interesting in its implications for the teaching of literature."[1] The latter point seems to me plausible; in a rather oblique fashion I shall address some of those implications here. But I am not convinced that de Man was convinced that the rejection was "justified," even if it did prove paradoxically fortunate for the future life and influence of the essay. In one sense I thoroughly approve of de Man's decision to begin with the anecdote of the committee's decision. It is not possible to be sufficiently suspicious of "the value / Of well-gowned approbation / Of literary effort," and of this the committee's judgment is an exemplary reminder. In another sense, however, I find the decision to begin with the anecdote disingenuous, although interesting in its implications, in the barely disguised pride it takes in evidence of "well-gowned' institutional disapprobation.

It is evidence that de Man would have had some difficulty multiplying. In 1982 he was widely considered the state of the art, and few committees or journals would have so obligingly provided him with proof of the institutional form of the resistance to theory on which his essay, at least in part, depends. Recourse to the anecdotal or personal is not characteristic of de Man in general, and he can be forgiven for making good rhetorical and polemical use, which he does, of an opportunity so happily provided. But the anecdotal is significant, as de Man himself notes, only if it is "systematic" (RT 7), which the committee's decision manifestly was not. Yet de Man treats it as if it were, for the simple reason that it allows him to exaggerate the extent of the resistance to theory as he understands and practices it, which he can then explain in equally exaggerated claims for its "threatening" or "subversive" powers (RT 5, 8). (For "theory," read poststructuralism; rival theoretical positions are implicitly denigrated as either literary history or literary criticism.) The argument is efficient but circular. To the extent that it is concerned with "resistance" in any empirical or verifiable sense—which, admittedly, is not much—it is purely anecdotal.

De Man is concerned, however, with what he calls "social and historical (that is to say ideological) reality" (RT 11). He defines his theoretical enterprise in formal terms, as the "introduction of linguistic terminology in the metalanguage about literature" (RT 8), yet he credits theory, "more than any other mode of inquiry, including economics," with the power to expose "ideological mystifications" (RT 11), with political purpose and efficacy. The resistance to theory that would dismiss it as "pure verbalism, as a denial of the reality principle in the name of absolute fictions," is itself an ideological mystification (RT 10). For de Man, opponents of theory merely state "their fear at having their own ideological mystifications exposed by the tool they are trying to discredit" (RT 11). In what is perhaps the most memorable passage in the essay—it is de Man at his bravado best—opponents of the linguistic emphasis in contemporary theory are characterized as "very poor readers of Marx's *German Ideology*" (RT 11), presumably on the basis that language or the "materiality of the signifier" is synonymous with the material determinants of ideological production itself. A "few feeble allusions to the sonorous vibration of language in air and space" do not, however, a materialist make,[2] and there is apparently more than one way to misread *The German Ideology*.

De Man's 1982 claims for the threat posed by theory have been much rehearsed, are still much rehearsed, and this despite the fact that a former colleague and fellow poststructuralist is a past president of the very organization that de Man gives as an instance of the resistance to theory in its institutional form. Indeed, claims for the subversive force of theory, in relation to both its object of study and the cultural context in which it functions, are now so routinely advanced that, should "The Resistance to Theory" be rewritten today, it could only be titled "The Triumph of Theory." Thus, even if one were to concede de Man his 1982 characterization of the theoretical scene—and it is a generous concession: he speaks of remarkably diverse individuals and trends as united in the "broad, though negative, consensus . . . [that] is their shared resistance to theory" (RT 6–7)—the essay now reads like a document from before the Flood. Today, if any consensus obtains in the diversity of theoretical endeavors, it is precisely de Man's claim for the political and ideological efficacy of theory, the now thoroughly orthodox contention that theory is somehow innately subversive. Here one might cite as evidence not only the institutional prestige still enjoyed by poststructuralism proper, but any number of theoretical positions that have been effectively colonized by it. Contemporary psychoanalytic or psycholinguistic theories, for example, in which the operations of desire are said to be in excess of the possibility of containment or control, testify to the enduring influence of poststructuralism, as do various feminisms, particularly those of Continental inspiration, in which *jouissance,* the erotics of *écriture,* is said to disrupt "patriarchal" claims to discursive mastery or truth. "Post-" or revisionist marxisms, moreover, which contend that literary form disrupts or "internally distanciates" ideological formulations, recuperate poststructuralist premises, all the more effectively for advertising themselves as a critique of poststructuralism. The word *consensus,* both here and in de Man's essay, homogenizes a great deal. Yet if there is in fact a new orthodoxy, a contemporary counterpart to the 1982 "consensus that brings . . . extremely diverse trends and individuals together," it is the now ubiquitous notion that a text's (usually suspect) ideological messages do not finally "hang together,"[3] which is exactly the thesis that "The Resistance to Theory" helped to establish.

It is by no means certain, however, that the thesis can survive its success, or, more accurately, that it can continue to command conviction given its success. There is at best something problematic in the institutional approbation with which it has been met, something oxymoronic in the regularity with which it is advanced. From which D. A. Miller concludes: "[E]ven if it were true that literature exercises a destabilizing function in our culture," as poststructuralism contends, "the current consensus that it does so does not."[4] This seems to me very much to the point. Things have not fallen apart, at least not in any way that heralds liberation, and this despite the fact that the pages of *PMLA* now routinely assure us that the center cannot hold. In 1982 "The Resistance to Theory" asked what ideological anxieties the resistance to theory betrays, what work of ideological demystification, ideological subversion, theory performs. Of which today it might be asked: What ideological comfort is gained, what ideological ends are served, by the now ubiquitous contention that theory is innately subversive?

It is a contention that has survived—indeed, that has found positive sustenance in—Ortwin de Graef's discovery of a hitherto suppressed portion of the de Man corpus, collaborationist writings that must now inform our reading of the later accomplishment. I write "must inform," though de Man himself, or at the least the de Man of the much-quoted conclusion to "Shelley Disfigured," would disagree:

> *The Triumph of Life* warns us that nothing, whether deed, word, thought or text, ever happens in relation, positive or negative, to anything that precedes, follows or exists elsewhere, but only as a random event whose

power, like the power of death, is due to the randomness of its occur-
rence. It also warns us why and how these events then have to be reinte-
grated in a historical and aesthetic system of recuperation that repeats
itself regardless of the exposure of its fallacy.[5]

For the "late" or "mature" de Man, the categories of "late" and "early" are
themselves implicated in the "fallacy" of aesthetic recuperation, in the
ideologically suspect transformation of "random" events into narrative
teleologies. Yet even in those defenses of de Man that are intent on main-
taining the enduring value and intellectual power of the work of the
mature theoretician—of which "Shelley Disfigured" is a distinguished
example—the categories "early" and "late" are everywhere operable. Geof-
frey Hartman, for one, argues that "in the light of what we now know" de
Man's work "appears more and more as a deepening reflection on the
rhetoric of totalitarianism," and so functions in the context of the entirety
of the corpus as "a belated, but still powerful, act of conscience."[6] The
argument is attractive, yet as de Man might have noted, it betrays precisely
the passion for "aesthetic recuperation," narrative "totalization," that the
"mature" theorist regards as ideologically suspect.

My own argument, my own sense of the relation that obtains between
the wartime journalism and the theoretical writings, is less "attractive" than
Hartman's, although also motivated in its own way by a qualified respect
for the informing impulse of the later work. By less attractive I mean that I
shall argue for a continuity between the journalism of the early 1940s and
the accomplishment of the mature theoretician, which is explicitly a conti-
nuity of collusion, complicity in the operations of power. By qualified
respect for the informing impulse of the later work, I mean that the conti-
nuity is the unwitting and paradoxical product of a desire to be discon-
tinuous. Not that the mature work is given to fascism or anti-Semitism,
although the early work, de Man's defenders notwithstanding, strikes an
opportunistic bargain with both. On the contrary, the failure of the mature
work is its inability to conceive of a modality of power that is not overtly
fascistic, that is not in fact overt, but that is all the more powerful for its
powers of dissemination, for its strategic refusal of centralization, localiza-
tion. I have called this a continuity of collusion, but there is an important
distinction to be made. The collaborationist journalism of the early 1940s
constitutes a massive ethical and political failure; the complicity of the
post-1953 writings involves what de Man characterizes as the blindness of
an insight.

It is possible, then, to accept Hartman's characterization of the later
work "as a belated act of conscience," but to give "belated" a somewhat
different inflection: the work is belated in the sense that it resists a modality
of power with which the *Le Soir* articles openly collude, but which is largely
(although by no means totally) irrelevant to the specific historical context
in which it gained such general currency. "The Resistance to Theory"
claims for itself subversive power vis-à-vis "ideological aberrations" (RT

11)—aberrations that are never historicized—even as it works toward the reproduction of an ideology of power to which it remains effectively blind. Likewise, essays that have been written in defense of de Man (I focus on two in what follows: Derrida's "Like the Sound of the Sea Deep Within a Shell: Paul de Man's War," and J. Hillis Miller's untitled *Times Literary Supplement* piece)[7] tend to rehearse the strategy of "The Resistance to Theory," and hence the blindness of its insight.

The defenses are very much of a piece. The belated discovery of de Man's wartime journalism has provided little more than the occasion for recommending (once again) the politics of the nonteleological, the non-selfsame, the nontotalizing, and so for celebrating, implicitly or explicitly, our distance from all things modern. To express the difference schematically: Pound and Eliot are poets of proper names and fixed addresses; poststructuralism is a critique of the very notion of the proper. Consider, in this context, de Man's reflections on Locke's reflections on the "properties" of gold, on the difficulties involved in any attempt at "predication or definition by property":

> Like the blind man who cannot understand the idea of light, the child who cannot tell the figural from the proper keeps recurring throughout eighteenth-century epistemology as barely disguised figures of our universal predicament. For not only are tropes, as their name implies, always on the move—more like quicksilver than like flowers or butterflies which one can at least hope to pin down and insert in a neat taxonomy—but they can disappear altogether, or at least appear to disappear. Gold not only has a color and a texture, but it is also soluble. "For by what right is it that fusibility comes to be a part of the essence signified by the word *gold,* and solubility but a property of it? . . . That which I mean is this: that these being all but properties, depending on its real constitution, and nothing but powers either active or passive in reference to other bodies, no one has authority to determine the signification of the word *gold* (as referred to such a body existing in nature) . . ." (*Essay Concerning Human Understanding,* bk. 3, chap. 9). Properties, it seems, do not properly totalize, or, rather, they totalize in a haphazard and unreliable way. It is indeed not a question of ontology, of things as they are, but of authority, of things as they are decreed to be. . . . We have no way of defining, of policing, the boundaries that separate the name of one entity from the name of another; tropes are not just travellers, they tend to be smugglers and probably smugglers of stolen goods at that.[8]

Tropes may be unreliable, but evidently they can be relied on to acknowledge themselves as such. If the child who cannot tell the literal from the figural is a "barely disguised" figure of "our universal predicament," then the figural is a more or less transparent figure for its own universal unreliability; if we have "no way of defining, of policing, the boundary" between the literal and the figural, we can nevertheless police the boundaries between figures. Tropes are "more like quicksilver than flowers or butterflies" because "quicksilver" is a better figure—a hierarchical distinction that already presupposes the operations of the poststructuralist police—for the resistance of tropes to policing. There is, it turns out, little difficulty involved in "predication or definition by property"; the ease with which figures acknowledge their own unreliability argues a tropological mobility that is already pinned down and inserted into a taxonomy.

Pound would see in this "universal predicament" little more that an apology for economic exploitation. The celebration of catachresis (a highly valorized term in the poststructuralist lexicon) presupposes an economy of chrematistics, a connection de Man himself seems to intuit. He characterizes tropes not just as "travellers" but as "smugglers," and "probably smugglers of stolen goods at that." This is the ethos of Odysseus Polytropos—the man who succeeds, by virtue of a form of portative violence, polytropic language, in appropriating the goods of others—although here "the prototype of the bourgeois individual" functions as a figure for transgression. It is not accidental, of course, that de Man focuses on Locke's reflections on the solubility of gold. Poststructuralism is opposed, as it were, to all fetishizations of the gold standard, to all attempts to determine meaning or value on the basis of a subtending presence. For Michael Ryan this argues a certain compatibility between poststructuralism and marxism:

> Another prototypical kind of "diaphoristics" or economy of forces is decipherable in Marx's description of exchange value. Exchange value is a concrete social relation, but it has no sensible existence outside of the play of differences between commodities or the difference of forces between capital and labor. One cannot study the "truth" of exchange value as the thing itself revealed in its presence without recourse to a differential system that breaks up presence into an economy of forces and deploys the "thing itself" along a chain of referential serial relations. In a foreshadowing of Derrida's more philosophic critique of substantialism, Marx says repeatedly that capital and exchange value are not substantial things, but instead "relations." As in physics, "insubstantial" force permits matter to congeal, and that substance of matter does not lend itself to being a primordial ground in the philosophic sense, because it is an effect of a differential of force.[9]

But Derrida's "more philosophic critique of substantialism" is more than just "more philosophic"; it is radically dehistoricizing. The capitalist evacuation of presence is precisely that—capitalist—and if one "cannot study the 'truth' of exchange value as the thing itself revealed in its presence," an economy in which exchange value enjoys priority over use value, in which the logic of difference supersedes the presence of "substantial things," nevertheless has its "primordial ground" in real economic exploitation. The evacuation of presence is not simply an escape from logocentric illusions, but the already accomplished means by which an economy of "serial relations" or difference "forgets" its material grounding. Poststructuralism, however, defines itself against an archaic metaphysics of presence. It thus risks serving both as an apology for things as they are (recall the celebration of "usury" as an "interdicted" value) and as an assurance that they cannot be otherwise (any attempt to overcome the logic of *différance* can only betray complicity in the old metaphysical illusions). Perry Anderson accuses poststructuralism of suffering from "a poverty of strategy,"[10] but it may be that all this is strategic enough. In any case, poststructuralism, in taking arms against the regime of the transcendental signified, refigures what is as the subversive.

I begin with the relation of de Man's early journalism to the mature accomplishment, a topic already much explored by de Man's defenders. The standard argument is roughly as follows: if the *Le Soir* articles are given to a celebration of unity, teleology, and coherence, the mature accomplishment valorizes indeterminacy, dissemination, irony; if the *Le Soir* articles advance a rhetoric of totalitarianism, the mature accomplishment is a retroactive critique of the same. But the obvious discontinuities belie the persistence of a radically essentialized understanding of power, as if fascism somehow exhausted the field of ideological aberrations.[11] And even if fascism were prototypical, a critique that is conducted exclusively on the level of rhetoric—or theory, which, "more so than any other mode of inquiry, including economics," possesses the power to unmask "ideological aberrations"—merely rehearses the aestheticization it alleges to demystify. Fascism "sees its salvation in giving the masses not their right, but a chance to express themselves"; poststructuralism sees its subversive power in giving the academy (and nothing but the academy, of which more presently) the power to deconstruct the same. The reversal is perfectly symmetrical, but as poststructuralism itself insists, symmetrical reversals are ideologically suspect.

In the second section, I focus on Ernesto Laclau and Chantal Mouffe's *Hegemony & Socialist Strategy: Towards a Radical Democratic Politics,* which attempts to translate the implicit political agenda of poststructuralism into a blueprint for praxis. Like Derrida's "Structure Sign and Play in the Discourse of the Human Sciences," *Hegemony & Socialist Strategy* defines itself against the "totalizing" force exerted by "ends" and "centers," and thus, according to the logic of the homology that virtually governs poststructuralist thought, totalitarianism itself. Yet if recourse to a center or end is invariably totalizing, if totalization is invariably totalitarian, then marxism is structurally indistinguishable from fascism. The failure to distinguish between the two is inconsistent with poststructuralism's own p.r., but it is crucial to its ideological project. As Terry Eagleton observes: "No simple binary opposition can be established between 'ideology'— conceived as relentlessly closed and seamlessly self-identical—and *écriture*. Deconstruction's failure to dismantle such an opposition is the surest sign of its own ideological character, and of its collusiveness with the liberal humanism it seeks to embarrass."[12]

Now all this might seem contradictory (hardly a damning charge from a poststructuralist perspective, but one I nevertheless choose to address). Can poststructuralism be accused both of collusion with the fascist aestheticization of the political it alleges to critique and of the liberal humanism it seeks to embarrass? Fascism conceives of itself as different in kind from liberalism, and liberalism in turn routinely invokes the specter of fascism, particularly National Socialism, in order to forestall each and every critique of itself. But not all alternatives to liberalism necessarily involve the return of the old enslavement, and it is altogether too easy to take comfort—and a cold comfort it is—in the negative "pretext that we do not have (too many) police breathing down our necks or that our labour is not (too) exploited."[13] In our very efforts to keep the police at bay (or to define ourselves negatively against the police state), we may have succeeded only in reconciling ourself to a rather different form of policing. Such, in any case, is my argument in the third and final section. If poststructuralism colludes with the liberal humanism it seeks to embarrass, it is not therefore without what I shall insist on calling, perhaps unwisely, totalitarian implications.

Symmetrical Reversals

I have accused de Man of failing to historicize his understanding of the operations of power, but this is to invoke a category that de Man himself has done much to problematize. In "The Resistance to Theory," for example, he argues that "literary history, even when considered at the furthest remove from the platitudes of positivistic historicism, is still the history of an understanding of which the possibility is taken for granted" (RT 7). The very term "literary history" betrays a redundancy, as a history or historiography that assumes the possibility of its own mode of understanding is already and always literary. "No one in his right mind," de Man concedes, "will try to grow grapes by the luminosity of the word 'day'"— that is, no one in his or her right mind will "confuse the materiality of the signifier with the materiality of what it signifies"—"but it is very difficult not to conceive of the pattern of one's past and future existence as in accordance with temporal and spatial schemes that belong to fictional narratives and not to the world." This does not mean, as de Man is careful to note, "that fictional narratives are not part of the world and of reality; their impact upon the world may well be all too strong for comfort," a point that his own anti-Semitic fiction, "Les Juifs dans la littérature actuelle" (*Le Soir*, March 4, 1941), which seeks to pass itself off as literary history, makes abundantly and painfully clear. And it is precisely this "confusion of linguistic with natural reality, of reference with phenomenalism" (RT 11), that the mature de Man comes to define as ideological.

It is obvious from the *Le Soir* articles, however, that de Man did not always possess, or at least did not always publicly profess, a sense of the discontinuity that obtains between life and its "aesthetic recuperation." "La littérature française devants les événements" (January 20, 1942), for example, speaks of the "particular pleasure" one derives from reading books—including the works of French collaborators: Robert Brasillach's *Notre Avant-Guerre,* Bertrand de Jouvenal's *Après la défaite,* and Alfred

Fabre-Luce's *Journal de la France*—in which a part of "our own experience is reflected" ("le plaisir tout particulier qu'on ressent à lire ces livres dans lesquels une partie de notre expérience propre se trouve reflétée").[14] The formulation presupposes that adequacy of the aesthetic to experience; else-where, experience is said to assume the purposiveness and coherence of aesthetic representation:

> This is the first element that may interest visitors [to an exhibition on the history of Germany]: to have a clearer vision of the very complex history of a people whose importance is fundamental to the destiny of Europe. They will be able to see that the history of Germany is governed by a fundamental factor: the will to unite the set of regions that have a like racial structure but that adversaries have incessantly endeavoured to divide.

De Man's review of the exhibition ("L'Exposition 'Histoire d'Allemagne' au Cinquantenaire," *Le Soir,* March 16, 1942) fails to distinguish adequately between "l'histoire très complexe d'un peuple" and its "aesthetic recuperation." "Le destin de l'Europe" is indistinguishable from "dessein," "design" in its explicitly narrative or aesthetic sense; the signifying medium that is the exposition is one with the concrete experience it signifies: "Ce sont là des facteurs historiques que chacun, désireux de comprendre la raison profonde des événements actuels, doit connaître. Il les verra comme une réalité concrète dans le schéma que cette exposition lui présente." There is no tension between the lived immediacy of historical experience and the structural principle that renders experience intelligible. The visitor to the exposition is given knowledge as experience, experience as knowledge:

> There is another reason for which Germany's historical destiny both past and future cannot leave us indifferent: and that is because we depend on it directly. . . . None can deny the fundamental importance of Germany for the life of the West as a whole. One must see this obstinacy that resists subjugation as more than a simple proof of national steadfastness. The whole continuity of western civilization depends on the unity of the people who are its center. [Toute la continuité de la civilisation occiden-tale dépend de l'unité du peuple qui en est le centre.]

Nazi Germany is the principle of both structural and historical intel-ligibility.

This "early" celebration of teleology, continuity, and unity is nothing if not remote from the "late" accomplishment:

> I would never have by myself undertaken the task of establishing such a collection and . . . I confess that I still look back upon it with some misgivings. Such massive evidence of the failure to make the various individual readings coalesce is a somewhat melancholy spectacle. The fragmentary aspect of the whole is made more obvious still by the hypo-tactic manner that prevails in each of the essays taken in isolation, by the continued attempt, however ironized, to present a closed and linear argu-

ment. This apparent coherence *within* each essay is not matched by a corresponding coherence *between* them. Laid out diachronically in a roughly chronological sequence, they do not evolve in a manner that easily allows for dialectical progression or, ultimately, for historical to- talization.[15]

Yet if the later work is remote from the earlier, "early" and "late" stand in a relation of binary opposition, and the later work regards the binary as ideologically suspect. Indeed, the later work, the later refusal of teleology, continuity, and unity, is itself the symmetrical inversion of the earlier, and hence subject to critique on its own terms.

De Man characterizes this refusal, however, not as a such but as "mas- sive evidence of failure," which might seem an excessively modest way of speaking of one's own work. But like the "failure" to write the kind of essay that would have met with the approval of the MLA Committee on Research Activities—that is, an essay of sufficient banality—"failure" is here, as in Eliot, a curiously valorized term. The absence of "dialectical progression" or "historical totalization," the injunctions against expecta- tions of coherence and continuity: all this reads as an index of the author's rigor, a sign that he is "at the furthest remove from the platitudes of positivistic historicism." True, the preface to *The Rhetoric of Romanticism* is rather more generous to the possibility of historical understanding than is de Man's wont. It sensibly acknowledges that "one is all too easily tempted to rationalize personal shortcoming as theoretical impossibility," and it notes, albeit condescendingly, that "especially among younger scholars there is ample evidence that the historical study of romanticism is being successfully pursued" (*RR* viii–ix). Yet however ample the evidence, his- torical studies are pursued at the cost of a massive theoretical blindness: "One feels at times envious of those who can continue to do literary history as if nothing had happened in the sphere of theory, but one cannot help but feel somewhat suspicious of their optimism" (*RR* ix). Certainly de Man himself does not "do" history, literary or otherwise, at least not in this sense, and the "optimism" of those who persist in trying provokes his suspicions. But unless theoretical rigor is now synonymous with futility, the fetishization of failure should provoke ours. In any case, one cannot help feeling that there is a certain confusion here between a specific his- torical experience and the category of the historical itself, as if historical explanation were innately totalizing, and the totalizing innately total- itarian:

> Generic terms such as "lyric" (or its various sub-species, "ode," "idyll," or "elegy") as well as pseudo-historical period terms such "romanticism" or "classicism" are always terms of resistance and nostalgia, at the furthest remove from the materiality of actual history. If mourning is called a "chambre d'éternel deuil où vibrent de vieux râles" [as it is in Baudelaire], then this pathos of terror states in fact the desired consciousness of eter- nity and of temporal harmony as voice and as song. True "mourning" is less deluded. The most *it* can do is to allow for non-comprehension and

enumerate non-anthropomorphic, non-elegiac, non-celebratory, non-lyrical, non-poetic, that is to say, prosaic, or, better, *historical* modes of language power. (*RR* 262)

The pure randomness of history—"nothing, whether deed, word, thought or text ever happens in relation, positive or negative, to anything that precedes, follows or exists elsewhere"—can be known only in the reiteration of what it is not; "the materiality of actual history" can be felt only in its resistance to aesthetic phenomenalization.[16] De Man rejects narratives of historical determinism and causality, yet the rejection itself seems determined by an earlier, radically different understanding of history and its relation to the aesthetic.[17] Even when it most explicitly addresses questions of ideology and power—I am thinking of "The Resistance to Theory"; de Man did not live to write two essays that would have been central here, one on Kierkegaard as understood by Adorno, the other on Marx's *German Ideology*—the later work makes no concessions to historical specificity. It thus seems caught, at least when read in conjunction with the earlier political commitments, in a symmetrical and ahistorical reversal.

Evidence of this reversal, unlike that of the institutional form of the resistance to theory, might be multiplied almost indefinitely. To give but two examples: in contrast to the *Le Soir* articles, which tend to juxtapose the mystical nature of the German character and destiny against French intellectualism and self-consciousness, the mature work eschews the very category of the national. It is with some contempt that "The Resistance to Theory" speaks of "nationally rooted concerns" and "personally competitive" views of history and literature (*pace* Harold Bloom?), which it identifies with the "wish to hierarchize" various theoretical movements (RT 7). Or, in contrast to the "organic" relation between culture and national destiny celebrated in the *Le Soir* articles, the mature work, particularly "The Rhetoric of Temporality," provides a powerful critique of organicism and organic analogies. Yet rather than multiply evidence duly noted by others—the contention that "in the light of what we now know" de Man's work appears "more and more as a deepening reflection on the rehetoric of totalitarianism" relies on many of the same arguments—I prefer to question the assumption that the evidence necessarily speaks for the defense. The "mature" Eliot, no less than the "mature" de Man, provides a powerful critique of organicism and organic analogies. But is he too necessarily of the antifascist party?

Both "The Rhetoric of Temporality" and *Four Quartets*—to elaborate on the comparison in chapter 3—are opposed to any form of "aesthetic recuperation":

> There is, it seems to us,
> At best, only a limited value
> In the knowledge derived from experience.
> The knowledge imposes a pattern, and falsifies,
> For the pattern is new in every moment

> And every moment is a new and shocking
> Valuation of all we have been.[18]

In "The Epistemology of Metaphor," de Man argues that from "the recognition of language as trope, one is led to the telling of a tale, to the narrative sequence. . . . The temporal deployment of an initial complication, of a structural knot, indicates the close, though not necessarily complementary, relationship between trope and narrative, between knot and plot" (EM 21–22). But de Man is not in fact led to "the telling of a tale, to the narrative sequence." Rather, he insists on the resistance of "the materiality of actual history" to aesthetic recuperation, much as Eliot rejects narrative "pattern" as the falsification of experience. The "recognition of language as trope" issues in narrative only if trope is understood in its Aristotelian sense of an "eye for resemblances," and both de Man and Eliot are suspicious of the metaphorical habit of making equal what is different. Peter Brooks argues that narrative "brings into relation different actions, combines them through perceived similarities, [and] appropriates them to a common plot, which implies the rejection of merely contingent (or unassimilable) incident or action. Plot is the structure of action in closed and legible wholes; it thus must *use* metaphor as the trope of its achieved interrelations."[19] But it is precisely tropes of achieved interrelation, and the utopianism that informs them, that de Man and Eliot reject.

This shared rejection of totalizing tropes and discourses extends to what de Man terms "aesthetic phenomenalization." Literature, as an older discourse would have it, both delights and instructs, but for de Man the one is strictly incompatible with the other:

> The text as body, with all its implications of substitutive tropes always retraceable to metaphor, is displaced by the text as machine and, in the process, it suffers the loss of the illusion of meaning. The deconstruction of the figural dimension is a process that takes place independently of any desire; as such it is not unconscious but mechanical, systematic in its performance but arbitrary in its principle, like a grammar. This threatens the autobiographical subject [Rousseau] not as the loss of something that once was present and that it once possessed, but as the radical estrangement between the meaning and the performance of any text.[20]

This is not, perhaps, perfectly intelligible in isolation—it is the de Man of "Excuses (*Confessions*)," of which more presently—but the general principle should be clear enough: the "text as body," as phenomenal "performance," is always estranged from its cognitive force. Likewise, *Four Quartets* aims to be "poetry standing naked in its bare bones," or "poetry with nothing poetic about it,"[21] even as it too recommends a "Desiccation of the world of sense":

> Descend lower, descend only
> Into the world of perpetual solitude,
> World not world, but that which is not world,

> Internal darkness, deprivation
> And destitution of all property,
> Desiccation of the world of sense.
> (CP 174)

For Eliot the operable distinction is between the natural and supernatural orders, and any confusion between the two issues in the ersatz religion of a Pater. For de Man the operable distinction is between the cognitive and the phenomenal, and any confusion between the two issues in "aesthetic formalization" or aestheticism, which it is the signal accomplishment of literature to void.

De Man does grant the phenomenal a limited place in literary experience: "[T]he phenomenality of the signifier, as sound, is unquestionably involved in the correspondence between the name and the thing named." But because the correspondence is conventional rather than phenomenal, language is

> epistemologically highly suspect and volatile, since its use can no longer be said to be determined by considerations of truth or falsehood. . . . Whenever the autonomous potential of language can be revealed by analysis, we are dealing with literariness and, in fact, with literature as the place where this negative knowledge about the reliability of linguistic utterance is made available. The ensuing foregrounding of material, phenomenal aspects of the signifier creates a strong illusion of aesthetic seduction at the very moment when the actual aesthetic function has been, at the very least, suspended. . . . Literature involves the voiding, rather than the affirmation, of aesthetic categories. One of the consequences of this is that, whereas we have been accustomed to reading literature by analogy with the plastic arts and with music, we now have to recognize the necessity of a non-perceptual, linguistic moment in painting and music, and learn to *read* pictures rather than to *imagine* meaning. (RT 10)

In "Hegel on the Sublime" de Man draws yet another consequence from this: the aestheticizing habit of "reading literature by analogy with the plastic arts and with music" easily degenerates into Goebbels's celebration of the "plastic art of the state,"[22] the cult of the führer as *artifex*. (Eliot draws a somewhat different, although not unrelated, conclusion. The habit of "reading literature by analogy with the plastic arts and with music" easily degenerates into the aesthetic religion of a Pater or the aesthetic humanism of an Arnold.)[23] De Man's thesis finds its fullest elaboration in the work of Philippe Lacoue-Labarthe, who argues that Nazism is continuous with, rather than a betrayal of, the deepest impulses of aesthetic humanism.[24] De Man never fully develops the connection, but it nevertheless informs, as his defenders quite properly note, his critique of aesthetic ideology.

It is difficult to know, however, how resistance to "tropes of achieved interrelatedness" can function, at least in the context in which the mature de Man worte, as anything other than an apology for the fragmentation, at once social and psychic, that is simply our daily experience of late capitalism. Nor is it clear how any further "desiccation of the world of sense" can do more than confirm us in the Cartesian settlement. For Marx, sensory perception is itself historical:[25]

> Private property has made us so stupid and partial that an object is only *ours* when we have it, when it exists for us as capital or when it is directly eaten, drunk, worn, inhabited, etc., in short, *utilized* in some way. But private property itself only conceives these various forms of possession as *means of life,* and the life for which they serve as means is the *life* of *private property*—labour and the creation of capital.
>
> Thus *all* the physical and intellectual senses have been replaced by the simple alienation of *all* these senses; the sense of *having*. The human being had to be reduced to this absolute poverty in order to be able to give birth to all his inner wealth.[26]

The revolution may not come about through an improvement in sensual enjoyment, but it will be accompanied by it. Private property is the impoverishment of the senses; its abolition will herald "the complete *emancipation* of all the human qualities."[27] Marx experiences the full utopian force of this sensuous consciousness—the condition to which the romantic symbol aspires—even as he insists on the priority of the economic transformation that will issue in it. De Man, however, dismisses the symbol, the utopian adumbration of sensuous consciousness, as the expression of innately reactionary values. The "belated" critique of aesthetic ideology, the attempt to explode the anachronistic analogy between literature and the plastic arts,[28] merely serves to reconcile us to an already realized sensory impoverishment.

"The unthinkable structure"

The tendency within poststructuralist thought to identify the operations of power with the most conspicuous of its manifestations—the "center" that "governs" the "free play" of elements within a structure, the telos that "commands" the temporality of narrative or historical unfolding—finds its fullest theoretical articulation in Derrida's "Structure, Sign, and Play in the Discourse of the Human Sciences," an essay that did much to establish his reputation in the United States:

> The function of this center [the center as construed by "Western science and Western philosophy"] was not only to orient, balance, and organize the structure—one cannot in fact conceive of an unorganized structure—but above all to make sure that the organizing principle of the structure would limit what we might call the *play* of the structure. By orienting and organizing the coherence of the system, the center of a structure permits the play of its elements inside the total form. And even today the notion of a structure lacking any center represents the unthinkable itself.[29]

Like de Man, who attributes structurally analogous functions to "summation" and "dialectical progress," Derrida associates the "organizing and orienting" force of a center with teleolgical mastery and the like, concepts he views as implicated in the metaphysics of presence. "It could be shown," he asserts but does not show, "that all the names related to fundamentals, to principles, or to the center have always designated an invariable presence—*eidos, archē, telos, energeia, ousia*" (SSP 279). Like de Man, moreover, Derrida assumes that a relation of homology exists between the formal organization or analysis of discursive structures and specific political positions and practices. To repeat the now familiar example: what is susceptible to "totalization" in a formal sense is at least potentially "totalitarian" in the political sense. The *Cantos*, "the sacred poem of the Nazi-fascist millennium," argues against the homology, as does Mussolini's conceptualization (or refusal thereof) of fascism. But even if one were to concede de Man and Derrida their point, a historically specific homology cannot be given a symmetrical and ahistorical reversal. Derrida claims that "even today the notion of a structure lacking any center represents the unthinkable itself," today being a day like any other in the long and monological history of western metaphysics. It may be, however, that today power operates all the more insidiously for its refusal of centers, and that a "structure lacking any center" is best characterized not as "unthinkable" but as strategically resisting thought, as a modality of power that would not be known as such.

Derrida himself thinks the "unthinkable":

> Totalization can be judged impossible in the classical style: one then refers to the empirical endeavour of either a subject or a finite richness which it can never master. There is too much, more than one can say. But non-totalization can also be determined in another way: no longer from the standpoint of a concept of finitude as relegation to the empirical, but from the standpoint of the concept of *play*. If totalization no longer has any meaning, it is not because the infiniteness of a field cannot be covered by a finite glance or a finite discourse, but because the nature of the field—that is, language and a finite language—excludes totalization. The field is in effect that of *play*, that is to say, a field of infinite substitutions only because it is finite, that is to say, because instead of being an inexhaustible field, as in the classical hypothesis, instead of being too large, there is something missing from it: a center which arrests and grounds the play of substitutions. (SSP 289)

The "unthinkable" that is here complexly thought is a structure liberated from the determining presence of a center, from determinism itself, save that intrinsic to language, which "excludes totalization." The center "classically" or conventionally understood "arrests and grounds the play of substitutions"; it remains theoretically committed to the possibility of totalization, the empirical richness of the field it fails to master notwithstanding. The Derridean "decentering" of structure, however, releases "the play of substitutions" from "the basis of a fundamental immobility and a reassuring certitude" (SSP 279). It is theoretically innocent of the possibility of totalization (and hence totalitarian implications) not on the basis of a richness it fails to master, but by virtue of an absence it refuses to regret.

Derrida's decentering of the concept of structure would thus seem to include the hitherto "interdicted" or excluded (SSP 279), yet it remains a polemic for a nontotalizing inclusiveness predicated on a practice of exclusion. What is excluded here is any principle of exclusion or totalization, any force or factor that would determine the structural "play" of elements, with the exception of language, "which excludes totalization." In one sense a polemic for inclusion that is predicated on a practice of exclusion suggests only the most familiar of poststructuralist paradoxes, recourse to the very concepts and strategies that it seeks to deconstruct. In another sense, however, the paradox merely rehearses the most routine of liberal gestures, the exclusion of "totalizing" discourses and practices—marxism and other "totalitarianisms"—from the "free play" of "free subjects" within its open field, with the paradoxical justification that all such discourses are themselves predicated on relations of exclusion. Liberalism understands this as the condition of its subjects' freedom or free play. It might be more accurately characterized, however, as the principle of its own structural self-perpetuation. There is no center or force that "grounds and arrests" the "free play" of elements within its "open field" (here one might cite the "incidental" categories of class, race, gender, sexuality). There is, therefore, no principle on which a challenge to the liberal myth of unrestricted mobility might be grounded.

All of this finds its logical culmination in the thesis of Laclau and Mouffe: "the social doesn't exist," not even in so ostensibly benign or modest a form as an "open field":

> Let us insist once again: to be something is always not to be something else (to be A implies not to be B). This banality is not what we are asserting, as it is situated in a *logical* terrain entirely dominated by the principle of contradiction: *not being* something is simply the logical consequence of being something different; the positivity of being dominates the totality of the discourse. What we affirm is something different: *that certain discursive forms, through equivalence, annul all positivity of the object and give a real existence to negativity as such.* The impossibility of the real—negativity—has attained a form of presence. As the social is penetrated by negativity—that is, by antagonism—it does not attain the status of transparency, of full presence, and the objectivity of its identities is permanently subverted. From here onward, the impossible relation between objectivity and negativity has become constitutive of the social. Yet the impossibility of the relation remains: it is for this reason that the coexistence of its terms must be conceived not as an objective relation of frontiers, but as reciprocal suvbversion of their contents.[30]

None of the various forms of antagonism that constitute the social is determinative, as "the coexistence of terms must be conceived not as an objective relation of frontiers, but as reciprocal subversion of their contents." "Society is not," therefore, "totally possible," but "neither is it totally impossible. This allows us to formulate the following conclusion: if society is never transparent to itself because it is unable to constitute itself as an objective field, neither is antagonism entirely transparent, as it does not manage totally to dissolve the objectivity of the social" (*HSS* 129). A society that is "unable to constitute itself as an objective field"—there is no possibility of a *tertium quid,* a resolutive future for antagonism—can never be "totalized" or reduced to totalitarianism; by the same token, antagonisms that are never "entirely transparent" cannot achieve the purposiveness of class conflict or degenerate into anarchy. The project of "towards a radical democratic politics" occupies the middle ground, the paradigmatic liberal position:

> The discourse of radical democracy is no longer the discourse of the universal; the epistemological niche from which "universal" classes and subjects spoke has been eradicated, and it has been replaced by a polyphony of voices, each of which constructs its own irreducible discursive identity. This point is decisive: there is no radical and plural democracy without renouncing the discourse of the universal and its implicit assumption of a privileged point of access to "the truth." (*HSS* 191–92)

A "polyphony" or parliamentary multiplicity of voices, equal access to representation without the assumption of "a privileged point of access to the truth": what is this but an attempt to revive the promise of bourgeois liberalism in its insurgent or revolutionary phase?

But Laclau and Mouffe do in fact assume a "privileged point of access to 'the truth.'" If "radical democracy" is a "polyphony of voices," if each voice "constructs its own discursive identity," then discursivity itself is the "privileged point of access to 'the truth,'" even if that truth is only the renunciation of the discourse of universal truth. There are no objective class interests, and hence no objectively or potentially revolutionary classes, prior to their discursive manifestations; yet this hypertextualization of social antagonism is not meant to exclude marxism.[31] "Radical democracy" includes the " socialist dimension," the "abolition of capitalist relations of production," even as it "rejects the idea that from this abolition there necessarily follows the elimination of . . . other inequalities" (*HSS* 192); thus Laclau and Mouffe define their project as both "*post*-Marxist" and "post-*Marxist*" (*HSS* 4). The refusal to collapse all forms of oppression into some totalizing notion of the economic is appropriate in principle, but it in no way follows that the project is thus "*post*-Marxist." Vulgar economism is a betrayal, not a fulfillment, of marxism: "[T]he determining factor in human history is, in the final instance, the production and reproduction of immediate life," a process that involves not only "the production of the means of existence" but "the production of human beings themselves, the propagation of the species."[32] Issues of race, gender, and sexuality are not mere epiphenomena; they cannot be folded back into the economic as the sole provenance of the "real politics." But neither do they function in the manner in which they have been appropriated by the academy, as so many rarefied, quasi-autonomous academic disciplines. The current celebration of the play of mutually incompatible elements—the decoupling of, say, gender from class— merely reinforces the separation of spheres that under-writes the liberal settlement. But therein lies the advantage of defining one's project against a thoroughly demonized notion of "totalization." A characteristically liberal play of differences is easily refigured as the radical.

It is not my intention here to launch a polemic against what I take to be the paradoxes of liberal ideology; rather, it is to make the perhaps obvious point that even if the concept of structural centers or centered structures is "as old as the *Epistēmē*—that is to say, as old as Western science and Western philosophy" (*SSP* 278), longevity itself is not an argument against a contextually or historically specific reading. Foucault's understanding of the operations of "panoptic" or "disciplinary" power, for example, sug-gests a distinctly sinister analogue to the poststructuralist celebration of structure without center. Disciplinary power is "not possessed as a thing, or transferred as a property"; rather, it is "relational," and the normalizing coercion it exerts is innocent of the "organizing and orienting" force of a center.[33] Or consider Jean Baudrillard's analysis of the logic of consumer capitalism, which suggests the demonic obverse of the poststructuralist celebration of the nonteleological. The principle that legitimizes the order of production and consumption—people "discover a posteriori and almost miraculously that they need what is produced and offered on the mar-ketplace"—masks the "internal finality" of an order that recognizes no teleology other than its own perpetuation.[34] Or, finally, there is Fredric Jameson, who explicitly argues the continuity between the practices of postnational consumer capitalism and the decentered universe of post-structuralist theory.[35] Poststructuralism is strictly contemporary with an unprecedented growth in the power of international banking capital; since the 1970s the global financial system has achieved a degree of autonomy from real production, and from any control that even the most advanced capitalist state might seek to exert over it, that is unprecedented in the history of capitalism. (The closest rival would be the period 1890–1929, which also witnessed an unprecedented growth in the dominance of fi-nance capital.)[36] Poststructuralism is perfectly at home in this world of system without center, signs without signifieds, yet center and end remain privileged targets of poststructuralist attack, or the "unthinkable" structure lacking any center remains the privileged ambition of poststructuralist politics. This is not to posit a rigid homology between poststructuralism and the decentered, disembodied world of late capitalism, for if the one were reducible to the other, the hold the former continues to exercise over the collective (academic) imagination—again, postmodernism is effec-tively poststructuralism by another name—would be inexplicable. Rather, the appeal, which is utopian in its own way, is of an altogether different order. Poststructuralism/postmodernism allows us to accommodate ourselves to things as they are under the guise of a subversive attack on the status quo. It is a utopianism without efficacy; it collapses rather than exacerbates the tension between what is and what should be.

"The best legacies"

The essay de Man was commissioned to write by the Committee on Research Activities of the Modern Language Association was to be called "Literary Theory: Aims and Methods," a title that now seems hopelessly quaint, especially when juxtaposed against "The Resistance to Theory," which is easily the sexier of the two. The initial title presupposes that theory can have "aims," teleological ambitions and efficacy; the conjunction recognizes "aims" as related to methodological assumptions and procedures but also distinct from them. There is a sense, however, in which the paper de Man did write reads as a critique of the implications of the title of the paper he was asked to write. By this I mean that "The Resistance to Theory" progressively assimilates the category of "aims" to "method," teleology to means. What emerges at the conclusion of the essay is an understanding of theory that has as its aim only the perpetual worrying of its own methodological (im)possibility. The "rigor" for which de Man is alternately celebrated and condemned is very much in evidence here. "The Resistance to Theory" is a rigorous or etymologically "radical" questioning of first principles, methodological presuppositions. The essay is at pains to distinguish itself, for example, from what it terms "literary history," which is "still the history of an understanding of which the possibility is taken for granted" (RT 7), and "aesthetics," which, "ever since its development just before and with Kant," is "a phenomenalism of a process of meaning and understanding" that "may be naive in that it postulates (as its name indicates) a phenomenology of art and of literature which may well be what is at issue" (RT 7–8). Yet if "The Resistance to Theory" assumes nothing, least of all the possibility of the activity or discipline that is its subject, its radical questioning of methodological presuppositions is at the expense of a radicalism of an altogether different sort—the potential of the title "Literary Theory: Aims and Methods," a radical aim or purpose, a teleology.

It is a commitment to aims and purposes that informs the "most recurrent objection" to theory, which "considers it as pure verbalism, as a denial of the reality principle in the name of absolute fictions, and for reasons that are . . . ethically and politically shameful" (RT 10). But because these aims are themselves determined by, "subservient" to, the very medium their proponents dismiss as "pure verbalism," theory exposes the ideological mystification that governs any and all resistance to it.[37] Hence the perfectly closed economy: resistance confirms the subversive power of the theory it seeks to resist, and the subversive power of theory manifests itself in exposing the ideological mystification that informs the resistance to it. This is to blur the distinction between resistance and collaboration, but it is not the only indignity resistance is to suffer. For if de Man first speaks of resistance as "hostility directed against theory in the name of ethical and political values," as a relation between theory and a position external to it, resistance soon comes to be defined as but a displaced symptom "of a resistance inherent in the theoretical enterprise itself" (RT 12), as a resistance already within. Resistance suffers a double devaluation. It is both self-defeating, as it can only confirm what it seeks to resist, and redundant, as it is already anticipated by, inscribed within, the enterprise it seeks to challenge from without. "Rather than asking why literary theory is threatening," de Man ultimately suggests, "we should perhaps ask why it has such difficulty going about its business. . . . Such insecurity about its own project calls for self-analysis . . ." (RT 12).

Interminable self-analysis, as it happens, for it is a question, finally, not of one methodological choice over another but that of acceding to "the universal theory of the impossibility of theory" (RT 19), to an enterprise that keeps on going because it goes nowhere. De Man does distinguish between methodological choices, but only in terms of the rigor with which they confront the futility of their own ambitions. He sees in "the contemporary theoretical scene," for instance, "an increased stress on reading as a theoretical problem" (RT 17), of which he approves, but a "stress" that is only a more "effective" form of the resistance to its own enterprise: "It turns out that the resistance to theory is in fact a resistance to reading, a resistance that is perhaps at its most effective, in contemporary studies, in the methodologies that call themselves theories of reading but nevertheless avoid the function they claim as their object" (RT 15). De Man's specific examples are *Rezeptionsästhetik,* which he views as continuous with "traditional hermeneutic models that do not allow for the problem of the phenomenalism of reading and therefore remain uncritically confined within a theory of literature rooted in aesthetics" (RT 18), and speech act–oriented theories of reading, which "read only to the extent that they prepare the way for the rhetorical reading they avoid" (RT 19). But like the child who cannot tell the literal from the figurative, the specific is again a synecdoche for a universal predicament, a generalized failure. "[E]ven if a 'truly' rhetorical reading that would stay clear of any undue phenomenalization" or "grammatical or performative codification of the text could be conceived," it too would "avoid and resist" the very reading it advocates (RT 19). "Truly" or "technically correct rhetorical" readings are "not necessarily impossible," and de Man insists that they are the proper ambition of literary theory: "They are, always in theory, the most elastic theoretical and dialectical model to end all models and they can rightly claim to contain within their own defective selves all other defective models of reading-avoidance, referential, semiological, grammatical, performative, logical, or whatever" (RT 19). Rhetorical readings contain *in ovo* all other defective forms of their own defective selves, and de Man frankly acknowledges that they are "totalizing (and potentially totalitarian)" (RT 19). Happily, however, they totalize only the refusal of totalization that is theory. They are "universals" only in the sense that they are "consistently defective models of language's impossibility to be a model language" (RT 19).

De Man ultimately characterizes this situation in terms of undecidability, as the elision of a binary opposition:

> Nothing can overcome the resistance to theory since theory *is* itself this resistance. The loftier the aims and the better the methods of literary theory, the less possible it becomes. Yet literary theory is not in danger of going under; it cannot help but flourish, and the more it is resisted, the more it flourishes, since the language it speaks is the language of self-resistance. What is impossible to decide is whether this flourishing is a triumph or a fall. (RT 19–20)

The difficulty theory has going about its business translates into business as usual, both for the life of theory (a comforting conclusion for those of us who teach it for a living) and for the life of the culture that is its context. "Lofty" aims and methods are ultimately irrelevant to a "flourishing" that is ambiguously either (or both) "a triumph or a fall," for theory is in danger of going neither "under" nor anywhere. But perhaps a "different kind" of aim, lofty or otherwise, is surreptitiously reinscribed in the fetishization of failure. De Man accepts the inevitability of resistance to theory in one form or another, and what I would argue we do best to resist—here and in any number of de Man's essays—is the curious tendency to valorize failure, to make of it an index of intellectual integrity and rigor. De Man asks: Why does theory have such difficulty going about its business? Does that difficulty constitute "a triumph or a fall"? We might ask: What does that difficulty actively produce? What does the "failure," which is precisely the failure to distinguish between failure and success, succeed in accomplishing?

The most relevant answer here would be the defense of Paul de Man. The strategy by which de Man defends theory against the charge that it is "ethically and politically shameful" becomes the orthodox strategy by which de Man is defended against his own "ethically and politically shameful" journalism. In Derrida's "Like the Sound of the Sea Deep Within a Shell," for example, the categories of accuser and accused grow indistinct, and the "failure" of the journalist becomes an argument for the "flourishing" of the theorist:

> To judge, to condemn the work or the man on the basis of what was a brief episode, to call for closing, that is to say, at least figuratively, for censuring or burning his books is to reproduce the exterminating gesture of which one accuses de Man of not having armed himself against sooner with the necessary vigilance. It is not even to draw a lesson that he, de Man, learned to draw from the war. (SSD 651)

De Man's judges are judged and found guilty. To condemn de Man is not only to rehearse the "exterminating gesture" of which he stands accused—accused, it should be noted, only of not having armed himself against it sooner—but to compound de Man's own error by failing to learn the lesson of Paul de Man. The psychologism to which "The Resistance to Theory" is occasionally given—"The attack [on theory] reflects the anxiety of the aggressors rather than the guilt of the accused" (RT 10)—also taints Derrida's "Like the Sound of the Sea Deep Within a Shell," and it is everywhere operable in J. Hillis Miller's *Times Literary Supplement* defense of de Man. What, then, is the lesson of the "failure" of Paul de Man? Simply the "flourishing" of de Man, the obligation to read and reread de Man:

> After the period of sadness and hurt, I believe that what has happened to us was doubly necessary. First as a fated happening: it had to happen one day or another and precisely because of the deserved and growing influence of a thinker who is fascinating enough that people always want to learn more—from him and about him. Second, it had to happen as a salutary ordeal. It will oblige all of us, some more than others, to reread, to understand better, to analyze the traps and the stakes—past, present, and especially future. Paul de Man's legacy is not poisoned, or in any case no more than the best legacies are if there is no such thing as a legacy without some venom. (SSD 650)

The sadness and hurt are genuine (for many, myself included) but they are hardly the point. Nothing has really "happened to us," or at least our own "salutary ordeal" is not the most relevant of the "ordeals" with which the *Le Soir* journalism is to be identified. Something might have happened, the belated discovery of de Man's early writings might have occasioned something, yet Derrida's argument seeks to ensure that nothing much will happen, that nothing should happen. Far from "poisoning" de Man's "legacy," or "poisoning" it only to the extent that it now joins company with the "best legacies," the "scandal" merely confirms an already "deserved and growing influence."

Derrida does have a point: "to call for a closing, that is to say, at least figuratively, for censuring or burning his books" is not a response with which I would care to be identified (nor is it a response that I would identify, even "figuratively," with the very different "exterminating gesture" of which de Man stands accused). Yet even if one were to concede Derrida his premise—and it too is a generous concession: I am not aware that there has been a generalized call for book burning, figurative or otherwise—his argument remains implicated in an untenable opposition between the "open" and the "closed." Derrida defines his position against those who would "call for a closing," much as "Structure, Sign, and Play" defines the "unthinkable structure lacking any center" against structure as it is conventionally or "classically" conceived. "People will learn" he writes, "to reread the books, and *once again* the newspapers, and *once again toward that which opens itself up there*. To do so, one will need in the first place, and more than ever *in the future*, the lessons of Paul de Man" (SSD 591). The ease with which the "ordeal" is rendered "salutary," the efficiency with which "scandal" becomes a vindication of the work it might be expected to question, suggests, once again, an openness that is finally closed. Like the "ordeal" occasioned by Watergate, which also came to vindicate the system it might have been expected to question, scandal functions as part of the "routine self-maintenance" of a system in which every "fall" or failure becomes evidence of a "flourishing."[38] Early in his essay Derrida argues that repetition, the "cushioning" of the shock of the new, is necessarily constitutive of experience as such:

> Something *happens* only on the condition that one is not expecting it. Here of course I am speaking the language of consciousness. But there would also be no event *identifiable as such* if some repetition did not come along to cushion the surprise by preparing its effect on the basis of some experience of the unconscious. (SSD 593)

Later in his essay he characterizes "what has happened," the shock of our new knowledge, as a "fated happening" (SSD 650), as a necessity in some sense internal to de Man's own project. Derrida is convincing when he speaks "the language of consciousness": experience is identifiable as experience only on the basis of the repetition that necessarily empties any individual experience of its unique content. But a "fated happening" speaks the language of "ideology," the confusion of "linguistic" and "natural" reality, and "fate" is apparently intent on guaranteeing the enduring value of de Man's legacy in particular and poststructuralist thought in general. In "Hegel on the Sublime" de Man is critical of the "recuperative" strategy that "allows for a mediated passage or crossing between negative or positive valorization." He gives as an example Pascal's famous *pensée* on human grandeur—"In a word, man knows that he is miserable. Thus, he is miserable since that is what he is. But he is very great inasmuch as he knows it"—in which "an absolute lack" is transformed into "an absolute surplus."[39] The orthodox defense of de Man involves much the same strategy and is subject to critique on much the same grounds: an "economy" that transforms the absolute "failure" of the wartime journalism into an absolute "flourishing," an argument for the enduring value of the legacy of which it is a part, is "recuperative" in the extreme. "*Toward that which opens itself up there*": can an openness immune even to the shock of collaborationist politics be open to anything other than its own self-perpetuation?

Again, the revelations concerning de Man's wartime activities could have occasioned something, if only what Derrida terms an investigation into "ideologico-institutional practices having to do with certain themes" relevant to de Man's wartime writings. "What," Derrida asks in this context, "is the press in the culture and politics of this century?" (SSD 592). But only "elsewhere," where he will have "more time and more space" (SSD 591), can these issues receive their proper due. In the context of the pages of *Critical Inquiry* devoted to de Man's journalism, which literally give Derrida the last word, he is obliged to set them "aside" (SSD 592). The issues are relegated to the periphery, however, only to reemerge as Derrida's central line of defense:

> To my knowledge, at the moment I write, this war ["Paul de Man's War," the subtitle of Derrida's piece] presents itself as such, it is *declared* in newspapers, *and nowhere else,* on the subject of arguments made in the

newspapers, *and nowhere else,* in the course of the last world war, during
two years almost a half century ago. (SSD 591)

The news here is newspapers themselves. The continuity between the war
declared against de Man in newspapers and the newspaper articles de Man
wrote during the war is newsworthy, Derrida seems to suggest, even if the
actual content of de Man's newspaper articles, arguments made "during
two years almost a half century ago," is old news. "Paul de Man's War"
begins to read like the war declared on de Man, who emerges at the
conclusion of Derrida's argument, in a passage already quoted, as more
sinned against than sinning: "To judge, to condemn the work or the man
on the basis of what was a brief episode . . . is not even to draw a lesson
that he, de Man, learned to draw from the war." Derrida's conflation of
two "exterminating" gestures—the war launched against de Man in con-
temporary newspapers and de Man's newspaper articles during the war—
reveals virtually nothing about the "ideologico-institutional practices" of
the press in this century. It reveals a great deal, however, about the
"ideologico-institutional practices" of a theoretical position that could
conflate the two, that could posit "ideologico-institutional practices" as
historically unspecific or undetermined.

J. Hillis Miller's *Times Literary Supplement* article, which is largely con-
tinuous with Derrida's *Critical Inquiry* piece, argues that the "violence of
the reaction in the United States and in Europe to the discovery of Paul de
Man's writings of 1941–42 marks a new moment in the collaboration
between the university and the mass media. . . . It is an extremely in-
structive moment, one worth much sober reflection." These, the first and
last sentences of Miller's first paragraph, leave no doubt as to who the
villain of the piece will be. Like Derrida, but with far less circumspection,
Miller is intent on turning a war *"declared* in newspapers, *and nowhere else"*
into a war *on* newspapers *and nothing else:* "Most, though not all, of these
attacks have been written by academics who also write journalism. It is as
though these professors had somewhat abruptly discovered the power of
the press in this area, just as the young de Man discovered the power of the
press in wartime Belgium." The word that figures so dramatically in Mil-
ler's first sentence—"collaboration"—is never once applied, at least in any
way that is allowed to stick, to de Man's wartime activities:

> The argument, implied or overt, goes as follows, in a crescendo of distor-
> tions. First error: it is asserted that de Man's wartime writings are fascist,
> collaborationist, antisemitic through and through [What is the opposite
> of this: a little anti-Semitic? Not at all anti-Semitic?], and that he was
> himself a fascist, collaborator, and antisemite.

"All these propositions are false," Miller assures his reader (and for a
poststructuralist, he is curiously sure of the opposition between true and
false); the "facts are otherwise." And the facts discredit only those intent on
seizing the moment to discredit poststructuralism. "What is the most terri-
fying in this argument," Miller maintains, "is the way it repeats the well-

known totalitarian procedures of vilification it pretends to deplore. It repeats the crime it would condemn." The war declared on de Man rehearses the crime it would condemn—here we have a virtual parody of poststructuralist repetition without origin—although there is no crime to repeat.

Miller's use of the word "collaboration" in the first sentence of his article virtually guarantees that any reflection we might get on the "ideologico-institutional" practices of the contemporary press will not be sober. If there is any "sober reflection" to be had, Miller's article can only be its object, not its source; what is of interest here is not the alleged "collaboration" between the university and the "mass media," by which Miller seems to mean the nonacademic press, but the academic contempt for journalism, for the dissemination of the debate over de Man beyond, say, the pages of *Critical Inquiry* or *TLS*. I choose the word "dissemination," which nowhere figures in Miller's article, with reason: it is conventionally one of the most celebrated of terms in the poststructuralist lexicon, a central premise of the "subversion thesis." Within discourse circulated within an academic coterie, dissemination, tropological "excess," is said to function as a principle of "subversion," as the systematic undoing of discursive claims to mastery or truth. Dissemination of discourse beyond the academy, however, motivates Miller's call for "sober truth telling," "especially on the part of those journalists who are also professors." Hence, the "ideologico-institutional practices" by which the "powers and dangers" of discourse are themselves "controlled" (I am quoting Foucault) survive intact: ". . . [I]n every society the production of discourse is at once controlled, selected, organized and redistributed according to a certain number of procedures, whose role is to avert its powers and dangers, to cope with chance events, to evade its ponderous, awesome materiality."[40] For Miller "dissemination" is characteristically a principle of subversion, but one that is not to be disseminated beyond the academy, beyond those professionally charged with the custodianship of language. There is, then, nothing oxymornonic in the institutional success with which it has met. Dissemination so defined merely extends the conventional monopoly rights the academy has always claimed over the production and circulation of discursive "truth" to include the systematic undoing of the same. It in no way challenges the monopoly itself.

It is not, of course, Miller's intention to defend the monopoly. The ideological principles by which the academy conventionally organizes and distributes discourse—the "contemporary tissue of received opinion about literature, national identity, and culture" that finds institutional expression in departments of national literatures—are explicitly critiqued, for they too are a repetition of the error of Paul de Man:

> . . . "[A]esthetic ideology" and the nationalism associated with it have by no means disappeared. They are extremely widespread and powerful in Europe and America today, for example in the xenophobia in the United States that resists literary theory because it is a foreign import. What de Man called "aesthetic ideology" forms an important part of the contem-

porary tissue of received opinion about literature, national identity, and culture, both in the mass media and the university. It was what I was taught at college and university, and it is what we are all likely to say if we are not vigilant. Which of us can say he or she is free of it? And yet de Man's work and his historical placement shows it is both false and can lead to hideous political and historical consequences.

The university and the "mass media" are again caught in the act of "collaborating," although here the early de Man is acknowledged as something of a co-collaborator. (For Miller the xenophobia that explains the putative resistance to theory in the United States also explains the "war" declared on de Man by professors-turned-journalists.) But of the many charges that can be brought against de Man's wartime journalism, nationalism is not the most damning. It is also one of the few against which de Man might mount a plausible defense. Miller invokes the categories of "historical placement" and "historical consequences" in his reading of the *Le Soir* articles, but only to conflate two very different historical moments, to elide the category of "historical placement" in the very act of invoking it. He is thus without the resources to read either moment: either the historical moment in which he himself writes or that in which the young de Man wrote.

The conflation, which assumes the ahistorical constancy of ideological production, allows Miller to transform, in the most overt of "recuperative" gestures, the failure of the "early" de Man into an argument for the "flourishing" of the "late." "What is significant and instructive about the presence of this 'aesthetic ideology' in de Man's early writings," we are instructed, "is the confirmation it gives to one of his basic later insights about literature":

> Ideology is defined by de Man as "the confusion of linguistic with natural reality" [RT 11]. Of special importance are those linguistic constructions that depend on thinking in terms of oppositions, literal versus metaphorical language, man against woman, inside against outside, and so on. An example would be the way the nationalism that is so important a part of "aesthetic ideology" leads to defining one group in opposition to another. This can lead, as in the case of Nazi Germany, to the horror of the slaughter of the Jews in the attempt to create an Aryan nation purified of all "polluting" elements.

Miller's own argument—the "and so on" could easily be extended to include the opposition "early versus late"—requires precisely those "linguistic constructions that depend on thinking in terms of oppositions." The logic of opposition that structures Miller's argument contradicts the "lesson" it endeavors to confirm or "subverts" the subversive wisdom it seeks to define. To dwell on the incoherence is, however, to concede to Miller in particular, and the "subversion hypothesis" in general, the terms in which the debate over de Man is to be conducted. The relevant categories, those of "special importance," his essay invokes only to elide: "historical placement" and "historical consequences." For Miller is simply wrong historically—wrong in his reading of the literary and political nationalism of de

Man's *Le Soir* articles, wrong in his pronouncements on the relation of nationalism to the Holocaust, and wrong in his reading of the politics of contemporary nationalisms.

The *Le Soir* articles do, of course, invoke the concept of nationalism, in both a literary and a political context, although not simply, or not only, in the manner Miller's essay suggests. De Man does speak of the "mystical" nature of the German destiny and character, which he tends to juxtapose (or, as Miller would say, "define in opposition") to French intellectualism and self-consciousness. But here it is helpful to recall the obvious: the *Le Soir* journalism is deeply collaborationist, and a collaborator has, by definition, no meaningful investment in a politics or ideology of the oppositional. In the passage from "L'Exposition 'Histoire d'Allemagne' au Cinquantenaire" quoted earlier, for example, de Man argues that "one must see this obstinacy that resists subjugation," by which he means resistance to German occupation, as "more than a simple proof of national steadfastness." The "early" work, no less than the "late," reads as a critique of the ideology of the binary. The "opposition" to which the early de Man is opposed, however, is the "national steadfastness" that resists "Germany's historical destiny" on the mistaken premise that Nazi hegemony in Europe is opposed to individual national interests. (Italian Fascism was nothing if not nationalistic, yet Mussolini found it possible to form a pact with Hitler.) The work of a collaborator might logically serve as an argument for a politics of resistance and opposition, or for a reading of resistance and opposition as historically specific and ideologically variable practices. In Miller's article, however, de Man's journalism merely confirms the ahistorical premise, which is central to the "subversion hypothesis," that "thinking in terms of opposition" is bad. The significance Miller attributes to "aesthetic ideology" in de Man's journalism is thus curiously blind to the obvious: its failure is precisely the failure to oppose.

Curiously blind, in fact, to the form "aesthetic ideology" actually assumes in de Man's journalism, to the "ideological aberration" it seeks to explain:

> The article on "The Jews in Contemporary Literature" depends on the absurd and extremely dangerous notion that there is a specific national and racial character in French literature, a different one in German literature, and that the Jews have yet another specific identity. These ideas about the specificity of the German, French, Spanish, Flemish, Walloon and Dutch national characters recur in essay after essay in which there is nothing at all anti-Semitic or even explicitly political. . . .

There can be no doubt that the *Le Soir* articles frequently express essentialist ideas about the racial and national character of various literatures, but "The Jews in Contemporary Literature," the most terrible of the lot, is not among them. The strategy by which de Man defends contemporary literature against the charge of "Jewification"—the article begins by noting the pleasure "vulgar antisemitism" takes in characterizing postwar cultural phenomena as "dégénérés et décadents, parce que enjuivés"—is purely formal and aesthetic:

> [T]he reality is different. It seems that aesthetic evolutions obey very powerful laws that continue their action even when humanity is shaken by considerable events. The world war has brought about a profound upheaval in the political and economic world. But artistic life has been swayed relatively little, and the forms that we know at present are the logical and normal successors to what there had been before.

Miller speaks of de Man's "ideas about the individual organic development of the literature of each country according to intrinsic laws of its own." The de Man of "The Jews in Contemporary Literature," however, speaks of "les évolutions aesthétiques," which remain relatively immune even to the most "profound upheaval in the political and economic world." Writers who seem "degenerate and decadent"—de Man cites novelists of various nationalities and ethnicities, including Kafka, a Jew—are in fact orthodox, "not innovators who have broken with all past traditions, but mere continuers who are pursuing further the realist aesthetic that is more than a century old." De Man does suggest that Jews, by virtue of the "specific characteristics" of their spirit, "might have been expected" to play "a more brilliant role in this artistic production," particularly in the development of the "realist aesthetic," the novel, for which their alleged "cérébralité," "their capacity to assimilate doctrines while maintaining a certain coldness before them," would render them particularly suitable. "Mais la réalité est différente." The specific racial characteristics of the Jews have had no significant impact on the evolution of literature, which obeys a dynamic intrinsic to literature itself. Thus, happily,

> one sees that a solution of the Jewish problem that would aim at the creation of a Jewish colony isolated from Europe would not entail, for the literary life of the West, deplorable consequences. The latter would lose, in all, a few personalities of mediocre value, and would continue, as in the past, to develop according to its great evolutionary laws.

What Miller terms the "absurd and extremely dangerous notion that there is a specific national and racial character to literature" in no way explains the horror of this passage, although one might wish that de Man had entertained the opinions Miller attributes to him. For had he believed that the "solution of the Jewish problem" would entail some deplorable consequences—deplorable literary consequences, for he is concerned with no other—he might have thought "the solution" to be of some consequence. But because it in no way threatens literature and "its great evolutionary laws," what was soon to become the slaughter of millions—"The Jews in Contemporary Literature" was written in March 1941; the systematic deportation of Belgian Jews began in August 1942—is dismissed as the potential loss of a few literary personalities of "mediocre value."

If Miller is thus blind to the specific form "aesthetic ideology" assumes in this, the most terrible of the *Le Soir* articles, so too is he mistaken in the lesson he derives from it: "[T]he nationalism that is so important a part of 'aesthetic ideology' leads to defining one group in opposition to another. This can lead, as in the case of Nazi Germany, to the horror of the slaughter of the Jews." Here it is Miller who is led, no doubt by his commitment to binary opposition as the key to all ideological aberrations, to what Hannah Arendt terms a "hasty" explanation for the rise of modern anti-Semitism, which is the conventional "identification of antisemitism with rampant nationalism and its xenophobic outbursts." "Mais la réalité est différente." And the reality, again as formulated by Arendt, is "that modern antisemitism grew in proportion as traditional nationalism declined, and reached its climax at the exact moment when the European system of nation-states and its precarious balance of power crashed."[41] Arendt is not, of course, celebrating the phenomenon Miller condemns. She characterizes the connection between the growth of anti-Semitism and the decline of traditional nationalisms as "unfortunate." Nor is Miller's broad characterization of nationalism without validity. Nationalism can lead (indeed has led) "to defining one group in opposition to another" with hideous consequences. Arendt terms Nazism an "insane nationalism,"[42] but as de Man's "Exposition 'Histoire d'Allemagne'" amply illustrates, an "insane nationalism," a post- or pannational nationalism, is easily construed as compatible with individual national interests. Miller's "reading" of the Holocaust confirms a central premise of the "subversion hypothesis," or the hypothesis already explains all history, all "ideological aberrations," the Holocaust included. A hypothesis so unlimited in its explanatory power, so universal in its application, is itself, however, predicated on a resistance to history. Miller's defense of de Man fails in its obligations to the historical specificity of the horror that it seeks to understand, the historical recurrence of which it seeks to protect against.

It would be possible to elaborate the argument at greater length. Miller's perfunctory and inaccurate reading of the relation of nationalism to Nazism becomes, in turn, an equally perfunctory and inaccurate reading of nationalism in its contemporary context. Again, Miller's broad characterization is not without its validity. "'Aesthetic ideology' and the nationalism associated with it" have not in fact "disappeared." But are we to assume that all contemporary nationalisms are thus implicated in the ideology of fascism, which is apparently synonymous with "thinking in terms of opposition?" Are we to dismiss, say, the national aspirations of the Palestinian people on the basis of what could only be for Miller their mystified commitment to an ideology of the binary? The relevant question is not, however, whether "'aesthetic ideology' and the nationalism associated with it have disappeared," although it is highly relevant that Miller would consider this relevant. Rather, it is whether nationalism is not itself largely anachronistic, a residual form of political organization in a world increasingly dominated by the global interests of multinational business and finance capital. Miller's investment in citing nationalism as a relevant contemporary example of "aesthetic ideology" is obvious. The poststructuralist celebration of dissemination or the decentered can claim a subversive relation to its contemporary context only if power is localized or centralized, only if the center, conventionally or "classically" understood, continues to subtend various hierarchies. Or, to reverse the perspective, Miller's investment in eliding the operations of a power that is everywhere operable but nowhere localized is likewise obvious. If power is disseminated, decentered, poststructuralism is complicit in the socioeconomic arrangement it alleges to subvert. There is a sense, however, in which Miller's argument, or his rehearsal of de Man's argument, is already proof against all argument:

> It is fear of this power in "deconstruction" and in contemporary critical theory as a whole, in all its diversity, that accounts better than any other explanation for the unreasoning hostility, the abandoning of the canons of journalistic and academic responsibility, in the recent attacks on de Man, on "deconstruction" and on theory generally.

The "fear" Miller attributes to those who "attack" de Man is the fear de Man attributes to those who reproach "literary theory for being oblivious to social and historical (that is to say ideological) reality." Miller's defense of de Man recasts the vocabulary of de Man's defense of literary theory—"the resistance to theory" is now figured in the most explicit of military metaphors, as "war" and "attack"—but it is otherwise much the same argument. Nothing has happened.

Convention has it that the best defense is a good offense, and in this Miller is nothing if not conventional. His essay takes aim at the "well-known totalitarian procedures of vilification" in which de Man's enemies are said to engage. The condemnation is appropriate in principle, and Miller is correct in identifying totalitarianism with what Arendt terms the loss of "factuality":

> [T]he decision regarding success and failure under totalitarian circumstances is very largely a matter of organized and terrorized public opinion. In a totally ficititious world [a totalitarian world], failures need not be recorded, admitted, and remembered. Factuality itself depends for its continued existence upon the existence of the nontotalitarian world.[43]

But "totalitarian circumstances" are not the only ones under which decisions "regarding success and failure" are rendered inoperable or undecidable—recall the conclusion to "The Resistance to Theory": "What remains impossible to decide is whether this flourishing is a triumph or a fall"—and factuality does not necessarily "flourish" in a world innocent of the mechanisms conventionally identified with totalitarian regimes. Anti-Semitism, for example, in no way requires an overtly totalitarian elision of the facts:

> An ideology is really "holding us" only when we do not feel any opposition between it and reality—that is, when the ideology succeeds in determining the mode of our everyday experience of reality itself. How then would our poor German, if he were a good anti-Semite, react to this gap between the ideological figure of the Jew (schemer, wire-puller, exploit-

ing our brave men and so on) and the common everyday experience of his good neighbour, Mr. Stern? His answer would be to turn this gap, this discrepancy itself, into an argument for anti-Semitism: "You see how dangerous they really are? It is difficult to recognize their real nature. They hide it behind the mask of everyday appearance—and it is exactly this hiding of one's real nature, this duplicity, that is a basic feature of the Jewish nature." An ideology really succeeds when even the facts which at first sight might seem to contradict it start to function as arguments in its favour.[44]

Pound's anti-Semitism proved immune to any factual encroachments or corrections:

> If or when one mentions the Protocols alleged to be of the Elders of Zion, one is frequently met with the reply: Oh, but they are a forgery.
>
> Certainly they are a forgery, and that is the one proof we have of their authenticity. The Jews have worked with forged documents for the past 24 hundred years, namely ever since they had any documents whatsoever. And no one can qualify as a historian of this half century without having examined the Protocols. Alleged, if you like, to have been translated from the Russian, from a manuscript to be consulted in the British Museum, where some such document may or may not exist.[45]

A fact that might be expected to challenge anti-Semitism—the *Protocols of the Elders of Zion* is a forgery—actually serves to sustain and validate it. Neither Pound nor Hitler experienced any contradiction between the inauthenticity of the document, which both acknowledged, and the lesson they derived from it.[46] An ideology is really "holding us" only when we feel no contradiction between it and our experience of reality—when, say, an ethically and politically shameful past can be made to sustain and augment a distinguished reputation.

De Man made no public acknowledgment of, offered no public explanation for, his wartime activities. (The one quasi-public explanation he did provide, the 1955 letter to Harvard's Society of Fellows, was, to put it charitably, misleading.)[47] Instead, we are given "Excuses (*Confessions*)," which seeks to problematize what acts of explanation or expiation might mean:

> In order to come into being as text, the referential function [of the *Confessions*] had to be radically suspended. Without the scandal of random denunciation of Marion, without the "faits oiseux" of the *Confessions*, there could not have been a text. . . . Far from seeing language as an instrument in the service of a psychic energy, the possibility now arises that the entire construction of drives, substitutions, repressions, and representations is the aberrant, metaphorical correlative of the absolute randomness of language, prior to any figuration or meaning. It is no longer certain that language, as excuse, exists because of a prior guilt but just as possible that since language, as a machine, performs anyway, we have to produce guilt . . . in order to make the excuse meaningful. Excuses generate the very guilt they exonerate, although always in excess or by

> default. . . . No excuse can ever hope to catch up with such a prolifera-
> tion of guilt. On the other hand, any guilt . . . can always be dismissed
> as the gratuitous product of a textual grammar or a radical fiction: there
> can never be enough guilt around to match the text-machine's infinite
> power to excuse. (*AR* 298–99)

To have acknowledged guilt, de Man's defenders conclude, would only have been a more subtle means of denying it. An individual of less integrity (or theoretical rigor) might have been tempted by the bad faith of public explanation or expiation; not, however, the author of "Excuses (*Confessions*)." "At least in this case," Ortwin de Graef argues, silence was "morally more admirable":

> We should be aware that this line of reasoning [the argument of "Excuses
> (*Confessions*)" as it reflects on de Man's own refusal of "confession"] more
> than seems to entail that we are radically turning the tables by in fact
> affirming that, in this case at least, it is morally more admirable not to
> confess than to publicly testify to one's own "shameful past." I must say
> that I feel extremely reluctant about such a move, as it appears surrep-
> titiously to reintroduce the ideology of authenticity into a discourse of
> defacement, but at the same time I cannot afford not to pretend not to be
> forced to take such an interpretation into consideration.[48]

The moral heroism of de Man's silence finds its counterpart in the theoreti-cal heroism of de Graef's rigor. The latter is willing to risk everything—even theoretical naïveté, recourse to "the ideology of authenticity"—in his relentless fidelity to the eloquence of de Man's silence. (De Man himself came to abandon the pathos of "an authentically temporal predicament," the pathos of authenticity itself, in favor of the late "discourse of efface-ment.") De Graef's "reluctance" to advance such an argument (or to be carried away by it: "I cannot afford not to pretend not to be forced to take such an interpretation into account" hardly suggests agency) is easily un-derstandable, although not necessarily for the reasons he specifies. The ease with which public explanation is construed as an act of bad faith risks a great deal more than the charge of theoretical naïveté. De Man's defenders characteristically invite us to speculate on what his silence might have cost him. Perhaps a great deal; I cannot pretend to know. But again, de Man's personal anguish is not the most relevant of the "ordeals" with which the *Le Soir* journalism is to be identified, and whatever the personal toll, the silence cost him nothing professionally. Today, moreover, it reverberates to his credit: "at least in this case"—although poststructuralism purports to be suspicious of the exclusionary gesture of "the special case"—"silence is morally more admirable." But if so, the morally admirable is functionally indistinguishable from the professionally and personally expedient, and the "lesson" of "Excuses (*Confessions*)" is reducible to this: there never can be enough guilt around to impede the power of the poststructuralist text-machine to excuse.

The "facts" of de Man's wartime journalism have all been duly "recorded, admitted, and remembered," and it is with legitimate pride that Derrida notes "that no one . . . questioned the necessity of making these texts widely accessible and to do everything possible to permit a serious, minute, patient, honest study of them, as well as open discussion" (SSD 633). (Such openness is not always standard academic practice, even if it remains a defining academic ideal. As late as 1973 the Pound estate threatened legal action against a scholar for quoting from the radio broadcasts.[49] These too have been published in their entirety, although selected portions of the Pound corpus are still relatively difficult to obtain. It is not accidental that the *ABC of Reading* is more readily available than, say, *Jefferson and/or Mussolini*. Legal and economic control over a text remains a powerful tool in the management of a literary reputation.) The simple accessibility of the facts or texts "themselves" does not, however, exhaust the issue. There still remains, both within poststructuralist defenses of de Man and poststructuralism itself, the more vexed question of the relation of the facts to the discursive strategies that constitute or elide them as such.

Derrida's essay at first seems to admit the facts:

> On the one hand, the *massive, immediate, and dominant* effect of all these texts [de Man's *Le Soir* articles] is that of a *relatively* coherent ideological ensemble which, *most often and in a preponderant fashion*, conforms to official rhetoric, that of the occupation forces of the milieux that, in Belgium, had accepted the defeat and, if not state and government collaboration as in France, then at least the perspective of a European unity under German hegemony. (SSD 607)

This is an admirable, if somewhat baroque, statement of the crucial fact: de Man was a collaborator. But *"on the other hand,"* Derrida continues, "and within this frame, de Man's discourse is constantly split, disjointed, engaged in incessant conflicts" (SSD 607). There is evidently no fact, no political "effect," sufficiently "massive, immediate, and dominant" that a careful analysis of discursive strategies cannot render problematic, cannot "internally distanciate," cannot make not "hang together." Derrida's reading, which is in no way bound by what the *Le Soir* articles seem to want to say, is undeniably "subversive" in relation to the texts that occasion it. It is anything but subversive, however, in terms of its own "massive, immediate, and dominant" political effect.

Here, for example, is Derrida on "The Jews in Contemporary Literature," a text that has proved as amenable as any other to ideological rehabilitation:

> To condemn vulgar antisemitism may leave one to understand that there is a distinguished antisemitism in whose name the vulgar variety is put down. De Man never says such a thing, even though one may condemn his silence. But the phrase can also mean something else, and this reading can always contaminate the other in a clandestine fashion: to condemn "vulgar antisemitism," *especially if one makes no mention of the other kind*, is to condemn antisemitism *itself inasmuch as* it is vulgar, always and essentially vulgar. De Man does not say that either. (SSD 607)

This might seem an unprecedented excursion into the realm of the counter-intuitive, but consider the following statement, which may also leave one to understand that its author was anti-Semitic: "[R]easons of race and religion combine to make any large number of free-thinking Jews undesir-able." The "massive, immediate, and dominant" effect of this seems clear enough, yet the phrase can always mean something else, and this reading can always contaminate the other in a clandestine fashion. To condemn "free-thinking Jews," *especially if one makes no mention of the other kind,* is to argue that reasons of race and religion combine to make a large number of *Orthodox* Jews desirable. Eliot does not say so, but his words have been taken to mean, or have been made to mean, precisely that.[50] And while nothing, perhaps, can prohibit so willful a "contamination"—an interpre-tive strategy in no way unique to poststructuralism—"contamination" does not seem the appropriate term.

On the contrary, poststructuralism is an ideology of ideological decon-tamination, a now thoroughly routinized procedure for "saving the text" from its suspect ideological investments. It thus takes its place within the "defensively recuperative" relation to "authoritative texts" that is at the heart of western humanism.[51] Plato banishes poets from his Republic, but subsequent apologies for poetry are not therefore embarrassed to invoke his authority in their behalf. Plato was himself a poet (or so the conven-tional argument goes); the dialogues contain the most striking of meta-phors, and a dialogue is itself an innately dramatic form. The saying undoes the authority of the thing said, although it never impinges on the authority of Plato himself. Or if Plato privileges speech over writing, this in no way prevents poststructuralism from invoking the authority of Plato in the cause of a generalized grammatology. The celebration of the logos as pure presence, as voice welded to the immediate certainty of consciousness, is contaminated (or so Derrida's argument goes) by the mediation of the writing it eschews. The writing undoes the authority of speech, although it never impinges on the authority of the Platonic texts themselves. The early humanists followed Plutarch in rehabilitating a failed literalism in the mode of allegorical interpretation. The most unabashedly erotic and physi-cal of intrigues had only to be recast as moral, philosophical, or naturalistic parables for their authority to be preserved unscathed.[52] Poststructuralism completes the humanist project by recovering a failed philosophical au-thority as "allegories of reading." Literature may no longer be the abode of eternal truth, but it nevertheless remains "the place where . . . negative knowledge about the reliability of linguistic utterance is made available" (RT 10). Derrida rejects Pound's faith in any "beyond" to metaphor—the *propre,* the "clean," the "pure," is always implicated in, "contaminated" by, the figurative:

> That appeal to the criteria of clarity and obscurity would suffice to
> confirm . . . [that the] entire philosophical delimitation of metaphor
> already lends itself to being constructed and worked by "metaphors."
> How could a piece of knowledge or a language be properly clear or

obscure? Now, all the concepts which have operated in the definition of metaphor always have an origin and an efficacity that are themselves "metaphorical," to use a word that this time, rigorously is no longer suitable to designate tropes that are as much defining as defined.[53]

But if language can never be "properly clear or obscure," if the appeal to the criterion of clarity or obscurity is itself metaphorical, literature is not thereby "contaminated." Rather, the stabilizing gesture that insists that all language is given to the instability, the refusal of proper place and name, that is metaphor is also the gesture that releases literature from the fixity of its ideological burden.

A reading that is "subversive" in relation to its textual object yet reactionary in terms of its own "massive, immediate, and dominant" political effect: nowhere is the paradox more in evidence than in Miller's reflections on "The Jews in Contemporary Literature":

> Strangely [de Man] mentions Kafka along with Hemingway and Lawrence as three great and exemplary modern authors. Other essays . . . praise Proust as a major writer. Did de Man not know Kafka was a Jew, or could the mention of Kafka here be an example of the kind of double-talk one learns to practice under a totalitarian regime? In an essay written at the end of his life de Man, in one of the two references to Leo Strauss in his writings, praises Strauss for having understood "double-talk, the necessary obliqueness of any persecuted speech that cannot, at risk of survival, openly say what it means to say" [RT 107]. To suggest that this may explain the oddness of de Man's essay on the Jews in no way exonerates him from responsibility for whatever support his essay may have given to the then developing German policy that led seventeen months later to the first deportations of Jews from Belgium to the death camps. But it is important to note that the essay itself is by no means straight party-line antisemitism.

Miller advances a rather attenuated version of the "subversion hypothesis." De Man remains culpable for the support his essay *may* have given to the developing German policy (although only a reader untrained in the rigors of rhetorical analysis *could* have found support for this policy in de Man's complex "double-talk"), yet whatever the essay "means to say," it is nevertheless deemed at least partially innocent of its overt ideological content ("the essay itself is by no means straight party-line antisemitism"):

> The evidence suggests that he stupidly wrote the deplorable essay ["The Jews in Contemporary Literature"] to please his employers and keep his job, putting in as much "double-talk" as he dared. According to the letter he wrote Renato Poggioli when he was a Junior Fellow at Harvard, and he had been anonymously denounced, he quit writing for *Le Soir* in November of 1942 when "Nazi thought control" made it impossible for him any longer to express himself freely. This seems to have been the moment when Nazi propaganda control was extended from the political to the cultural parts of *Le Soir,* for which of course de Man wrote and which had until then been free of direct censorship.

Miller credits de Man both with a principled decision to quit *Le Soir* when it was no longer possible "to express himself freely" once "Nazi propaganda control" was extended to his own journalistic sphere, and with the subversive inclusion of "double-talk" in an article written under compulsion. It is clear that both cannot be true, or both can be true only in the context of a "double-talk," a discursive strategy, that has little to do with the kind "one learns to practice under a totalitarian regime." The "suspect" ideological burden of "The Jews in Contemporary Literature" hangs together well enough: its "dominant, immediate, and massive effect" is more or less "straight party-line antisemitism." The "subversion hypothesis" does have relevance here, but only as it might be applied to Miller's article, which is utterly innocent of its ideological burden, which is precisely the "subversion hypothesis." Miller invokes "double-talk" in the context of "the necessary obliqueness of any persecuted speech that cannot, at risk of survival, openly say what it means to say," which is the perilous condition of factuality under totalitarian regimes. Miller's broader point, however, is that discourse never can say what it seems to mean, mean what it thinks it says, which is the perilous condition of factuality, at least as it is rendered discursively, under the current theoretical regime. "Totalitarian" control over the dissemination of discourse does involve a loss of factuality, which can entail horrifying consequences. But there are any number of ways of controlling or eliding the "decision regarding success and failure," and the current fetishization of dissemination is to be counted among them.

This seems to me the relevant issue in the debate over the wartime activities of Paul de Man: not what "resistance to theory" the "attack" on de Man evinces, but what "resistance to factuality," to history, the defense of de Man entails. Perhaps the most serious charge that can be brought against de Man is his failure to acknowledge the facts, to address the issue of his wartime activities publicly, and the poststructuralist defense of de Man does neither de Man nor poststructuralism any favor in "rehearsing" his failure, in refusing, as de Man himself puts it in "The Resistance to Theory," to "call the cat a cat" (RT 4). This is to assume, however, that the poststructuralist defense acknowledges de Man's elision of the facts, or at least his strategic omission of the facts, as a failure, which it does not. De Man's refusal of public explanation or expiation, far from being a "fact" that might reflect on his integrity, merely questions the motives of those who would posthumously attack him. Thus we read in Derrida: "If there are some who want to organize a trial in order to judge him, de Man, they must remember that he, de Man, is dead and will not answer in the present" (SSD 593), although we characteristically read in Derrida that no one ever speaks in or from the "present." Or we read in Miller: "The real target is not de Man himself. He is dead, beyond the reach of attack. The real aim is to discredit that form of interpretation called 'deconstruction,'" although we now everywhere read that all authors, the very category of the author, died some time ago. Defenses of de Man might be expected to explain this public silence, or at least to suffer a degree of embarrassment on its account. But as they seem little troubled by the actual facts of de Man's wartime activities—let me repeat a fact that I still find extraordinary: Miller's article reserves the word "collaborator" exclusively for de Man's critics—so also are they unembarrassed by the subsequent silence in which he enveloped those facts. Proof against both the facts and their suppression: if the future of factuality is contingent on this "nontotalitarian" world, on this alleged critique of totalitarian practices, its future is limited.

NOTES

Chapter 1

1. T. S. Eliot, *After Strange Gods* (New York: Harcourt, Brace, 1934), p. 47.

2. Perry Meisel, *The Myth of the Modern: A Study of British Literature and Criticism After 1850* (New Haven: Yale University Press, 1977); Andrew Ross, *The Failure of Modernism: Symptoms of American Poetry* (New York: Columbia University Press, 1986).

3. On anti-Semitism as a grotesque or perverse utopianism, see Max Horkheimer and Theodor W. Adorno, *Dialectic of Enlightment,* trans. John Cumming (New York: Continuum, 1993), pp. 168–208. Jameson argues that it "is increasingly clear in today's world (if it had ever been in doubt) that a Left which cannot grasp the immense Utopian appeal of nationalism (any more than it can grasp that of religion or of fascism) can scarcely hope to 'reappropriate' such collective energies and must effectively doom itself to political impotence." Fredric Jameson, *The Political Unconscious: Narrative as a Socially Symbolic Act* (Ithaca, N.Y.: Cornell University Press, 1981), p. 298. Eliot and Pound stand as testimony to the immense utopian appeal of religion and fascism, respectively.

4. Gilbert Allardyce, "What Fascism Is Not: Thoughts on the Definition of a Concept," *American Historical Review* 84, no. 2 (April 1979): 367–88.

5. Stanley G. Payne, *Fascism: Comparison and Definition* (Madison: University of Wisconsin Press, 1980), p. 4.

6. Ernst Nolte, *Three Faces of Fascism: Action Française, Italian Fascism, National Socialism,* trans. Leila Vennewitz (New York: Holt, Rinehart, and Winston, 1966); hereafter cited by page in the text.

7. Geoffrey H. Hartman, *Criticism in the Wilderness: The Study of Literature Today* (New Haven: Yale University Press, 1980), p. 100.

8. Juan Linz, "Totalitarianism and Fascist Regimes," in *Handbook of Political Science: Macropolitical Theory,* ed. Fred I. Greenstein and Nelson W. Polsby, 5 vols. (Reading, Mass.: Addison-Wesley, 1975), 3:270–72; see also Payne, *Fascism: Comparison and Definition,* pp. 101, 75.

9. Payne, *Fascism: Comparison and Definition,* p. 74.

10. This is especially true in the case of Fascist Italy. Doug Thompson, for example, characterizes fascism as "an extreme form of conservatism" and argues that Mussolini's regime "created little if anything that was new"; see *State Control in Fascist Italy: Culture and Conformity, 1925–43* (Manchester: Manchester University Press, 1991), pp. vi, xi. The inclusion of anticonservatism among the fascist "negations" ignores the fact that fascist regimes characteristically came to power with the tacit consent or collusion of older conservative elites.

11. Walter Benjamin, "The Work of Art in the Age of Mechanical Reproduction," in *Illuminations,* trans. Hannah Arendt (New York: Schocken Books, 1969), p. 241.

12. Slavoj Žižek, *For They Know Not What They Do: Enjoyment as a Political Factor* (London: Verso Books, 1991), p. 186.

13. And, at least in the case of Nazi Germany, the racial. But as I argue in chapter 2, the strategic translation of questions of economic injustice into racial villainy serves to preserve the status quo.

14. Peter F. Drucker, "Fascism as the End of Economic Man," in *The Place of Fascism in European History,* ed. Gilbert Allardyce (Englewood Cliffs, N.J.: Prentice-Hall, 1971), pp. 49–66.

15. Benito Mussolini, "The Political and Social Doctrine of Fascism," as quoted in Charles F. Delzell, ed., *Mediterranean Fascism, 1919–1945* (New York: Walker and Company, 1971), p. 100.

16. A. James Gregor, *Italian Fascism and Developmental Dictatorship* (Princeton: Princeton University Press, 1979), pp. 32–33. My entire reading of Italian syndicalism is taken from Gregor.

17. Although it is not quite my intention to rehearse the rather old-fashioned thesis that fascism somehow "saved" capitalism—as old, in fact, as Mussolini's defection from orthodox socialism—my argument is clearly sympathetic to it. But then some rudimentary distinctions between fascisms must be drawn. Pre-Nazi Germany was not an economically or industrially retarded society. If the bourgeoisie had not yet completed, it was clearly going about the business of realizing its historic mission. There is a sense here, however, in which extremities meet. Germany was a major but anomalous power: no other nation of comparable status was without an empire or felt itself so unjustly deprived of international prestige. Hitler was thus free to play on intense nationalist aspirations. Pre-Fascist Italy, by contrast, was largely agrarian and artisan; it considered itself the victim of the plutocratic, capitalist powers of the North. Mussolini was also free, albeit for different reasons, to play on intense nationalist aspirations. A great deal depends, moreover, on what one takes to be the "capitalist minimum," the "lowest common denominator" of the "legitimately" capitalist. Alan Milward, for example, rejects the thesis that fascism somehow saved capitalism, even as he notes that Nazi Germany respected the right to private property and profit. All of which raises the obvious issue: What is the "capitalist minimum" if not the right to private property and profit? Hitler did subject the economy, as Milward also notes, to various forms of state control. After 1936, when the main drive toward re-armament began, economic production was increasingly subordinated to a military agenda. But this

was not the quasi-socialist collectivism promised by the founding Twenty-Five Points of the National Socialist Workers' party, and a militarized economy in no way implies a noncapitalist one. See Alan S. Milward, "Fascism and the Economy," in *Fascism: A Reader's Guide,* ed. Walter Laqueur (Berkeley: University of California Press, 1976), pp. 379–412. It is sometimes argued that fascism could not have saved capitalism, if only because fascism was itself defeated by capitalist forces. But this is to assume that capitalist powers never war among themselves.

The average gross hourly wage for German workers rose from the index figure of 94.6 in 1933 to 100 in 1936 and 108.6 in 1939, but it remained far below the 1929 index figure of 129.5; given the increase in the cost of living and in wage deductions over the same period of time (which rose from less than 10 percent to more than 20 percent), the income at the disposal of workers fell dramatically, despite the increase in production (in 1938 it was 25 percent above the 1929 level) and the average productivity of labor (which increased by approximately 10 percent). Under such conditions the mass of profits shot upward: from RM 15.4 billion in 1929 to RM 18 billion in 1932 and RM 20 billion in 1938 (these figures refer to all forms of profit, including commercial and bank profits and undistributed company profits). The Nazi prohibition against strikes and the compulsory tying of workers to jobs—itself compelling evidence, as Ernest Mandel notes, of the capitalist nature of the National Socialist state—prevented the German proletariat from exploiting market conditions that might have permitted it to better its lot. In Italy real wages declined from an index figure of 56 in 1922 to 46 in 1938. Italian workers also lost the right to strike, although various social programs, such as the Opera Nazionale Dopolavoro (the National Institute for Leisure Time), were apparently intended as compensation. (The institute provided workers with the opportunity to play billiards, engage in sports, and the like.) All figures are taken from Ernest Mandel, *Late Capitalism,* trans. Joris De Bres (London: New Left Books, 1975), pp. 159–62.

18. Gregor, *Italian Fascism,* p. 33.

19. Mussolini, as quoted in Delzell, *Mediterranean Fascism,* p. 92. I take the terms "pragmatists" and "fundamentalists" from Richard Plant, *The Pink Triangle: The Nazi War Against Homosexuals* (New York: Henry Holt, 1986), p. 162.

20. See, for example, Barrington Moore, "Fascism as the Heritage of Conservative Modernization," in Allardyce, *The Place of Fascism,* pp. 127–43; and Ernst Nolte, "Fascism as an Antimodernist Revolt," ibid., pp. 144–61.

21. Benito Mussolini, "Orientamenti e problemi," in *Opera Omnia di Benito Mussolini,* ed. Edoardo and Duilio Susmel, 36 vols. (Florence: La Fenice, 1951–63), 11:283.

22. Mussolini quoted in John Weiss, "Fascism as the Extremism of the Right," in Allardyce, *The Place of Fascism,* p. 121.

23. Horkheimer and Adorno, *Dialectic of Enlightenment,* p. 173.

24. This is a focus that David Harvey argues defines our postmodernity; see *The Condition of Postmodernity: An Enquiry into the Origins of Cultural Change* (Cambridge: Basil Blackwell, 1980), p. 102.

25. Slavoj Žižek, *The Sublime Object of Ideology* (London: Verso Books, 1989), pp. 5–6; hereafter cited by page in the text.

26. Žižek notes that the camps were "an invention of 'liberal' England, dating from the Boer war," and that they "were also used in the USA to isolate the Japanese population, and so on" (ibid., p. 50). The "and so on" might easily be extended to include our own historical moment: "ethnic cleansing," a term that has

only recently gained currency, echoes with the most sinister of historic memories. And lest we are tempted, once again, to relegate those atrocities to the other people, recall the fate of HIV-positive Haitians seeking refuge in the United States. Yet to assume that the death camps are not therefore the product of specific sociopolitical formulations is to make the possibility of historical explanation contingent on the stability of the opposition between the liberal-democratic and the fascist-dictatorial state. Not that the two can be conflated. Jeffrey Mehlman, for instance, takes issue with Pound's *Jefferson and/or Mussolini,* which he characterizes as a "maddeningly wrong-headed" attempt "to neutralize—if not deconstruct—the opposition between the father of democracy and the fascist leader. ('The heritage of Jefferson . . . is HERE, NOW, in the Italian peninsula at the beginning of the second decennio, not in Massachusetts or Delaware')." Yet if Pound's act of protodeconstruction is "maddeningly wrong-headed"—and it is—so too is the temptation simply to dismiss it as such. *Jefferson and/or Mussolini* is not an indulgence in rhetorical ingenuity, and if our relation to fascism, to repeat an earlier point, is to progress beyond ritual condemnation, its celebration of Il Duce as Jefferson reborn must be taken in earnest. After all, Roosevelt was compared to Mussolini, and fascist elements were discerned in the New Deal. See Jeffrey Mehlman, "Writing and Deference: The Politics of Literary Adulation," *Representations* 15 (Summer 1986): 8–9; on the comparison between Roosevelt and Mussolini, see Nolte, *Three Faces of Fascism,* pp. 8–9.

27. See John Weiss, "Fascism as the Extremism of the Right," in Allardyce, *The Place of Fascism,* p. 122.

28. Ezra Pound, Canto XC, in *The Cantos of Ezra Pound,* rev. ed. (New York: New Directions, 1991).

29. As Nolte observes: "The unmistakable thrust of her [Arendt's] book, *The Origins of Totalitarianism* [1951], was to equate Nazism and Stalinism and to subsume Italian Fascism, along with Franco's Spain and Horthy's Hungary, under the rubric of mere authoritarianism. This approach prevailed in western historical writing during the next decade, even though it was subjected to numerous variations. That the concept of fascism was accorded at most a subordinate role is obviously attributable to its unmistakably distrubing implications for western society at a time when the virtues of western democracy seemed so evident." Ernst Nolte, "The Problem of Fascism in Recent Scholarship," in *Reappraisals of Fascism,* ed. Henry A. Turner, Jr. (New York: New Viewpoints, 1975), p. 26. On the role of the early volumes of *Das Argument* in exposing "the legitimatory function of the totalitarianism theory in the context of the Cold War," see Anson G. Rabinbach, "Toward a Marxist Theory of Fascism and National Socialism: A Report on Developments in West Germany," *New German Critique,* no. 3 (Fall 1974): 127–53.

30. Laclau and Mouffe argue that it is "the 'people' (in the sense of *plebs* rather than *populus*), the barely organized and differentiated masses, who dominate the barricades of 1789 and 1848, the Chartist agitation in England and the Mazzinian and Garibaldian mobilizations in Italy." But it is "the unions or nascent social-democratic parties, first in Germany and England and then in the rest of Europe, which establish themselves with increasing solidity in the last third of the century." They continue:

> This break has frequently been interpreted as the transition to a moment of higher political rationality on the part of the dominated sectors: in the first half of the century the amorphous character of "democracy," its lack

of roots in the economic bases of society, made it essentially vulnerable and unstable, and prevented it from constituting itself into a steadfast and permanent trench in the struggle against the established order. Only with the disintegration of this amorphous "people," and its replacement with the solid social base of the working class, would popular movements achieve the maturity that allowed them to undertake a long-term struggle against the dominant classes. Nevertheless, this mythical transition to a higher stage of social maturity resulting from industrialization, and to a higher lever of political efficacy in which the anarchic outbursts of the "people" would be replaced by the rationality and solidity of class politics, could only appear as a bad joke to Rosenberg, who wrote . . . while Spain burned, Hitler was preparing for the *Anschluss,* and Mussolini was invading Ethiopia. For Rosenberg this closing up along class lines constituted on the contrary the great historical sin of the European labour movement.

Ernesto Laclau and Chantal Mouffe, *Hegemony & Socialist Strategy: Towards a Radical Democratic Politics* (London: Verso, 1985), pp. 149–50; hereafter cited by page in the text. Laclau and Mouffe conclude: "[C]lass opposition is incapable of dividing the totality of the social body into two antagonistic camps, of reproducing itself *automatically* as a line of demarcation in the political sphere" (p. 151). The argument presupposes the more than relative autonomy of the political, which is characteristic of contemporary critiques of marxist "reductionism" in general. But then Mussolini argued much the same: "[A]bove all Fascism denies that class-war can be the preponderant force in the transformation of society" ("The Political and Social Doctrine of Fascism," in Delzell, *Mediterranean Fascism,* p. 100). The horror in which the fascist denial of "the rationality and solidity of class politics" issued does not seem an effective argument against the priority that Marx attributes to class antagonism.

31. Jean-François Lyotard, *The Postmodern Condition: A Report on Knowledge,* trans. Geoff Bennington and Brian Massumi (Minneapolis: University of Minnesota Press, 1984), p. 82.

32. Fredric Jameson, *Postmodernism, or, The Cultural Logic of Late Capitalism* (Durham, N.C.: Duke University Press, 1991), p. 333. My entire reading of the contemporary "war on totality" is indebted to Jameson.

33. On bourgeois "ex-nomination," see Roland Barthes, *Mythologies,* trans. Annette Lavers (New York: Granada, 1976), pp. 137–38.

34. "Much of what passes for a spirited defense of difference is, of course, simply liberal tolerance, a position whose offensive complacencies are well known but which has at least the merit of raising the embarrassing historical question of whether the tolerance of difference, as a social fact, is not the result of social homogenization and standardization and the obliteration of genuine social difference in the first place" (Jameson, *Postmodernism,* p. 341).

35. Eve Kosofsky Sedgwick, *Epistemology of the Closet* (Berkeley: University of California Press, 1990), p. 23. Alan Liu notes that when high-postmodernist cultural critics invoke details, they "are never more than throwaway markers, representations, 'symbols' of a contest enacted in the *name* of detail but greater than any particular detail. . . . [T]he very facility with which they process interchangeable details argues their greater commitment to 'struggle,' 'resistance,' 'opposition,' 'subversion,' 'transgression,' as abstract, perfect forms of contest"; see "Local Tran-

scendence: Cultural Criticism, Postmodernism, and the Romanticism of Detail," *Representations* 32 (Fall 1990): 97–98.

36. Mandel, *Late Capitalism,* p. 507.

37. Jameson, *Postmodernism,* p. 343.

Chapter 2

1. These languages included Italian, French, Spanish, Provençal, Latin, and Greek, which Pound knew well; German and Old English, in which he was competent; Chinese, which he never fully mastered; and Japanese, Hindi, and Egyptian, of which he was almost entirely ignorant. See Burton Raffel, *Ezra Pound: The Prime Minister of Poetry* (London: Archon Books, 1984), pp. 61–62.

2. See Hugh Kenner, *The Pound Era* (Berkeley: University of California Press, 1971), p. 196.

3. Ernest Fenollosa, *The Chinese Written Character as a Medium for Poetry,* ed. Ezra Pound (New York: Arrow Editions, 1936), p. 9.

4. Ezra Pound, *Literary Essays of Ezra Pound,* ed. T. S. Eliot (London: Faber and Faber, 1954), p. 259; hereafter cited by page in the text as *LE.*

5. Matthew Arnold, *On Translating Homer* (New York: Chelsea House, 1983), p. 21.

6. Jacques Derrida, *Positions,* trans. Alan Bass (Chicago: University of Chicago Press, 1981), p. 20.

7. Jacques Derrida, "Violence and Metaphysics," in *Writing and Difference,* trans. Alan Bass (Chicago: University of Chicago Press, 1978), p. 83.

8. Karl Marx, *Grundrisse: Foundations of the Critique of Political Economy,* trans. Martin Nicolaus (New York: Penguin Books, 1973), p. 221.

9. Ibid., p. 145.

10. Ezra Pound, *The Cantos of Ezra Pound,* rev. ed. (New York: New Directions, 1991); hereafter cited in the text.

11. This is a much-simplified version of the thesis of Jean-Joseph Goux, *Les Monnayeurs du langage* (Paris: Galilee, 1984); see also Richard Sieburth, "In Pound We Trust: The Economy of Poetry/The Poetry of Economics," *Critical Inquiry* 14, no. 1 (Autumn 1978): 142–72.

12. Max Horkheimer and Theodor W. Adorno, *Dialectic of Enlightenment,* trans. John Cumming (New York: Continuum, 1972), p. 43. The characterization of Odysseus as "the individual responsible to himself" is Pound's; see Ezra Pound, *Guide to Kulchur* (1938; rpt. New York: New Directions, 1970), p. 38; hereafter cited by page in the text as *GK.*

13. Lauro Martines, *Power and Imagination: City-States in Renaissance Italy* (New York: Vintage Books, 1980), p. 85. In 1252, thirteen years before Dante's birth, Florence began minting the florin. On the "economy" of the *Divine Comedy,* see R. A. Shoaf, *Dante, Chaucer, and the Currency of the Word: Money, Images, and Reference in Late Medieval Poetry* (Norman, Okla.: Pilgrim Books, 1983).

14. Ezra Pound, *Personae,* rev. ed. (New York: New Directions, 1971), p. 196; hereafter cited by page in the text as *P.*

15. Jürgen Habermas, *Legitimation Crisis,* trans. Thomas McCarthy (Boston: Beacon Press, 1975), p. 78.

16. Leonardo Bruni, quoted in Glyn P. Norton, *The Ideology and Language of Translation in Renaissance France and Their Humanist Antecedents* (Geneva: Librairie Droz, 1984), pp. 41–42, n. 51.

17. Derrida, *Positions,* p. 20.

18. Gianfranco Folena, "'Volgarizzare' e 'tradurre,'" in *La traduzione: saggi e studi,* ed. Centro per lo studio dell' insegnamento all'estero dell'italiano (Trieste: Lint, 1973), p. 68. See also Eugene Vance's contribution to the "Roundtable on Translation" in Jacques Derrida, *The Ear of the Other: Otobiography, Transference, Translation,* ed. Christie V. McDonald, trans. Peggy Kamuf (New York: Schocken Books, 1985), pp. 135–42; and Vance's "Edmund Spenser, Troy, and the Humanist Ideology of Translation," in *Mervelous Signals: Chaucer's "Troilus and Criseyde"* (Lincoln: University of Nebraska Press, 1986), pp. 311–51.

19. Derrida, *Positions,* p. 20.

20. Vance, *Mervelous Signals,* pp. 119–22; my entire discussion here is indebted to Vance.

21. Ibid., pp. 119–22.

22. On Erasmus' *De Copia* and the Renaissance ideal of verbal "copiousness" in general, see Terence Cave, *The Cornucopian Text: Problems of Writing in the French Renaissance* (Oxford: Clarendon Press, 1979), pp. 3–34. On Erasmus' translation of *logos* in John 1, see Marjorie O'Rourke Boyle, *Erasmus on Language and Method in Theology* (Toronto: University of Toronto Press, 1977), pp. 1–31.

23. This Derridean contention is "translated" here by Barbara Johnson; see her essay "Taking Fidelity Philosophically," in *Difference in Translation,* ed. Joseph F. Graham (Ithaca, N.Y.: Cornell University Press, 1985), p. 145. It is difficult to know, however, how "classical notions of translation"—if the "classical" includes, say, the Roman—could be predicated on the priority of the signified, as Roman translators tended to assume an audience familiar with (that is, fluent in the language of) the original. Roman translations were "perceived as an exercise in comparative stylistics, since they were freed from the exigencies of having to 'make known' either the form or the content *per se,* and consequently did not need to subordinate themselves to the frame of the original"; Susan Bassnett-McGuire, *Translation Studies* (New York: Methuen, 1990), p. 45.

24. Benedict Anderson, *Imagined Communities: Reflections on the Origins and Spread of Nationalism,* rev. ed. (London: Verso, 1991), p. 13.

25. Anderson, *Imagined Communities,* p. 39.

26. Jacques Derrida, *Dissemination,* trans. Barbara Johnson (Chicago: University of Chicago Press, 1981), pp. 71–72.

27. See Hugh Kenner, "Blood for the Ghosts," in *New Approaches to Ezra Pound,* ed. Eva Hesse (Berkeley: University of California Press, 1969), p. 337.

28. Divus uses a text that contains a twice-repeated line ("diogenes Laertiade, polumekhan Odusseu") that is now considered an interpolation. He apparently mistakes the second "diogenes" for "digenes," which becomes Pound's " A second time? why? man of ill star." See Jean-Michel Rabaté, *Language, Sexuality and Ideology in Ezra Pound's "Cantos"* (Albany: State University of New York Press, 1986), pp. 67–68.

29. On Ulysses' failure to name and his inability to contain himself within the limits of the known or named world, see Giuseppe Mazzotta, *Dante, Poet of the Desert: History and Allegory in the Divine Comedy* (Princeton: Princeton University Press, 1979), pp. 89–90.

30. *Inferno* 26.90–99, in Dante Alighieri, *The Divine Comdey,* ed. Charles S. Singleton (Princeton: Princeton University Press, 1970); all subsequent references are to this edition.

31. M. D. Chenu, *Nature, Man, and Society in the Twelfth Century: Essays on New*

Theoretical Perspectives in the Latin West, trans. Jerome Taylor and Lester Little (Chicago: University of Chicago Press, 1968), p. 187.

32. Philip Kuberski, "Ego, Scriptor: Pound's Odyssean Writing," *Paideuma* 14, no. 1 (Spring 1985): 32.

33. Herbert Schneidau, *Ezra Pound: The Image and the Real* (Baton Rouge: Louisiana State University Press, 1969), p. 143.

34. Ezra Pound, *ABC of Reading* (1934; rpt. London: Faber and Faber, 1961), p. 46; hereafter cited by page in the text as *ABC*.

35. Ezra Pound, *Confucius: "The Unwobbling Pivot," "The Great Digest," "The Analects"* (New York: New Directions, 1969), p. 192; hereafter cited by page in the text as *Con*.

36. John Dryden, *The Poems of John Dryden,* ed. James Kinsey, 4 vols. (Oxford: Oxford University Press, 1958), 3:1059. On the role translation played in the development of a national literature, see Susan Staves, "Pope's Refinement," *The Eighteenth Century: Theory and Interpretation* 29, no. 2 (Spring 1988): 145–63.

37. For example: the French *translation;* the German *Übertragung* and *Übersetzung;* the Italian *translatio, metaphora, translatore,* and *transferimento;* and the Spanish *traslatico, traslado,* and *traslación.* See Marc Shell, *Money, Language, and Thought: Literary and Philosophical Economies from the Medieval to the Modern Era* (Berkeley: University of California Press, 1982), p. 85.

38. Ezra Pound, *The Letters of Ezra Pound, 1907–1941,* ed. D. D. Paige (New York: New Directions, 1971) p. 91; hereafter cited by page in the text as *L*.

39. Franco Moretti, *Signs Taken for Wonders: Essays in the Sociology of Literary Forms,* rev. ed., trans. Susan Fischer, David Forgacs, and David Miller (London: Verso, 1988). p. 303.

40. I mean the *Poetics* in its most influential translations. Aristotle opposes metaphor only to "ordinary" or "current" usage; the now conventional opposition with the "proper" is the product of later (mis)translations. See Paul Ricoeur, *The Rule of Metaphor: Multi-Disciplinary Studies of the Creation of Meaning in Language,* trans. Robert Czerny (Toronto: University of Toronto Press, 1977), p. 20.

41. As Andrew Parker, among others, has noted, "The basic principles of Pound's economic theories derive almost without exception from Aristotle's classic treatise on government, the *Politics*"; see Andrew Parker, "Ezra Pound and the 'Economy' of Anti-Semitism," *boundary 2* 11, nos. 1–2 (Fall–Winter 1982–83): 105.

42. Ezra Pound, *Selected Prose: 1909–1965,* ed. William Cookson (New York: New Directions, 1973), p. 311; hereafter cited by page in the text as *SP*.

43. Georg Simmel, *The Philosophy of Money,* trans. T. Bottomore and D. Frisby (London: Routledge and Kegan Paul, 1978), p. 251. Peter Nicholls notes that although there is no evidence that Pound read Simmel, his analysis of the relation of economic to aesthetic values has much in common with Pound's; see Peter Nicholls, *Ezra Pound: Politics, Economics and Writing* (Atlantic Highlands, N.J.: Humanities Press, 1984), pp. 28–29.

44. George Puttenham, *The Arte of English Poesie* (Kent, Ohio: Kent State University Press, 1970), 3.16.

45. Ezra Pound, *Ezra Pound Speaking: Radio Speeches of World War II,* ed. Leonard W. Doob (Westport, Conn.: Greenwood Press, 1978), p. 284; hereafter cited by page in the text as *EPS*.

46. Goux, *Les Monnayeurs du langage,* p. 131.

47. Fenollosa, *The Chinese Written Character as a Medium for Poetry,* pp. 25, 8.

48. Ezra Pound, *Collected Early Poems of Ezra Pound,* ed. Michael John King (New York: New Directions, 1976). Submitted to *Poetry* in 1912, first published in *Collected Shorter Poems* (1968), the poem is an epilogue to what Pound calls "my five books containing mediaeval studies, experiments and translation"—that is, *The Spirit of Romance, Canzoni, Ripostes, The Sonnets and Ballate of Guido Cavalcanti,* and *The Canzoni of Arnaut Daniel.*

49. See Frederick K. Sanders, *John Adams Speaking: Pound's Sources for the Adams Cantos* (Orono: University of Maine Press, 1975).

50. John Driscoll, *The China Cantos of Ezra Pound* (Uppsala: Almqvist and Wiksell, 1983), pp. 28–29.

51. On the violence that attended the imposition of *cheng ming* in China, a phenomenon that both Pound and his critics tend to aestheticize, see Xuefei Jin, "Universalization in Modern English and American Poetry: With Particular Reference to China" (Ph. D. diss., Brandeis University, 1990).

52. Roland Barthes, *Writing Degree Zero,* trans. Annette Lavers and Colin Smith (New York: Hill and Wang, 1968), p. 24.

53. Robert M. Rennick, "The Nazi Name Decrees of the Nineteen Thirties," *Names* 18, no. 1 (March 1970: 65–88.

54. Parker, "The 'Economy' of Anti-Semitism," p. 118.

55. Jacques Derrida, *"Speech and Phenomena" and Other Essays on Husserl's Theory of Signs,* trans. David B. Allison (Evanston, Ill.: Northwestern University Press, 1973), p. 148; and idem, *Of Grammatology,* trans. Gayatri Chakravorty Spivak (Baltimore: Johns Hopkins University Press, 1976), p. 80. Both of these passages are quoted by Parker in "The 'Economy' of Anti-Semitism."

56. Roland Barthes, *Mythologies,* trans. Annette Lavers (Frogmore: Paladin, 1976), p. 101.

57. Stephen Owen, *Traditional Chinese Poetry and Poetics: Omen of the World* (Madison: University of Wisconsin Press, 1985), p. 34.

58. Derrida, *Of Grammatology,* p. 92.

59. Anderson, *Imagined Communities,* p. 44; on the invention of printing and its lack of revolutionary impact in China, see p. 44, n. 21.

60. Herbert N. Schneidau, *Sacred Discontent: The Bible and Western Tradition* (Berkeley: University of California Press, 1977), pp. 3, 11.

61. D. A. Miller, *The Novel and the Police* (Berkeley: University of California Press, 1989), p. 100.

62. Max Weber, *The Protestant Ethic and the Spirit of Capitalism,* trans. Talcott Parsons (New York: Scribner, 1965), p. 53.

63. Ezra Pound, *Jefferson and/or Mussolini* (1935; rpt. New York: Norton, 1970), p. 77; hereafter cited by page in the text as *JM.*

64. Kenneth Burke, *The Rhetoric of Religion: Studies in Logology* (Boston: Beacon Press, 1961), p. 3; see also Rabaté, *Language, Sexuality and Ideology,* p. 157.

65. On this theme, see Philip Furia, *Pound's Cantos Declassified* (University Park: Pennsylvania State University Press, 1984).

66. Plato, *Republic* 9, in *Plato: The Collected Dialogues,* ed. Edith Hamilton and Huntington Cairns (Princeton: Princeton University Press, 1961), p. 819.

67. Kenner, *The Pound Era,* p. 469.

68. Rabaté, *Language, Sexuality and Ideology,* pp. 148–49.

69. This point is convincingly argued by Rabaté, to whom I am indebted for this entire discussion; see ibid., pp. 148–49.

70. Published in *Paideuma* 8, no. 3 (Winter 1979): 456.

71. Nicholls, *Ezra Pound: Politics, Economics and Writing*, p. 123.

72. Massimo Bacigalupo, *The Forméd Trace: The Later Poetry of Ezra Pound* (New York: Columbia University Press, 1980), p. x.

73. Gérard Genette, *Figures* (Paris: Éditions du Seuil, 1966), p. 209. On the romantic literalization of this space, see Patricia A. Parker, *Inescapable Romance: Studies in the Poetics of a Mode* (Princeton: Princeton University Press, 1979), p. 165.

74. Samuel Taylor Coleridge, *The Poems of Samuel Taylor Coleridge*, ed. Ernest Hartley Coleridge (London: Oxford University Press, 1971), p. 180.

75. Ricoeur, *The Rule of Metaphor*, p. 221.

76. John Stuart Mill, "What Is Poetry?," in *Essays on Poetry*, ed. F. Parvin Sharpless (Columbia: University of South Carolina Press, 1976), pp. 14, 12.

77. Lewis Hyde, *The Gift: Imagination and the Erotic Life of Property* (New York: Vintage Books, 1979), p. 230; hereafter cited by page in the text.

78. Mill, *Essays on Poetry*, p. 36.

79. Peter D'Epiro, "Whose Vanity Must Be Pulled Down?," *Paideuma* 13, no. 2 (Fall 1984): 247–52; Jerome J. McGann, "The *Cantos* of Ezra Pound, the Truth in Contradiction," *Critical Inquiry* 15, no. 1 (Autumn 1988): 15.

80. Bollingen Prize Committee quoted in Noel Stock, *The Life of Ezra Pound* (New York: Pantheon Books, 1970), p. 426.

81. Christine Froula, *A Guide to Ezra Pound's Selected Poems* (New York: New Directions, 1982), p. 201.

82. Pound quoted in Stock, *The Life of Ezra Pound*, p. 414.

83. Spinoza quoted in Ezra Pound, "Gists from uncollected Prose,"; cited in Peter Makin, *Pound's Cantos* (London: George Allen and Unwin, 1985), p. 85.

84. Pound quoted in Stock, *The Life of Ezra Pound*, p. 414.

85. "The strangeness and point of lyric can be seen when we note that the speaker in lyric by contrast to the speakers in drama (all of whom are named) and the speakers in epic narrative (all of whom are named except the narrator) is only equivocally named, has in effect a sponsor (the author) but no name, is prior to or posterior to name, is an orphan voice. The name of the speaker in lyric is inferential or intuitive"; Allen Grossman, "Summa Lyrica: A Primer of the Commonplaces in Speculative Poetics," *Western Humanities Review* 44, no. 1 (Spring 1990): 7. Homer's Odysseus is, however, something of an exception in epic narrative: he tends to withhold or misrepresent his name.

86. On the *Cantos* as a poem written "on credit"—on the "future tense of money" or the £/Pound—see Richard Sieburth, "In Pound We Trust: The Economy of Poetry/The Poetry of Economy," *Critical Inquiry* 14, no. 1 (Autumn 1987): 142–72.

87. Bruce Robbins, "The Representation of Servants," *Raritan* 4, no. 2 (1987): 59.

88. See Leo Bersani, *The Culture of Redemption* (Cambridge, Mass.: Harvard University Press, 1990), p. 74: "The rhetorical criticism associated with Derrida and, more properly, de Man, has much to say about the deconstructive effects of the figural on political and moral assertions, and very little to say about the strategic nature of its own analytic enterprise. The decision to treat history as rhetoric must itself be deconstructed—which is of course to say *re*constructed—as a profoundly reactionary move: it deliberately ignores how networks of power can be independent of the subversive effect presumably inherent in their own discursive practices. The resistance of language to its own performance provides insufficient friction to

curtail the operational efficiency of even the most 'mystified' (but powerful) linguistic performance."

89. The Fasci di Combattimento came into being in March 1919; the program of this "fascism of the first hour" is published in Charles F. Delzell, ed., *Mediterranean Fascism: 1919–1945* (New York: Walker and Company, 1971), pp. 7–11. The official program of the party, which was published in June of the same year, is somewhat less radical; instead of calling for the confiscation of 85 percent of war profits, for example, the new program recommended only the sequestering of profits that were "left unproductive." See Delzell, *Mediterranean Fascism,* p. 14. On the Twenty-Five Points of Hitler's National Socialist Workers' party, see Stanley G. Payne, *Fascism: Comparison and Definition* (Madison: University of Wisconsin Press, 1980), p. 52.

90. Peter Nicholls notes that between 1930 and 1934 Pound contributed to *Morada, Front, Left Review, Little Magazine, Left Front,* and *New Quarterly;* see Nicholls, *Ezra Pound: Politics, Economics and Writing,* pp. 234–35, n. 1.

91. Max Horkheimer, "Die Juden und Europa," quoted in Douglas Kellner, *Critical Theory, Marxism, and Modernity* (Baltimore: Johns Hopkins University Press, 1989), p. 67.

92. The open letter from Joseph Goebbels appeared in the *Lokal-Anzeiger* of April 11, 1933; quoted in Philippe Lacoue-Labarthe, *Heidegger, Art and Politics,* trans. Chris Turner (London: Basil Blackwell, 1990), pp. 61–62.

93. In a novel Goebbels wrote in his youth; quoted in Lacoue-Labarthe, *Heidegger,* p. 62.

94. Mussolini quoted in Doug Thompson, *State Control in Fascist Italy: Culture and Conformity, 1925–43* (Manchester: Manchester University Press, 1991), p. 120.

95. Lacoue-Labarthe, *Heidegger,* p. 64.

96. Ezra Pound, "The Italian Score," *New English Weekly,* May 23, 1935, p. 107.

97. Nicholls, *Ezra Pound: Politics, Economics Writing,* p. 53.

98. BBC interview with D. G. Bridgson, quoted in William Cookson, *A Guide to the Cantos of Ezra Pound* (New York: Persea Books, 1985), p. xxi.

99. Lester Little, *Religious Poverty and the Profit Motive in Medieval Europe* (Ithaca, N.Y.: Cornell University Press, 1978), p. 56.

100. Calvin quoted in Hyde, *The Gift,* p. 130.

101. Moretti, *Signs Taken for Wonders,* pp. 37–38.

102. Goux, *Les Monnayeurs du langage,* p. 131.

103. David Harvey, *The Condition of Postmodernity: An Inquiry into the Origins of Social Change* (Oxford: Basil Blackwell, 1980), pp. 260–62, 194.

104. Rudolph Hilferding, *Finance Capital: A Study of the Latest Phase of Capitalist Development* (London: Routledge and Kegan Paul, 1981). In monopoly capitalism, unlike competitive capitalism, the link between personal wealth and ownership is tenuous; many owners make their capital available to single control. The limits set by personal fortunes and capabilities are overcome. Monopoly capitalism makes possible the increase of monopolistic organizations within each capitalist country, the internationalization of all capital, and the division of the world into competing spheres of economic influence—the age of imperialism, as Lenin terms it.

105. Jean-Paul Sartre, *Anti-Semite and Jew,* trans. George J. Becker (New York: Schocken Books, 1948), pp. 23–24.

106. *Schwundgeld* is a tax on money in the sense that "a stamp (costing, say, 1¢)

must be attached to a dollar bill at regular (say, monthly) intervals in order to keep the signified worth of the dollar at 'face value'; if, for example, no stamps were attached during the course of a year, the dollar would be worth only 88¢. Such a system is designed to keep money unhoarded and in rapid circulation, for consumers will want to spend it before having to pay 12¢ per dollar per year"; Parker, "The 'Economy' of Anti-Semitism," p. 108.

107. Stuart Ewen, *All Consuming Images: The Politics of Style in Contemporary Culture* (New York: Basic Books, 1988), pp. 159–60.

108. Fredric Jameson notes that "the symbol is the instantaneous, the lyrical, the single moment in time; and this temporal limitation perhaps expresses the historical impossibility in the modern world for genuine reconciliation to endure in time, for it to be anything more than a lyrical, accidental present"; see Fredric Jameson, *Marxism and Form: Twentieth-Century Dialectical Theories of Literature* (Princeton: Princeton University Press, 1971), p. 72. But it is precisely this temporal limitation that Pound refuses to accept. If money "melts" at the "same rate" as the goods it renders intelligible, the romantic symbol is given a properly temporal dimension.

109. Pound quoted by C. David Heyman, *Ezra Pound: The Last Rower* (New York: Viking, 1976), p. 236.

110. Italy, though considerably less racist than Hitler's Germany, was racist nonetheless. Of a Jewish Italian population numbering approximately forty-five thousand in 1938, some ten thousand eventually ended up in Nazi concentration and death camps. Doug Thompson argues that "far from being an imported invention from Germany," racism was "endemic in Fascism, probably from the start, and in large sections of Italian society for much longer. The attitudes to, and treatment of, the indigenous people of Libya and Ethiopia by the colonial regime, but also much nearer home, of the Slav and German minority populations in the Italian north-east, all of whom were continually reminded, often in harsh or even savage ways, of their inferior status within the Italian state, bear eloquent testimony to this fact"; see Doug Thompson, *State Control in Fascist Italy: Culture and Conformity, 1925–43* (Manchester: Manchester University Press, 1991), pp. 141–45.

111. Pound quoted in Heyman, *Ezra Pound: The Last Rower,* p. 75.

112. Ezra Pound, "Orientation and News Sense," *New English Weekly,* January 5, 1933, pp. 273–74.

113. Mussolini quoted in Delzell, *Mediterranean Fascism,* pp. 23–24.

114. See Mussolini's speech of October 4, 1934:

> The present crisis means the end of liberal capitalism, the economic system which emphasized the individual profit motive, and marks the beginning of a new economy which stresses collective interests. These collective interests will be achieved . . . through the corporate system which is based on the self-regulation of production under the aegis of the producers. . . . When I say producers, I do not mean only employers, I mean workers also. . . . Speaking to the people of Bari I said that the economic objective of the Fascist regime is greater social justice for the Italian people. What do I mean by greater social justice? I mean the guarantee of work, a fair wage, a decorous home, I mean the possibility of evolution and betterment. . . . If modern science, spurred on by the state, has solved the problem of multiplying wealth, science must now solve the other great problem, that of the distribution of wealth, so that the illogical, paradoxical, and cruel phenomenon of want in the midst of

plenty shall not be repeated. Toward this great goal all our energies and all our efforts must be bent.

Quoted in Earle Davis, *Vision Fugitive: Ezra Pound and Economics* (Lawrence: University Press of Kanas, 1968), p. 152.

115. Arno J. Mayer, *Why Did the Heavens Not Darken? The "Final Solution" in History* (New York: Pantheon Books, 1988), p. 7.

116. Parker, "The 'Economy' of Anti-Semitism," p. 114.

117. Benjamin, "The Work of Art in the Age of Mechanical Reproduction," p. 218.

118. Jacques Derrida, "Edmond Jabès and the Question of the Book," in *Writing and Difference*, p. 65.

119. Martin Heidegger, "Hölderlin und das Wesen der Dichtung," in *Erläuterungen zu Hölderlins Dichtung* (Frankfurt am Main: Vittorio Klostermann, 1951), pp. 43–44.

120. Jeffrey Mehlman, "Prosopopeia Revisited," *Romanic Review* 81, no. 1 (January 1990): 142.

121. Paul de Man, "The Task of the Translator," in *The Resistance to Theory*, rev. ed. (Minnesota: University of Minnesota Press, 1986), p. 103.

122. Jacques Derrida, "White Mythology," in *Margins of Philosophy*, trans. Alan Bass (Chicago: University of Chicago Press, 1982), pp. 215–16.

123. Parker, "The 'Economy' of Anti-Semitism," p. 115.

124. Jabès quoted in Derrida, "Edmond Jabès and the Question of the Book," p. 65.

125. Parker, "The 'Economy' of Anti-Semitism," p. 119. Maud Ellmann asks, "Could it be that Ezra the wanderer, Ezra the prophet, and indeed, Ezra the Pound, is the Semite incarnate?," in *The Poetics of Impersonality: T. S. Eliot and Ezra Pound* (Cambridge, Mass.: Harvard University Press, p. 89.

126. Robert Casillo, *The Genealogy of Demons: Anti-Semitism, Fascism, and the Myths of Ezra Pound* (Evanston, Ill.: Northwestern University Press, 1988), p. 240.

127. "This morning he [Pound] came up with a remark like this, over the Jewish question: 'It's too bad, and just when I had plans to rebuild the Temple in Jerusalem for them'"; from a conversation between Pound and James Laughlin, as recollected by Charles Olson, in *Charles Olson and Ezra Pound: An Encounter at St. Elizabeth's,* ed. Catherine Seelye (New York: Viking, 1975), p. 77.

128. Ezra Pound, *Gaudier-Brzeska: A Memoir* (1916; rpt. New York: New Directions, 1960), pp. 113–14.

129. Ibid., p. 81.

130. Michael Reck, "A Conversation Between Ezra Pound and Allen Ginsberg," *Evergreen Review* 55 (June 1968): 27–28.

Chapter 3

1. Northrop Frye, *T. S. Eliot: An Introduction* (Chicago: University of Chicago Press, 1963), pp. 98–99; hereafter cited by page in the text.

2. T. S. Eliot, *On Poetry and Poets* (London: Faber and Faber, 1957), p. 53; hereafter cited by page in the text as *OPP*.

3. T. S. Eliot, "A Note on Poetry and Belief," *The Enemy: A Review of Art and Literature* 1 (January 1927): 16–17. The earlier Eliot did hold that poetry could be separated from issues of belief and worldly interest. *The Sacred Wood* (1920), for

example, is almost exclusively aesthetic in its concerns, although the preface to the edition of 1928 explicitly registers its author's discontent with the limitations of its scope. And by the time of *After Strange Gods* (1934), Eliot is unwilling to grant the literary virtually any autonomy whatsoever. See T. S. Eliot, *The Sacred Wood: Essays on Poetry and Criticism*, 2d ed. (London: Methuen, 1928), p. viii; hereafter cited by page in the text as *SW*; and *After Strange Gods: A Primer of Modern Heresy* (London: Faber and Faber, 1934); hereafter cited by page in the text as *ASG*.

4. Fredric Jameson, *The Political Unconscious: Narrative as a Socially Symbolic Act* (Ithaca, N.Y.: Cornell University Press, 1981), p. 289.

5. T. S. Eliot, *The Complete Poems and Plays of T. S. Eliot* (London: Faber and Faber, 1969), pp. 136–37; hereafter cited by page in the text as *CP*.

6. Raymond Williams, *Culture and Society, 1780–1950* (New York: Harper and Row, 1966), pp. 241–42.

7. D. A. Miller, *The Novel and the Police* (Berkeley: University of California Press, 1988), pp. xi–xii.

8. Joel Fineman, "The Significance of Literature: *The Importance of Being Earnest*," *October* 15 (1981): 86.

9. Louis Menand, *Discovering Modernism: T. S. Eliot and His Context* (New York: Oxford University Press, 1987), p. 7.

10. Northrop Frye, *The Anatomy of Criticism: Four Essays* (Princeton: Princeton University Press, 1957), p. 18.

11. See Harold Bloom, *The Anxiety of Influence: A Theory of Poetry* (New York: Oxford University Press, 1973). Frye notes in *The Anatomy of Criticism* that his own work is largely an attempt to annotate Eliot's contention that the existing monuments of literature form an ideal order among themselves, and are not simply collections of individual writings (p. 18). *The Anxiety of Influence* might be read as an annotation of Eliot's contention that "every great work of poetry tends to make impossible the production of equally great works" (*On Poetry and Poets*, p. 64). On Bloom's misreading of Eliot—that is, on Bloom's debt to him—see Gregory S. Jay, *T. S. Eliot and the Poetics of Literary History* (Baton Rouge: Louisiana State University Press, 1983), pp. 67–79. According to F. O. Matthiessen (as reported by Joseph Summer), Eliot contemplated writing a book titled "The Fruitfulness of Misunderstanding," which was to argue that "many of the significant changes in poetry have occurred when a writer who is attempting to imitate another or others, through misunderstanding of his model or models creates inadvertently something new." The project was to include an examination of Eliot's own misunderstanding of French poets. See Joseph H. Summers, *The Heirs of Donne and Jonson* (New York: Oxford University Press, 1970), p. 129.

12. Michel Foucault, *The Order of Things: An Archaeology of the Human Sciences* (New York: Vintage Books, 1970), p. 56; hereafter cited by page in the text.

13. Samuel Taylor Coleridge, *The Collected Works of Samuel Taylor Coleridge,* ed. Kathleen Coburn and Bart Winer, 16 vols. (Princeton: Princeton University Press, 1972), 4:304.

14. T. S. Eliot, *Selected Essays*, 3d ed. (London: Faber and Faber, 1951), p. 21; hereafter cited by page in the text as *SE*.

15. T. S. Eliot, *For Lancelot Andrews: Essays on Style and Order* (1928; rpt. London: Faber and Faber, 1970), p. 7.

16. Robert Sencourt, *T. S. Eliot: A Memoir* (New York: Delta, 1973), pp. 74–75.

17. Hugh Kenner, *The Invisible Poet: T. S. Eliot* (New York: McDowell, Obolensky, 1959).

18. T. S. Eliot, *Notes Towards the Definition of Culture* (London: Faber and Faber, 1948), p. 52; hereafter cited by page in the text as *NTDC*.

19. T. S. Eliot, *The Idea of a Christian Society* (New York: Harcourt, Brace, 1940), p. 64. It should be noted, however, that Eliot's condemnation of Nazism is far from unequivocal. He characterizes his objections to Nazi "oppression and violence and cruelty," for example, as "objections to means and not ends" (p. 20), though he does not specify which of the Nazi "ends" he would, in theory, find acceptable.

20. T. S. Eliot, *The Waste Land: A Facsimile and Transcript of the Original Drafts Including the Annotations of Ezra Pound*, ed. Valerie Eliot (London: Faber and Faber, 1971), p. xviii.

21. T. S. Eliot, *To Criticize the Critic* (London: Faber and Faber, 1965), p. 7.

22. T. S. Eliot, contribution to the anthology *Revelation*, ed. John Baille and Hugh Martin (London, 1937), p. 2; quoted in Rossell Hope Robbins, *The T. S. Eliot Myth* (New York: Schuman, 1951), pp. 25–26.

23. Fredric Jameson, "Religion and Ideology: A Political Reading of *Paradise Lost*," in *Literature, Politics, and Theory: Papers from the Essex Conference, 1976–84*, ed. Francis Barker et al. (London: Methuen, 1986), pp. 37–38.

24. *Josiah Royce's Seminar, 1913–14: As Recorded in the Notebooks of Harry T. Costello*, ed. Grover Smith (New Brunswick, N.J.: Rutgers University Press, 1963), p. 76.

25. Eliot, *The Waste Land: A Facsimile*, p. 1.

26. Maud Ellmann, *The Poetics of Impersonality: T. S. Eliot and Ezra Pound* (Cambridge, Mass.: Harvard University Press, 1987), p. 51.

27. Elizabeth Drew, *T. S. Eliot: The Design of His Poetry* (New York: Scribners, 1949), p. 50. On Eliot's transformation of "Jew" into a common noun—"jew," which I have restored—see Melvin Wilk, *Jewish Presence in T. S. Eliot and Franz Kafka* (Atlanta: Scholars Press, 1986), p. 27.

28. On the "currants"/"current" pun, see Frye, *T. S. Eliot*, p. 67. On "Phoenician" as a euphemism, see Wilk, *Jewish Presence*, pp. 46–47, 52. Wilk cites a 1905 speech by Senator Simmons of North Carolina on the subject of immigration policy which warns against "the spawn of the Phoenician [Jewish] curse." "Spawned" is, of course, the verb Eliot uses to characterize Gerontion's birth.

29. T. S. Eliot, "A Comment," *Criterion* 14 (1935): 433.

30. Pierre Bourdieu, *Outline of a Theory of Practice*, trans. R. Nice (New York: Cambridge University Press, 1977), p. 84.

31. Williams, *Culture and Society*, pp. 295–97.

32. Thomas Hobbes, *Leviathan*, pt. 1. chap. 4; see C. B. Macpherson, *The Political Theory of Possessive Individualism: Hobbes to Locke* (Oxford: Oxford University Press, 1962).

33. Andrew Ross provides a reading of Eliot in terms of Lacanian *caption* in *The Failure of Modernism: Symptoms of American Poetry* (New York: Columbia University Press, 1986), p. 45.

34. Lewis Caroll, *Alice in Wonderland*, ed. Donald J. Gray (New York: Norton, 1971), p. 132.

35. Jacques Derrida, *Of Grammatology*, trans. Gayatri Chakravorty Spivak (Baltimore: Johns Hopkins University Press, 1976), p. 112.

36. Ferdinand de Saussure, *Course in General Linguistics,* ed. Charles Bally and Albert Sechehaye, trans. Roy Harris (La Salle, Ill.: Open Court, 1983), p. 115; hereafter cited by page in the text.

37. Karl Marx, *Capital: A Critique of Political Economy,* ed. Frederick Engels, trans. Samuel Moore and Edward Aveling, 3 vols. (New York: International Publishers, 1967), 1:52.

38. Paul Hirst, *On Law and Ideology* (Atlantic Highlands, N.J.: Humanities Press, 1979), p. 160.

39. John Locke, *An Essay Concerning Human Understanding,* ed. Peter N. Nidditch (Oxford: Oxford University Press, 1975), p. 404. On Locke, proper names, and private property, see Patricia Parker, " The (Self-) Identity of the Literary Text: Property, Propriety, Proper Place, and Proper Name in *Wuthering Heights,*" in *Identity of the Literary Text,* ed. Mario J. Valdés and Owen Miller (Toronto: University of Toronto Press, 1985), pp. 92–118.

40. T. S. Eliot, *Knowledge and Experience in the Philosophy of F. H. Bradley* (London: Faber and Faber, 1964), pp. 134, 137; hereafter cited by page in the text as *KE.*

41. Paul de Man, "Intentional Structure of the Romantic Image," in *The Rhetoric of Romanticism* (New York: Columbia University Press, 1984), p. 6. On the relation of Eliot's dissertation to poststructuralist poetics, see Walter Benn Michaels, "Philosophy in Kinkanja: Eliot's Pragmatism," *Glyph* 8 (1981): 182–83.

42. Louis Althusser, *Lenin and Philosophy,* trans. Ben Brewster (London: Monthly Review Press, 1971), p. 174.

43. Karl Marx, *The Eighteenth Brumaire of Louis Bonaparte* (New York: International, 1963), pp. 50–51.

44. Albert Cook, *Thresholds: Studies in the Romantic Experience* (Madison: University of Wisconsin Press, 1985), p. 15.

45. Percy Bysshe Shelly, "A Defense of Poetry," in *The Complete Works of Percy Bysshe Shelley,* ed. Roger Ingpen and Walter E. Peck, 10 vols. (New York: Gordian Press, 1965), 7:117.

46. Ibid., 7:109. On Shelley's relation to Saussure, see Paul H. Fry, *The Reach of Criticism: Method and Perception in Literary Theory* (New Haven: Yale University Press, 1983), p. 158.

47. Thomas Sprat, *History of the Royal Society* (1667); cited in Walter Jackson Bate, *From Classic to Romantic: Premises of Taste in Eighteenth-Century England* (New York: Harper and Row, 1961), p. 39.

48. But see the famous passage in *Prometheus Unbound* in Shelley, *Complete Works:*

> Language is a perpetual Orphic song,
> Which rules with Daedal harmony a throng
> Of thoughts and forms, which else senseless and shapeless were.
>
> (4.415–17)

49. T. S. Eliot, *The Use of Poetry and the Use of Criticism: Studies in the Relation of Criticism to Poetry in England,* 2d ed. (London: Faber and Faber, 1964), pp. 94–95; hereafter cited in the text as *UPUC.* Eliot is, of course, quoting from Shelley's *Defense.*

50. Walt Whitman, "Song of the Open Road," sec. 13, ll. 166–67, in *Leaves of Grass,* ed. Harold W. Blodgett and Sculley Bradley (New York: W. W. Norton, 1965).

51. John Stuart Mill, "What Is Poetry?," in *Essays on Poetry,* ed. F. Parvin Sharpless (Columbia: University of South Carolina Press, 1976), p. 12.

52. F. H. Bradley, *Ethical Studies* (Oxford: Oxford University Press, 1975), p. 404.

53. Ralph Waldo Emerson, "Self-Reliance," in *Selections from Ralph Waldo Emerson,* ed. Stephen E. Whicher (Boston: Houghton Mifflin, 1957), p. 149.

54. Ibid., p. 151.

55. Herbert F. Tucker, "Dramatic Monologue and the Overhearing of Lyric," in *Lyric Poetry: Beyond New Criticism,* ed. Chaviva Hošek and Patricia Parker (Ithaca, N.Y.: Cornell University Press, 1985), p. 231.

56. Ibid., p. 229.

57. Ibid., pp. 229–30.

58. Kenner, *Invisible Poet,* p. 3.

59. Robert Langbaum maintains that "we all" agree on the "divided self" reading; see his "New Modes of Characterization in *The Waste Land,*" in *T. S. Eliot in His Time: Essays on the Occasion of the Fiftieth Anniversary of The Waste Land,* ed. A. Walton Litz (Princeton: Princeton University Press, 1973), p. 98. Hugh Kenner advances "Dante or some analogue of Dante's" as one possibility among several in *The Pound Era* (Berkeley: University of California Press, 1973), p. 131. Eliot's own opinion, "an unidentified male companion," is contained in a letter to Kristian Smidt; quoted in Smidt's *Poetry and Belief in the Work of T. S. Eliot* (London: Routledge and Kegan Paul, 1961), p. 85.

60. W. K. Wimsatt, "'Prufrock' and 'Maud': From Plot to Symbol," *Yale French Studies* 9 (Spring 1952): 84–92.

61. William Shakespeare, *Hamlet* 2. 232–42, in *The Complete Works,* ed. Stanley Wells and Gary Taylor (Oxford: Clarendon Press, 1986).

62. Francis Barker, *The Tremulous Private Body: Essays on Subjection* (London: Methuen, 1984), p. 35.

63. Northrop Frye, *Fools of Time: Studies in Shakespearean Tragedy* (Toronto: University of Toronto Press, 1967), p. 29.

64. Samuel Johnson, "Preface" to The Plays of William Shakespeare, in *Samuel Johnson: Selected Poetry and Prose,* ed. Frank Brady and W. K. Wimsatt (Berkeley: University of California Press, 1971), p. 303; Fry, *The Reach of Criticism,* p. 27.

65. The classic modern formulation of this reversal of Aristotelian priorities is Forster's:

> "Character," says Aristotle, "gives us qualities, but it is in actions—what we do—that we are happy or the reverse." We have already decided that Aristotle is wrong and now we must face the consequences of disagreeing with him. "All human happiness and misery," says Aristotle, "take the form of action." We know better. We believe that happiness and misery exist in the secret life, which each of us lives privately, and to which (in his characters) the novelist has access. And by the secret life we mean the life for which there is no external evidence.

E. M. Forster, *Aspects of the Novel* (London: Edward Arnold, 1927), p. 113. Nothing could be further removed from the theory of "the objective correlative"; for Eliot a "life for which there is no external evidence" is an unrepresentable life.

66. Ian Watt, *The Rise of the Novel* (Harmondsworth: Penguin, 1963), p. 22; Michael Ragussis, *Acts of Naming: The Family Plot in Fiction* (New York: Oxford University Press, 1986), p. 5.

67. On the relation between *Hamlet* and "the culture of the book," see Paul Morrison, "'Noble Deeds and the Secret Singularity': *Hamlet* and *Phèdre,"* *Canadian Review of Comparative Literature / Revue canadienne de littérature comparée* 17, nos. 2–3 (June–September 1991): 263–88.

68. Miller, *The Novel and the Police,* p. 82.

69. Roman Jakobson, "Linguistics and Poetics," in *The Structuralists: From Marx to Lévi-Strauss,* ed. R. and F. DeGeorge (New York: Anchor Press, 1972), pp. 95, 102; James Joyce, *Ulysses,* ed. Hans Walter Gabler (New York: Vintage Books, 1986), p. 125.

70. Joel Fineman, "The Structure of Allegorical Desire," in *Allegory and Representation: Selected Papers from the English Institute, 1979–80,* ed. Stephen J. Greenblatt (Baltimore: Johns Hopkins University Press, 1981), p. 33.

71. Augustine, *The Confessions of St. Augustine,* trans. John K. Ryan (New York: Image Books, 1960), 4:11.

72. Maud Ellmann argues that the repeated assertion is a way of gaining time, of "prolonging the re-editions of desire" (*The Poetics of Impersonality,* p. 79).

73. Friedrich Nietzsche, *Beyond Good and Evil: Prelude to a Philosophy of the Future,* trans. Walter Kaufmann (New York: Vintage, 1966), p. 93.

74. On the source of the name Prufrock, see Kenner, *Invisible Poet,* p. 3; on "seaside girls" and turn-of-the-century advertising, see Thomas Richards, *The Commodity Culture of Victorian England: Advertising and Spectacle, 1851–1914* (Stanford: Stanford University Press, 1990), p. 241.

75. F. Scott Fitzgerald, *The Great Gatsby* (New York: Scribner's, 1953), pp. 120, 182.

76. Miller, *The Novel and the Police,* p. xii.

77. Kenner, *Invisible Poet,* p. 10.

78. René Descartes, *Philosophical Works,* trans. Elizabeth S. Haldane and G. R. T. Ross (New York: Dover, 1931), p. 157. On the relation of "Gerontion" to Descartes, see Ellmann, *The Poetics of Impersonality,* pp. 82–84.

79. On this ancient pseudoseparation of body and soul, see Barker, *The Tremulous Private Body,* p. 63.

80. Kenner, *Invisible Poet,* p. 134.

81. Derrida, *Of Grammatology,* p. 108.

82. Sir Philip Sidney, *An Apology for Poetry,* in *Critical Theory Since Plato,* rev. ed., ed. Hazard Adams (New York: Harcourt Brace Jovanovich, 1971), p. 155.

83. Fineman, "The Significance of Literature," p. 89.

84. Michael A. Bernstein, *The Tale of the Tribe: Ezra Pound and the Modern Verse Epic* (Princeton: Princeton University Press, 1980), pp. 39–40.

85. T. S. Eliot, "'Ulysses,' Order, and Myth," first appeared in *The Dial* (November 1923); I am quoting from the essay as it is reproduced in *Criticism: The Foundations of Modern Literary Judgment,* rev. ed., ed. Mark Schorer, Josephine Miles, and Gordon McKenzie (New York: Harcourt, Brace, and World, 1958), p. 270; hereafter cited by page in the text.

86. Franco Moretti, *Signs Taken for Wonders: Essays in the Sociology of Literary Forms,* rev. ed., trans. Susan Fischer, David Forgacs, and David Miller (London: Verso, 1988), p. 211.

87. Ibid., p. 213.

88. The relevance of Plato's reading of the myth of Philomel in the *Phaedo* is noted in David Ward, *T. S. Eliot Between Two Worlds: A Reading of T. S. Eliot's Poetry and Plays* (Boston: Routledge and Kegan Paul, 1973), p. 97.

89. Moretti, *Signs Taken for Wonders,* pp. 220–21.

90. Thom Gunn, "From the Highest Camp," in *Selected Poems: 1950–1975* (London: Faber and Faber, 1979), p. 39.

91. On the "homeopathic" strategies of modernism, see Fredric Jameson, "Seriality in Modern Literature," *Bucknell Review* 18 (1970): 63–80.

92. Roman Jakobson, "Two Aspects of Language," in *Selected Writings,* 4 vols. (The Hague: Mouton, 1971), 2:251.

93. D. A. Miller, "Sontag's Urbanity," in *The Lesbian and Gay Studies Reader,* ed. Henry Abelove, Michèle Aina Barale, and David M. Halperin (New York: Routledge, 1993), p. 218.

94. Ross, *The Failure of Modernism,* p. 43.

95. Michel Foucault, "What Is an Author?," in *Textual Strategies: Perspectives in Post-Structuralist Criticism,* ed. Josué V. Harari (Ithaca, N.Y.: Cornell University Press, 1979), p. 141. See also Ross, *The Failure of Modernism,* p. 43.

96. Jean Baudrillard, *For a Critique of the Political Economy of the Sign,* trans. Charles Levin (St. Louis: Telos Press, 1981), p. 105.

97. Oscar Wilde, "The Decay of Lying," in *Complete Works of Oscar Wilde* (New York: Harper and Row, 1989), pp. 977–78.

98. *Paradiso* 10.27, in Dante Alighieri, *The Divine Comedy,* ed. Charles S. Singleton (Princeton: Princeton University Press, 1970); all Dante citations are to this edition.

99. Jessie L. Weston, *From Ritual to Romance* (Garden City, N.Y.: Doubleday, 1957), pp. 14–16.

100. Ibid., p. 16.

101. G. Ferraro, *Il linguaggio del mito;* quoted in Moretti, *Signs Taken for Wonders,* p. 219.

102. On this comparison, see Moretti, *Signs Taken for Wonders,* p. 219.

103. Frye, *Anatomy of Criticism,* pp. 123–25.

104. Barker, *The Tremulous Private Body,* p. 32.

105. Claude Lévi-Strauss, *The Savage Mind* (Chicago: University of Chicago Press, 1966), p. 234; hereafter cited by page in the text.

106. Max Horkheimer and Theodor W. Adorno, *Dialectic of Enlightenment,* trans. John Cumming (New York: Continuum, 1972), pp. 12–13; hereafter cited by page in the text.

107. The passage alludes to Dante's Ugolino—"io senti' chiavar l'uscio di sotto / a l'orribile torre" (*Inferno* 33.46–47)—whose fate also parodies what I have called "corporate identity": Ugolino's cannibalism of his children is a travesty of the sacrifice of the Eucharist.

108. William Wordsworth, *Lyrical Ballads* (1798), ed. W. J. B. Owen, rev. ed. (Oxford: Oxford University Press, 1969), pp. 159–60.

109. Stephen Kern, *The Culture of Time and Space: 1880–1918* (Cambridge, Mass.: Harvard University Press, 1983), p. 260.

110. Martin Heidegger quoted in David Harvey, *The Condition of Postmodernity: An Enquiry into the Origins of Social Change* (Cambridge: Basil Blackwell, 1980), p. 208.

111. Eliot, *The Waste Land: A Facsimile,* p. 3.

112. Walter Benjamin, "Theses on the Philosophy of History," in *Illuminations,* ed. Hannah Arendt, trans. Harry Zohn (New York: Schocken Books, 1969), p. 256.

113. T. S. Eliot, "Mr. Middleton Murry's Synthesis," *Monthly Criterion* 6 (October 1927): 344.

114. Paul de Man, "The Rhetoric of Temporality," in *Blindness and Insight: Essays in the Rhetoric of Contemporary Criticism*, rev. ed. (Minneapolis: University of Minnesota Press, 1983), p. 208; hereafter cited by page in the text.

115. T. S. Eliot, as quoted in Helen Gardner, *The Composition of Four Quartets* (London: Faber and Faber, 1978), p. 176.

116. On the naming of Dante, see John Freccero, "Manfred's Wounds and the Poetics of the *Purgatorio*," in *Centre and Labyrinth: Essays in Honour of Northrop Frye*, ed. Eleanor Cook et al. (Toronto: University of Toronto Press, 1983), pp. 69–82.

117. William V. Spanos, "Hermeneutics and Memory: Destroying T. S. Eliot's *Four Quartets*," *Genre* 11, no. 4 (Winter 1978): 523–74.

Chapter 4

1. Paul de Man, "The Resistance to Theory," in *The Resistance to Theory* (Minneapolis: University of Minnesota Press, 1986), p. 3; hereafter cited in the text as RT.

2. Fredric Jameson, *The Political Unconscious: Narrative as a Socially Symbolic Act* (Ithaca, N.Y.: Cornell University Press, 1981), p. 45.

3. D. A. Miller, *The Novel and the Police* (Berkeley: University of California Press, 1988), p. xi.

4. Ibid.

5. Paul de Man, "Shelley Disfigured," in *Deconstruction and Criticism*, ed. Harold Bloom et al. (New York: Seabury, 1979), p. 69. Compare this to the personal (and, given the recent disclosures, prophetic and disturbing) reflections in the foreword to the revised second edition of *Blindness and Insight*: "I am not given to retrospective self-examination and mercifully forget what I have written with the same alacrity I forget bad movies—although, as with bad movies, certain scenes or phrases return at times to embarrass and haunt me like a guilty conscience"; Paul de Man, *Blindness and Insight: Essays in the Rhetoric of Contemporary Criticism*, rev. ed. (Minneapolis: University of Minnesota Press, 1983), p. xii.

6. Geoffrey Hartman, "Blindness and Insight," *New Republic*, March 7, 1988, p. 31. See also the final sentence of his "Looking Back on Paul de Man"—"De Man's critique of every tendency to totalize literature or language, to see unity where there is no unity, could be a belated, but still powerful, act of conscience"— in *Reading de Man Reading*, ed. Lindsay Waters and Wlad Godzich (Minneapolis: University of Minnesota Press, 1989), p. 23.

7. Jacques Derrida, "Like the Sound of the Sea Deep Within a Shell: Paul de Man's War," *Critical Inquiry* 14 (Spring 1988): 590–652; hereafter cited by page in the text as SSD; J. Hillis Miller, untitled essay in *Times Literary Supplement*, June 17–23, 1988; because of the brevity of the article, no page references are given. See also J. Hillis Miller, "An Open Letter to Professor Jon Wiener," in *Responses: On Paul de Man's Wartime Journalism* (Lincoln: University of Nebraska Press, 1989), pp. 334–42.

8. Paul de Man, "The Epistemology of Metaphor," in *On Metaphor*, ed. Sheldon Sacks (Chicago: University of Chicago Press, 1978), pp. 16–17; hereafter cited by page in the text as EM.

9. Michael Ryan, *Marxism and Deconstruction: A Critical Articulation* (Baltimore: Johns Hopkins University Press, 1982), p. 16.

10. Perry Anderson, *In the Tracks of Historical Materialism* (Chicago: University of Chicago Press, 1984), p. 28.

11. Terry Eagleton made this point some time ago: "[T]o select Stalinism and fascism as prototypes of the ideological is drastically reductive and essentialistic. For it is simply false to believe that all ideologies, in some structurally invariant manner, rely as profoundly upon apodictic truth, metaphysical groundedness, teleological vision and the violent erasure of difference as these brutally extreme models would suggest"; see *The Function of Criticism: From "The Spectator" to Post-Structuralism* (London: Verso, 1984), pp. 101–2.

12. Ibid., p. 102.

13. Philippe Lacoue-Labarthe, *Heidegger, Art and Politics*, trans. Chris Turner (Oxford: Basil Blackwell, 1990), p. 103.

14. Photocopies of de Man's articles in *Les Cahiers du Libre Examen, Le Soir*, and *Het Vlaamsche Land* began to circulate soon after the news of their existence broke; they have since been published as *Wartime Journalism, 1939–1943* (Lincoln: University of Nebraska Press, 1989).

15. Paul de Man, *The Rhetoric of Romanticism* (New York: Columbia University Press, 1984), p. viii; hereafter cited by page in the text as *RR*.

16. By "the materiality of actual history" de Man seems to mean little more than pure matter, which suggests a materialism fundamentally opposed to the marxist insistence on the priority of, or ultimate determination by, the means of production. The grounding of materialism in matter rather than production belongs to a tradition of bourgeois ideology that extends from eighteenth-century materialism through nineteenth-century positivism. It is to this tradition—and not, as "The Resistance to Theory" would have it, anything issuing from Marx's *German Ideology*—that de Man belongs. On "materialisms" that fetishize matter, see Jameson, *The Political Unconscious*, pp. 45–46.

17. I am explaining or locating de Man's late work in relation to the early collaborationist writings, but my argument does not finally depend on this structure: in other words, although I think it plausible to speak of the "informing impulse" of the later work, my point is not finally motivational. The post-1953 work is inadequate in its understanding of the operations of power, however that inadequacy might be explained.

18. T. S. Eliot, *Four Quartets*, in *The Complete Poems and Plays of T. S. Eliot* (London: Faber and Faber, 1969), p. 178; hereafter cited by page in the text as *CP*.

19. Peter Brooks, *Reading for the Plot: Design and Intention in Narrative* (New York: Knopf, 1984), p. 91.

20. Paul de Man, *Allegories of Reading Figural Language in Rousseau, Nietzsche, Rilke, and Proust* (New Haven: Yale University Press, 1979), p. 298; hereafter cited by page in the text as *AR*.

21. From a lecture Eliot delivered in New Haven in 1933; quoted in F. O. Matthiessen, *The Achievement of T. S. Eliot: An Essay on the Nature of Poetry*, 3d ed. (New York: Oxford University Press, 1958), pp. 89–90.

22. De Man quotes this passage from Goebbels's novel *Michael* in "Hegel on the Sublime," in *Displacement: Derrida and After*, ed. Mark Krupnik (Bloomington: Indiana University Press, 1983), p. 149.

23. *Four Quartets* may suggest Pater's aesthetic, if only by virtue of its title, but

Eliot's stated ambition was "to get *beyond poetry*, as Beethoven, in his later work, strove to get *beyond music.*" Eliot adds the crucial qualification: "We shall never succeed. . . ."; quoted in Matthiessen, *The Achievement of T. S. Eliot, pp. 89–90.*

24. *Lacoue-Labarthe, Heidegger, Art and Politics,* p. 64.

25. And so it is for Eliot as well: the thesis identified with the phrase "dissociation of sensibility" is an attempt, however unconvincing, to understand sensory perception in historical terms.

26. Karl Marx, "Private Property and Communism," in *Early Writings,* trans. T. B. Bottomore (New York: McGraw Hill, 1964), pp. 159–60.

27. Ibid., p. 160.

28. For a sympathetic account of this impulse in de Man, see William Flesch, "De Man and Idolatry," in *Tainted Greatness: Antisemitism and Cultural Heroes,* ed. Nancy A. Harrowitz (Philadelphia: Temple University Press, 1994), pp. 237–52.

29. Jacques Derrida, "Structure, Sign, and Play in the Discourse of the Human Sciences," in *Writing and Difference,* trans. Alan Bass (Evanston, Ill.: Northwestern University Press, 1987), pp. 278–79; hereafter cited by page in the text as SSP.

30. Ernesto Laclau and Chantal Mouffe, *Hegemony & Socialist Strategy: Towards a Radical Democratic Politics* (London: Verso, 1985), pp. 128–29; hereafter cited by page in the text as *HSS.*

31. For a critique of this position to which my own argument is indebted, see Barbara Foley, "Marxism in the Poststructuralist Moment: Some Notes on the Problem of Revising Marx," *Cultural Critique,* no. 15 (Spring 1990): 35.

32. Karl Marx, *Theories of Surplus Value,* trans. Renate Simpson (London: Lawrence and Wishart, 1969), I:276, cited in Foley, "Marxism in the Poststructuralist Moment," p. 35.

33. Michel Foucault, *Discipline and Punish: The Birth of the Prison,* trans. Alan Sheridan (New York: Vintage Books, 1979), p. 177.

34. Jean Baudrillard, *For a Critique of the Political Economy of the Sign,* trans. Charles Levin (St. Louis: Telos Press, 1981), p. 71.

35. Fredric Jameson, "The Ideology of the Text," *Salmagundi* (Fall 1975–Winter 1976): 204–46; see also his "Reification and Utopia in Mass Culture," *Social Text* 1 (Winter 1979): 130–48.

36. David Harvey, *The Condition of Postmodernity: An Enquiry into the Origins of Social Change* (Cambridge: Basil Blackwell Press, 1980), p. 194.

37. De Man maintains that "the tension between contemporary literary theory and the tradition of literary studies" is not "a mere historical conflict between two modes of thought that happen to hold the stage at the same time. If the conflict is merely historical, in the literal sense, it is of limited theoretical interest, a passing squall in the intellectual weather of the world. As a matter of fact, the arguments in favor of the legitimacy of literary theory are so compelling that it seems useless to concern oneself with the conflict at all" ("Resistance to Theory," pp. 11–12).

38. Miller, *The Novel and the Police,* pp. xii, 118.

39. De Man, "Hegel on the Sublime," p. 149.

40. Michel Foucault, "The Discourse of Language," in *The Archaeology of Knowledge and the Discourse on Language,* trans. A. M. Sheridan Smith (New York: Pantheon Books, 1972), p. 216.

41. Hannah Arendt, *The Origins of Totalitarianism,* rev. ed. (New York: Harcourt Brace Jovanovich, 1979), p. 3. Arendt argues that at the height of its development in the nineteenth century, the nation-state granted its Jewish inhabitants a

previously unprecedented "equality of rights" (p. 11). The entire argument of "The Jews, the Nation-State, and the Birth of Antisemitism" (pp. 11–53) is relevant.

42. Hannah Arendt, *Men in Dark Times* (San Diego: University of California Press, 1968), p. 43.

43. Arendt, *Origins of Totalitarianism*, p. 388.

44. Slavoj Žižek, *The Sublime Object of Ideology* (London: Verso, 1989), p. 49.

45. Ezra Pound, *Ezra Pound Speaking: Radio Speeches of World War II*, ed. Leonard W. Doob (Westport, Conn.: Greenwood Press, 1978), p. 283.

46. See Adolph Hitler, *Mein Kampf*, trans. Ralph Manheim (Boston: Houghton Mifflin, 1971), p. 307.

47. The letter, which remained confidential until 1987, was hardly the "public act" Derrida claims it to be; of its many half-truths and untruths, the claim that Henrik de Man was de Man's father (rather than his uncle) is the most curious. I return to the issue of the letter, or J. Hillis Miller's reading of it, later in this chapter.

48. Ortwin de Graef, "Silence to Be Observed: A Trial for Paul de Man's Inexcusable Confessions," *Yale Journal of Criticism* 3, no. 2 (Spring 1990): 219.

49. Alfred Kazin, "Homer to Mussolini: The Fascination and Terror of Ezra Pound," in *Ezra Pound: The Legacy of Kulchur*, ed. Marcel Smith and William A. Ulmer (Tuscaloosa: University of Alabama Press, 1988), p. 26; it was Kazin himself who was so threatened.

50. "It is difficult to construct a convincing case for Eliot's having been an anti-Semite. To hold a radical philosophy of this sort, and to permit a few ambiguities are, after all, different things. The notorious passage in *After Strange Gods* is capable of the interpretation that a community of *orthodox* Jews would be socially 'desirable' because of the strong social bonds established by Jewish solidarity"; see Roger Kojecky, *T. S. Eliot's Social Criticism* (London: Faber and Faber, 1971), p. 12. In a letter to J. V. Healy (May 10, 1940), Eliot glosses the passage from *After Strange Gods* in relation not to Orthodox Jews but to freethinking Christians, who, if "undesirable," are less "undesirable" that their Jewish counterparts: "By free-thinking Jews I mean Jews who have given up the practice and belief of their own religion, without having become Christians or attached themselves to any other dogmatic religion. It should be obvious that I think a large number of free-thinkers of any race to be undesirable, and the free-thinking Jews are only a special case. The Jewish religion is unfortunately not a very portable one, and shorn of its traditional practices, observances, and Messianism, it tends to become a mild and colourless form of Unitarianism. The free-thinking European, or American of European race, retains for the most part a good many of the moral habits and conventions of Christianity. If he does not retain them individually, still these habits survive to some extent in the community. The Jew who is separated from his religious faith is much more deracinated thereby than the descendants of Christians, and it is this deracinataion that I think dangerous and tending to irresponsibility." Eliot goes on to say that his "view does not imply any prejudice on the ground of race," but the letter itself argues otherwise. See Christopher Ricks, *T. S. Eliot and Prejudice* (London: Faber and Faber, 1988), p. 44.

Ricks defense of Eliot bears a marked resemblance to the poststructuralist defense of de Man: both involve a "mediated passage or crossing between positive and negative valorization." Although Ricks admits of no absolute failings in Eliot, he does concede that a line such as "Rachel *née* Rabinovitch ("Sweeney Among the Nightingales") may seem anti-Semitic; it may even be "natural" to "suspect" that it is. But suspicion is not knowledge, and to conclude that "Sweeney" is anti-Semitic is itself prejudicial (pp. 30–31). "It takes one to know one," as the saying goes; "it repeats the well-known totalitarian procedures of vilification it pretends to deplore," as J. Hillis Miller says of the attack on de Man. The question of prejudice is strategically transferred from the poem to the reader, and any potential failing in the former is rehabilitated as its success in exposing the deficiencies of the latter.

51. Joel Fineman, "The Structure of Allegorical Desire," in *Allegory and Representation: Selected Papers from the English Institute,* ed. Stephen J. Greenblatt (Baltimore: Johns Hopkins University Press, 1982), p. 28.

52. Ibid.

53. Jacques Derrida, "White Mythology: Metaphor in the Text of Philosophy," in *Margins of Philosophy,* trans. Alan Bass (Chicago: University of Chicago Press, 1982), p. 252.

Index

JAN 24 1997

DATE DUE

8.25			

Demco, Inc. 38-293